D1823640

Sustainable Management, Wertschöpfung und Effizienz

Series Editors

Gregor Weber, ecoistics.institute, Breunigweiler, Germany

Markus Bodemann, Warburg, Germany

René Schmidpeter, M3TRIX, Köln, Germany

In dieser Schriftenreihe stehen insbesondere empirische und praxisnahe Studien zu nachhaltigem Wirtschaften und Effizienz im Mittelpunkt. Energie-, Umwelt-, Nachhaltigkeits-, CSR-, Innovations-, Risiko- und integrierte Managementsysteme sind nur einige Beispiele, die Sie hier wiederfinden. Ein besonderer Fokus liegt dabei auf dem Nutzen, den solche Systeme für die Anwendung in der Praxis bieten, um zu helfen die globalen Nachhaltigkeitsziele (SDGs) umzusetzen. Publiziert werden nationale und internationale wissenschaftliche Arbeiten.

Reihenherausgeber:
Dr. Gregor Weber, ecoistics.institute
Dr. Markus Bodemann
Prof. Dr. René Schmidpeter, Center for Advanced Sustainable Management, Cologne Business School

This series is focusing on empirical and practical research in the fields of sustainable management and efficiency. Management systems in the context of energy, environment, sustainability, CSR, innovation, risk as well as integrated management systems are just a few examples which can be found here. A special focus is on the value such systems can offer for the application in practice supporting the implementation of the global sustainable development goals, the SDGs. National and international scientific publications are published (English and German).

Series Editors:
Dr. Gregor Weber, ecoistics.institute
Dr. Markus Bodemann
Prof. Dr. René Schmidpeter, Center for Advanced Sustainable Management, Cologne Business School

More information about this series at http://www.springer.com/series/15909

Zhangyuan He

Future Sustainable Urban Freight Network Design in the Large Cities and Megacities

Zhangyuan He
Business Studies & Economics
Universität Bremen
Bremen, Germany

This dissertation has been accepted by the doctoral committee (Dr. rer. pol.) at the Faculty of Business Studies & Economics at the University of Bremen, in September 2020. The date of the oral examination was August 4, 2020, and the examiners/reviewers were Prof. Dr. Hans-Dietrich Haasis, Prof. Dr. Herbert Kotzab, Prof. Dr. André Heinemann, and Dr. Ingrid Rügge. Zhangyuan He was a doctoral scholarship holder from the China Scholarship Council.

ISSN 2523-8620   ISSN 2523-8639 (electronic)
Sustainable Management, Wertschöpfung und Effizienz
ISBN 978-3-658-34202-9   ISBN 978-3-658-34203-6   (eBook)
https://doi.org/10.1007/978-3-658-34203-6

Responsible Editor: Anna Pietras
This Springer Gabler imprint is published by the registered company Springer Fachmedien Wiesbaden GmbH part of Springer Nature.
The registered company address is: Abraham-Lincoln-Str. 46, 65189 Wiesbaden, Germany

Acknowledgment

This book would not have been accomplished without the support of my advisors, colleagues, family, friends, and China Scholarship Council who sponsor this research.

I would like to take this opportunity to express my deep gratitude to Prof. Dr. Hans-Dietrich Haasis, my doctoral supervisor, for his guidances and encouragement that inspire me to always go one step further through hard times. Without his wisdom, patience, and support, I would never be able to develop this work as an independent researcher in such an efficient way. I also would like to specifically thank to Prof. Dr. Herbert Kotzab, my second doctoral supervisor, whose efforts greatly enhanced the quality and scope of this research.

I truly appreciate all the members and staff of the International Graduate School for Dynamics in Logistics (IGS) that have become part of life by sharing not just academic experiences but also by inspiring my path through their courage and effort. I would like to particularly thank Dr.-Ing. Ingrid Rügge, IGS managing director, for her support and advice since the beginning of my research. IGS has provided me with unique opportunities to enrich my investigative, professional, and personal skills. This was an intensive journey blessed with wonderful colleagues and friends. Besides, I would like to express my gratitude to the China Scholarship Council (CSC) for their financial support.

I also would like to specifically thank my parents for their selfless love and support. A very special thank you goes to my girlfriend, AN Lina, who always encourages me on stressful days and cares about me. I am grateful to all of you.

Abstract

Urban freight transport (UFT) plays a critical role in urban economic growth. City and freight have maintained a set of core relations since the city is an entity where production, distribution, and consumption movements are used and compete for scarce land. In fact, urban development and freight planning keep the relations of interaction and interdependence. Nevertheless, the links between urban development and urban freight transport have received less attention. In recent years, the notion of smart cities has increasingly become a solution to improve the sustainability and liveability of cities. Although the universal agreement of the definition is still lacking, academia has agreed that it radically influences the building allocation and urban transport network. Meanwhile, this concept promoted the application of innovative transport modes into the urban freight systems (e.g., autonomous vehicles and delivery drones), which challenge the network structure of conventional urban freight transport.

The impacts of spatial development on conventional urban freight network are particularly noticeable in large and megacities. As urban freight transport's long-term planning is rarely considered, which leads the logistics providers to employ short-term solutions to respond to urban challenges. These solutions include infrastructure expansions, freight fleets increasing, construction of the multi-tier urban freight system, etc. Although these solutions can improve the current city logistics system's performance in the short-term, they exacerbate the land-use conflict from the long-term view between the city and freight. This observation implies that these solutions are barriers to the sustainable transition for future large cities and megacities. In fact, urban freight transport strategy should be embedded in an overall sustainable development strategy with a long-term perspective (approximately 20–30 years). Therefore, the long-term planning of urban freight transport needs to consider large and megacities' tendencies systematically. Additionally, urban logistics providers intend to use distribution innovations to reduce the negative environmental externalities created by freight activities within urban areas, thereby promoting the transformation of sustainable urban freight transport. Nevertheless, they have paid less attention to the integrations of distribution innovations that operate together as a system and their impacts on the conventional urban freight system in large and megacities. Indeed, the integration of distribution innovations has increasingly become the endogenous trends of urban freight system. This integration has also challenged the network structure of the conventional urban freight network. Consequently, the long-term planning of sustainable urban freight transport needs to consider the trend extrapolations of large/megacities and the integration of distribution innovations, thereby designing an innovative urban freight network structure to respond to the future challenges.

The literature evidence reveals that the foresight research of sustainable urban freight transport is still lacking. Additionally, a considerable body of research has paid scant attention to the links between city development and urban freight planning, and the integration of urban distribution innovations. Given that, this work contributes to the closure of these gaps. The research methodology is composed of four steps are presented below: First, the method of the systematical literature review is used to identify the research gaps between the urban freight network design and urban distribution innovations, thereby developing the research framework. Subsequently, selecting the appropriate foresight research methods is adopted to strengthen the research framework. After that, the GE multifactorial analysis method is employed to discuss the applied status of eleven distribution innovations from the academic and enterprise dimensions. The concept of sustainable inner-urban intermodal transportation is proposed. Based on the above steps, morphological analysis is used to discuss both integrations of distribution innovations, namely operational integration and technological integration. Finally, the 2.x modular-sustainable urban freight system is developed to improve the flexibility and sustainability of future urban freight network.

This work is one of the studies that first integrated urban development and distribution innovations, providing a deep understanding of the long-term planning of sustainable urban freight transport. Concurrently, the 2.x-tier modular & sustainable urban freight network (2.x MSUFN) provides a systematical planning scheme for the sustainable transition of the conventional urban freight system.

Keywords: Sustainable urban freight transport, urban freight network design, urban distribution innovations, large city, megacity, urban spatial development, foresight research, morphological analysis, flexibility, sustainability

Contents

Abbreviations

2.x MSUFN	2.x-tier modular & sustainable urban freight network
AVs	Autonomous vehicles
CBs	Cargo-bikes
CL	City logistics
CLC	City logistics center
DDs	Delivery drones
DIs	Distribution innovations
DRs	Delivery robots
EVs	Electric vehicles
FS	Floating ship
LDPC	Last-mile delivery process of co-operation
LDPF	Last-mile delivery process of first-tier
LDPS	Last-mile delivery process of second-tier
MA	Morphological analysis
MD	Mobile depot
MEVs	Modular electric vehicles
PLs	Parcel lockers
SIUIT	Sustainable inner-urban intermodal transportation
SUFT	Sustainable urban freight transport
TTP	Transshipment transportation process
UFT	Urban freight transport

List of Figures

List of Tables

Introduction

1

1.1 Motivation of the Thesis

Economic growth necessitates flexible transportation to eases access to resources and trade markets (Rassafi and Vaziri 2005). Meanwhile, transportation is the main component of promoting social-intelligent approaches and economic development (Bamwesigye and Hlavackova 2019). Urban freight transport as the last step of the supply chain, playing a critical role in urban economic growth. Urban freight transport (UFT) has been defined a process and a system to collect, transport, and distribute goods within urban areas. According to the literature overview, some research has defined the term 'City Logistics (CL)' as the process for optimizing urban freight activities by stakeholders; it aims to decrease the primary negative of freight activities and balance the links with urban economic scale (e.g., Taniguchi et al. 1999; Taniguchi 2015; Savelsbergh and Van Woensel 2016). Nevertheless, a majority of scholars use the terms CL and UFT interchangeably, and their definitions are the same (e.g., Lagorio et al. 2016; Neghabadi et al. 2016). Moreover, the synonyms of UFT are also frequently used in this research field (e.g., urban logistics, city freight). In this work, the definition of UFT and CL is a process or a system describing freight activities within an urban enviornment.

In recent years, the notion of 'smart city' has increasingly become a popular topic in the academic field. This concept has arisen as a solution to improve the sustainability and liveability of cities based on the effective urban management of governance, energy, and transportation (Hammad et al. 2019; Ferraris et al. 2018). Considerable research focuses on applying innovative urban mobilities (e.g., autonomous vehicles and drones) to promote sustainable urban transport for smart cities. Although the smart city is based on the development of information and communications technology (ICT) and the internet of things (IoT), it also influences the urban spatial

© The Author(s), under exclusive license to Springer Fachmedien Wiesbaden GmbH, part of Springer Nature 2021
Z. He, *Future Sustainable Urban Freight Network Design in the Large Cities and Megacities*, Sustainable Management, Wertschöpfung und Effizienz, https://doi.org/10.1007/978-3-658-34203-6_1

development simultaneously. For example, it influences the zones, infrastructure allocations, and urban transport networks (Hammad et al. 2019; Tobey et al. 2019). The above analyses highlight that smart city's progress has challenged the urban spatial development and existed transportation network. It also implies that emerging transport modes and urban spatial development influence the performance of conventional urban freight transport, particularly on a long-term view. To this end, developing sustainable urban freight strategy remains a popular topic in the academic field.

The urban freight strategies can improve overall efficiency while mitigating negative externalities such as congestion and pollution (Rodrigue et al. 2016). Despite urban freight activities have continually contributed to cities' economic growth, they have created some adverse environmental impacts within urban areas. These negative externalities primarily consist of air pollution, congestion, and noise (Anderson et al. 2005; Wittlöv 2012). In fact, cities are responsible for more than 70% of global carbon dioxide emissions (UN-Habitat 2016), almost 5.5% of the total annual greenhouse gas emissions are generated by the logistics and transport sectors, around 57% of which are caused by road freight transport (Doherty and Hoyle 2009). To this end, some local authorities attempt to formulate/promote several new agenda for reducing the emission within urban areas. An example is that the European Commission calls for halving the use of "conventionally-fuelled" cars in urban transport by 2030, "phasing them out in cities by 2050" and essentially achieving "CO_2-free city logistics in major urban centers by 203" (European Commission 2011). The policy-supporting implies that green city logistics is a critical component for future urban construction. Additionally, congestion is also a major issue created by urban freight. The urban logistics vehicles account of 10–15% of vehicles equivalent miles traveled on urban streets (ALICE/ERTRAC Urban mobility WG 2015). Of these vehicles, only 42.6% of the miles traveled were full load, and approximately 25% were entirely or half-empty loaded (Bureau of Transportation and Statistics, Research and Innovation Technology 2009). These data reveal that the negative environmental externalities have primarily around the urban delivery vehicles and operation model. For responding to these externalities, urban logistics providers are intent on finding an appropriate internal approach to reduce these externalities. Besides optimizing operational strategy and improving the business model, applied distribution innovations are an efficient solution in promoting sustainable urban freight transport.

Urban distribution innovations refer to apply the emerging transport modes for developing new operational strategies and delivery concepts (He and Haasis 2019). For example, the usage of electric vehicles is capable of reducing the emission, thereby achieving the CO_2-free city logistics; The application of cargo-bikes contributes to relieving the congestion and emission in the last-mile delivery. Changing conventional freight modes is a central approach for city logistics providers to decrease the negative environmental externalities created by UFT. Besides the application of emerging transport modes, the providers have used ICT solutions and unit consolidation transportation to improve the sustainability of urban freight transport. ICT solution refers to the usage of internet communication technology to design new delivery strategies. An example is Wang Wang (2015) proposed a new city logistics service model based on cloud computing and mobile internet. Units consolidation transportation means that logistics providers consolidate urban commodities between the various companies and then deliver to consumers, but this consolidation is out of the urban consolidation center (UCC). In recent years, this topic has received more attention (e.g., Cepolina (2016); Lewandowski (2014); Moutaoukil et al. (2015)). Even though the fact that the extensive application of distribution innovations is an efficient solution for the logistics providers, these applications have radically influenced the conventional structure of urban freight network in the view of long-term planning. Meanwhile, urban development has also challenged the conventional urban freight system, as mentioned previously.

City and urban freight maintain a set of core relations, as the city is an entity where production, distribution, and consumption movements are used and compete for scarce land (Rodrigue et al. 2016). Nevertheless, a considerable body of research has paid scant attention to the connections between city development and urban freight planning (Cui et al. 2015). Indeed, the tendencies of urban development have exacerbated the challenges of city logistics system, particularly on the large and megacities around the world. These trends include urbanization, urban population growth, aging population increase, etc. All of these tendencies have been created by the rapid growth of the urban population. Meanwhile, urban population growth has also created the persistent issues and emerging urban challenges that are consist of urban growth, change in family patterns, increased residency in slums and informal settlements, challenges in providing urban service, climate change, exclusion, and rising inequality, insecurity, as well as the upsurge in international migration (UN-Habitat 2016). Although the fact that considerable research has considered the impacts of urban population growth on the city logistics system, from a long-term view, the links between urban development trends and city logistics planning are rarely considered.

It is noted that considerable research has paid more attention to the short-term planning of urban freight transport. However, the urban freight transport strategy should be embedded in an overall sustainable development strategy with a long-term perspective (approximately 20–30 years) (Wolfram 2004). From a long-term perspective, the exogenous trend (urban spatial development) is a barrier to the flexibility of conventional urban freight network, partially due to the city logistics providers use short-term solutions to respond to these trends. An example is that constructing more terminal/depots within urban areas or increasing the freight fleets to cope with delivery range growth created by urban sprawl. The distribution innovations, as the endogenous trends, can efficiently decrease the negative environmental externalities, thereby promoting sustainable urban freight transport. From a view of long-term planning, the integration of various distribution innovations that operated together as a system also radically influences the conventional structure of urban freight network. This observation implies that the foresight research on future sustainable urban freight system needs to comprehensively consider the exogenous and endogenous trends and their impact on the conventional urban freight network structure. The long-term planning of city logistics is capable of further promoting the flexibility and sustainability of future urban freight system. Nevertheless, the future urban freight network design has received less attention, particularly for the large and megacities. Given that, this work aims to contribute to addressing this gap. Figure 1.1 depicts the main aspects that motivate this research, and the relationship among them.

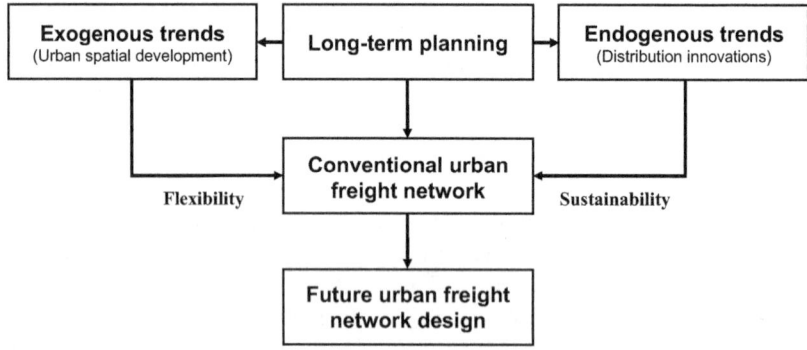

Figure 1.1 Research motivation

Why choose sustainable urban freight transport?
In the recent decade, sustainability is a popular topic in the research field of UFT. The term 'sustainable development' first gained significant prominence in the report *Our Common Future* (Brundtland Report) published by the *World Commission on Environment and Development*. The definition of sustainable development is "a development that meets the needs of the present without compromising the ability

of future generations to meet their own needs" (Brundtland et al. 1987). The dimensions of sustainability primarily include economic (e.g., economic performance), environmental (e.g., emissions, transport), and social (e.g., public policy, customer privacy) (Global Reporting Initiative 2013). Figure 1.2 depicts the concept and principles of sustainable development based on these three dimensions. The definition of sustainable urban transport includes six principles (May et al. 2001) that as following: (1) economic efficiency; (2)liveable streets and neighborhoods; (3) protection of the environment; (4) equity and social inclusion; (5) safety; and (6) contribution to economic growth.

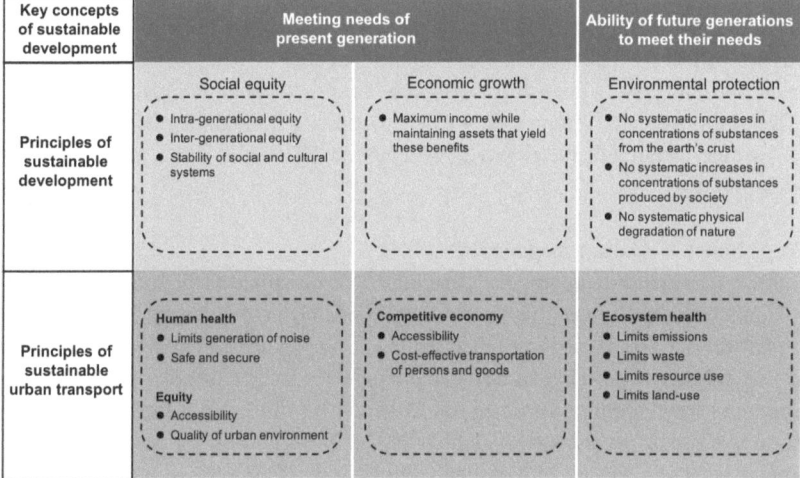

Figure 1.2 Concept & principles of sustainable development and sustainable urban transport. (Source: Adapted from Behrends et al. (2008))

As widely recognized that Urban transport is composed of passenger and freight transport. For sustainable development, UFT is one of the primary problems for cities to achieve sustainability due to cities' efforts to address the impacts that are often limited to urban and traffic planning (Behrends et al. 2008). Therefore, the approaches to sustainable urban freight transport (SUFT) have to go beyond strategic urban planning (Behrends et al. 2008). However, what is the definition of sustainable urban freight transport (SUFT) in the academical? Behrends et al. (2008) has defined that a SUFT system needs to fulfills all the following objectives:

- "to ensure the accessibility offered by the transport system to all categories of freight transport;
- to reduce air pollution, green house gas emissions, waste and noise to levels without negative impacts on the health of the citizens or nature;
- to improve the resource- and energy-efficiency and cost-effectiveness of the transportation of goods, taking into account the external costs and;
- to contribute to the enhancement of the attractiveness and quality of the urban environment, by avoiding accidents, minimising the use of land and without compromising the mobility of citizens."

Owing to city planning is focused principally on passenger transport, sustainable development measures mainly focus on passenger transport (Behrends et al. 2008). It led to that the freight transport issues at the city level are still not well understood, not quantified, and there is no methodology aimed explicitly at the analysis and planning of freight movements (Crainic et al. 2004; Behrends et al. 2008). Consequently, to achieve the sustainable development of cities, SUFT should take a long-term view of planning.

Why choose large and megacities?
Followed the urban demographic scale, the city is classified as the four types: small, medium, large, and megacity (metropolis). In which, large cities are defined as having between 5 and 10 million inhabitants and megacities as having 10 million or more inhabitants (UN-Habitat 2016). In recent decades, the urban population keeps a growing trend around the world. By 2015, 54% (4 billion) of the world's population lived in urban areas (UN-Habitat 2016). Nevertheless, by 2030, the world's urban population will reach more than 5 billion; by 2050, 68% of the world's population is projected to be living in the city (UN DESA 2018). The reason is city creates more employment opportunities, better conditions on health care and education, improved quality of life, as well as the perfect infrastructure, which have continuously motivated the people to migrate to the city. It leads to the numbers of both large and megacity worldwide appeared the distinctly rose. By 2015, both categories of the cities were 44 large cities, and 29 megacities (UN-Habitat 2016); by 2030, the world is projected to have 43 megacities(UN DESA 2018).

As mentioned previously, urban population growth has motivated city development while created persistent issues and challenges. With this in view, large and megacities will be confronted with more challenges and issues created by the urban population growth. For city logistics, the urban population ratio has maintained a degree of proportionality with the logistics performance index (LPI) (Rodrigue et al. 2016). This relation intimates that the trends of urban development created by the urban population growth have challenged the city logistics performance index. This challenge is exceptionally conspicuous in large and megacities.

Additionally, UN-Habitat (2016) has indicated that the large and megacities are, in some ways, leading edge of urbanization. This report also mentioned that "more dispersed patterns of urbanization in the form of suburbanization, peri-urbanization, or urban sprawl have constituted a significant trend over the last two decades." This trend has aggravated the challenges of city logistics in large and megacities in the long-term view. City logistics providers commonly employ short-term solutions to respond to these challenges, such as infrastructure (terminal/depot) expansion and freight fleets increase. Although the fact that these solutions can short-term increase both delivery frequency and distribution range within urban areas, they are in some ways to restrict the flexibility of the urban freight system from a view of long-term. Concurrently, these short-term solutions also aggravate the land-use conflict between the city and freight in the future large and megacities. Therefore, city logistics in large and megacities are urgent need a systematical strategy of long-term planning to cope with the future challenges of urban spatial development.

It is noteworthy that large and megacities are enormously influential in the global economy (UN-Habitat 2016). By 2016, the top 600 cities with a fifth of the world's population that generate 60% of global GDP (Dobbs et al. 2011). As a result of the city and freight maintaining a set of core relations (Rodrigue et al. 2016), the capability of city logistics influences urban economic growth and residential environment. Accordingly, long-term planning of city logistics on large and megacities can contribute to the urban economic growth and strengthen its global competitiveness.

Why choose network design?

For urban logistics, the network structure in large and megacities is distinct from that in small or medium-sized cities. Indeed, conventional urban freight network includes two types: the single-tier system and the two-tier system. The former refers to delivery circuits performed directly from the city logistics center (CLC), as depicted by Figure 1.3. The two-tier system constructed by the two components: CLC and shipping terminal/depot (Figure 1.3). The CLC constitutes the first tier of UFT and located in the urban suburbs. The second tier is formed by shipping terminals/depots, where the freight is coming from the CLCs. This process defined as transshipment transportation (Line-haul transportation) (Ehmke 2012). In terminal/depot, the goods from other external points possibly are transferred to and consolidated into vehicles that are adapted for utilization in dense city zones (Benjelloun and Crainic 2009). After the transshipment transportation, city logistics service providers pick up the commodities and deliver them to customers in terms of last-mile delivery (Ehmke 2012). In last-mile delivery, the shipping terminal/depot commonly uses the vehicles of relatively small capacity that can travel along any street in the city areas (Benjelloun and Crainic 2009; Ehmke 2012).

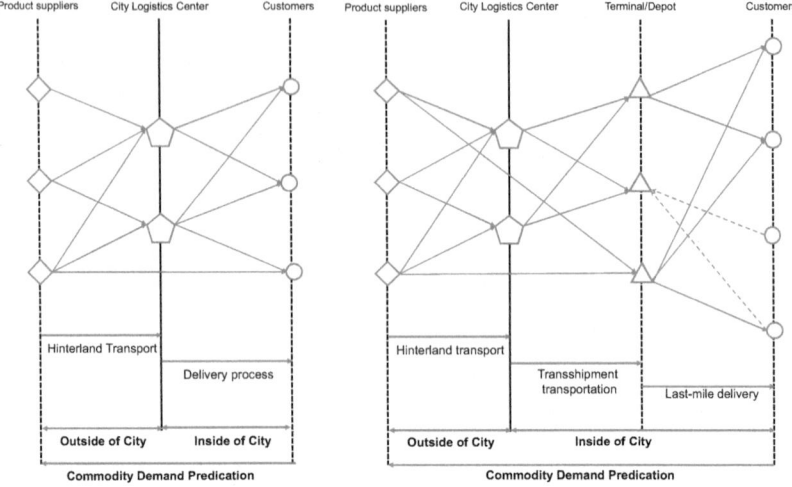

Figure 1.3 Single-tier & two-tier of urban freight system. (Based on Benjelloun and Crainic (2009); Ehmke (2012))

The single-tier system is regularly used in small or medium-sized cities, and the two-tier system is more suitable for large/megacity (Dablanc 2007; Benjelloun and Crainic 2009). The urban population density and urban delivery range are the main reference factors for the system selection. In the large/megacity, the single-tier system is incapable of satisfying the delivery demand and reducing the environmental externalities caused by freight activities, particularly in the aspects of congestion and contamination. Therefore, the logistics providers commonly adopt the two-tier system in the large and megacities. Additionally, the conventional freight network owned high stability. With the logistics expansion and urban sprawl, this feature increasingly appeared inflexibility and unsustainability in the aspect of the structural regulation. In recent decades, urban development and technological innovations have radically influenced the freight demands and logistics service requirements in city areas. For instance, urbanization has caused the urban sprawl to increase the urban delivery range, the rapid growth of the urban population increases the freight demands, and consumers' behavior changed (as B2C) requires efficiency and security of delivery. These exogenous challenges have aggravated the conflict between stability and inflexibility in urban freight network structure.

As mentioned previously, city logistics providers commonly employ short-term solutions to respond to these exogenous trends. In large and megacities, these solutions are generally based on the two-tier urban freight network. It is foreseeable that the conventional urban freight network is increasingly inflexible if increasing the number of second-tier infrastructures and freight fleets. From the view of economic sustainability, these solutions increase the operational costs that remain a barrier to further promoting sustainable urban logistics. Given this, an innovative network structure of SUFT should comprehensively take exogenous trends based on the long-term perspective. Despite the usage of urban distribution innovations is an efficient solution for logistics providers to reduce environmental externalities, the dispersed applications of distribution innovations challenge the conventional network structure. To this end, urban distribution innovations were discussed further in the following paragraphs.

Why choose urban distribution innovations?
The negative environmental externalities are primarily caused by transport vehicles. Consequently, logistics providers attempt to utilize emerging transport vehicles to reduce these externalities, thereby promoting environmental sustainability. For example, the extensive application of electric vehicles is able to decrease the emissions within urban areas; the project of delivery drones aims to reduce the congestion and to provide individualization logistics service. Although the fact that the implementations of distribution innovations are efficient solutions for promoting sustainable development, these applications have changed the urban delivery model and the conventional network structure of UFT. An example is *Yamato Transport Co.* (Japan) has been using a tram system for delivering goods to Arashiyama in Kyoto (Kikuta et al. 2012). Indeed, the model of "Road-tram-Road" is a three-tier system (Benjelloun and Crainic 2009). In this instance, the urban freight tram is operated with the cargo-bikes that is responsible for carrying goods to customers in last-mile delivery. This emerging freight model is based on the integration of different distribution innovations. The superiority of this integration is combining the merits of each innovation to improve logistics performance.

Indeed, logistics providers and technology companies have launched integration projects between different urban distribution innovations. For instance, *DHL*

Express piloted the *City Hub* concept (2017) that is the vehicles combined with a customized trailer carrying up to four containers, then use of DHL Cubicycles (a cargo-bike able to carry a container) to complete last-mile delivery (Deutsche Post DHL Group 2017). *Workhorse Group* have developed the *HorseFly UAV Delivery* system that is fully integrating with the electric/hybrid delivery trucks, while UPS has tested residential delivery with Drone launched from Atop Package Car (Workhorse Group 2016). Besides this operational integration, considerable technology enterprises have launched the projects of emerging urban freight vehicles. An example is *ZF Friedrichshafen AG* (Germany) proposed *Autonomous Depot* that is a robotic vehicle equipped with the parcel lockers The previous examples indicate that conventional trucks or vans are not the main transport modes in future urban logistics. Nevertheless, considerable research has paid scant attention to the impacts of these integrations on the urban freight network structure. Consequently, it is vital to consider the transformation of transport modes comprehensively for the long-term planning of SUFT.

1.2   Research Questions

Although the fact that SUFT is a popular topic in the research field of city logistics, much research is based on the conventional urban freight network to resolve short-term problems. As mentioned previously, urban spatial development has challenged the performance of city logistics, particularly on the large and megacities around the world. Nevertheless, much less research has paid attention to the connections between urban development and city logistics planning (Cui et al. 2015). For responding to the urban challenges, the logistics providers in large and megacities commonly used short-term solutions in the conventional urban freight network. This observation reveals that logistics providers lack an integrated consideration of the urban spatial development and the urban freight network structure.

Additionally, the sustainable strategies of UFT generally employ emerging transport modes to reduce the environmental externalities created by freight activities. However, considerable research has paid scant attention to the integration of urban distribution innovations and their impacts on urban freight network structure. The above discussion identified that the research of SUFT lacks long-term planning on the network design, particularly for the large and megacities. To closure of this gap, this work aims to resolve the main research question as follows:

> *How to design a sustainable and flexible urban freight network to face future challenges in the large and megacities?*

With the aim of answering this question, further research issues need to be considered as listed below.

- What are the main topics that have been considered in the different network structures, and which topic involves distribution innovations?
- What distribution innovations have been researched in transshipment transportation and last-mile delivery?
- What is the relevance of the main topics on freight network design and distribution innovations?
- How to further promote sustainable urban freight network in future research?
- What is the stat of the art on foresight research, and which methods are suitable for the research of future sustainable urban freight transport?
- What are the exogenous and endogenous trends of SUFT?
- How to select appropriate methods for the long-term planning of SUFT?
- How to conduct the long-term planning of sustainable urban freight transport from future perspectives?
- What is the status of the applications and research of these innovations in sustainable urban freight transport?
- What are the restrictions and suitability of these innovations in urban freight transport?
- What is the future transport model in urban freight system?
- What are the future trends of large/megacities and their impacts on future urban freight system?
- What are the future trends of UFT and their impacts on urban freight network structure?
- How to combine and select distribution innovations to design appropriate freight strategies?
- How to design the network structure of urban freight system to promote its sustainability and flexibility further?

1.3   Guideline of the Research Methodology

To respond to the aforementioned research questions, this work adopts a qualitative approach to integrate multiple disciplines in a unified framework focusing on the conceptual, freight network structure and delivery strategy, while legislative and policy issues are not considered. Figure 1.4 shows the mix methods that have been used to accomplish the present research.

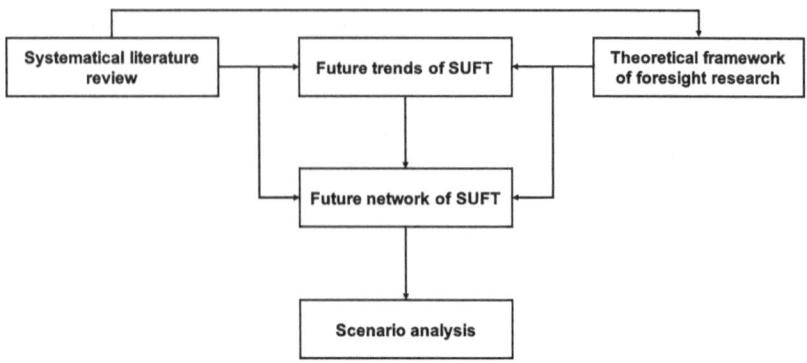

Figure 1.4 Research methodology mix

a) Systematic Literature Review
The systematic literature review (SLR) is one of the primary research methods in
this work. This method intends to identify the key concepts, possible research gaps,
and potential methodologies concerning the primary areas of interest for this work,
such as urban freight network planning, urban distribution innovations, and foresight
research methods. This work uses the Scopus database to detect the relevant articles
(conference and journal papers) that are published in the period of 2013–2018. As
mentioned before, the logistics providers are intended to find the appropriate internal approaches to accommodate the exogenous trends of urban spatial developm ent
and to enhance environmental sustainability. Despite the application of distribution
innovation is an efficient internal approach, the impacts of these innovations on the
conventional urban freight network are needed to analyze further. For this reason,
understanding the existing research gaps between the papers of urban freight network planning and distribution innovations is the critical component of promoting
this research. According to the identified research gaps, the research framework is
developed.

b) Theoretical Framework of Foresight Research
This research aims to develop long-term planning for sustainable urban logistics,
which connects to the field of foresight research. For addressing the central question, the appropriate methods of foresight research need to be selected for this work.
According to the general framework of foresight research, the theoretical framework
of foresight research on SUFT is designed by an integrated analysis between foresight methods and SUFT.

c) Future Trends of SUFT

The sort of distribution innovations is identified by the systematic literature review. After that, the innovations are summarized, discussed, and analyzed under the research framework, thereby developing the future freight models of SUFT. The objective of this step is to understand the feasible freight model for future SUFT.

d) Future Network of SUFT

Based on the developed model in the previous step, the selected research method is used to discuss further the integration of distribution innovation. Subsequently, the future urban freight network is designed through a comprehensive analysis of the future spatial tendencies on large and megacities.

e) Scenario Analysis

This step aims to evaluate the developed network model. Due to this work is based on the future perspective, scenario analysis is a suitable method for the evaluation. According to the scenario definition, three scenarios in the example city has set that correspond to three time-dimensions (now, 15 years later, and 30 years later). The control group is the conventional urban freight system in the example city. Followed the horizontal comparison between three time-dimensions, the future network model has systematically evaluated and further discussed it.

1.4   Thesis Structure According to the Research Questions

Chapter 1 introduces the motivations behind this work, the research questions, and the brief description of the methodologies used to address those questions. Chapter 2 describes state of the art resulted from the systematical literature review of urban freight network design and urban distribution innovations. According to the identified research gaps, the research framework has been developed to address the central research question. Chapter 3 presents the theoretical framework of foresight research on SUFT based on the previous chapter. The appropriate research methods have been selected and discussed to investigate the future urban freight network. Chapter 4 discusses the applied status of urban distribution innovations and their implemented restrictions. Following the discussion, the conceptual model of sustainable inner-urban intermodal transportation (SIUIT) was developed for the future urban freight system. Chapter 5 demonstrates the operational integration of distribution innovations. The morphological analysis has been used to determine the possible solutions for this integration. Connecting with the future spatial development on large and megacities, the model of 2.x modular-sustainable urban freight network has been designed. Chapter 6 indicates scenario analysis to analyze and evaluate the developed model, then the future research directions and limitations were discussed. In the end, Chapter 7 addresses the conclusions from this work.

Systematic Literature Review

2

2.1   Logical Arrangement of the Chapter

This chapter provides a systematic literature review with aspects of the network planning of UFT and urban distribution innovations. As mentioned previously, the logistics providers are intended to find appropriate internal approaches to accommodate with the exogenous trends as well as to reduce negative environmental externalities created by freight activities. The application of urban distribution innovation is an efficient solution for achieving these purposes of logistics providers. Despite the fact that multiple emerging transport modes have been used in the urban freight system, the accurate definition of term *distribution innovations* remains lacking. Additionally, the impacts of distribution innovations on conventional urban freight networks have received scant attention in the research field of SUFT. Therefore, a systematic literature review is essential to address these questions. Figure 2.1 depicts the logical structure of this chapter.

This chapter was published as an article[1] in the *International Journal of Physical Distribution and Logistics Management*. The content exposed in this chapter aims to resolve three sub-questions of this work as below:

- What are the main topics that have been considered in the different network structures, and which topic involves distribution innovations?
- What distribution innovations have been researched in transshipment transportation and last-mile delivery?

---

[1]He, Z (2020). The Challenges in Sustainability of Urban Freight Network Design and Distribution Innovations: A Systematic Literature Review, *International Journal of Physical Distribution and Logistics Management*, vol. 50 no. 6, pp. 601-640. https://doi.org/10.1108/IJPDLM-05-2019-0154, © Emerald Publishing Limited 2020

© The Author(s), under exclusive license to Springer Fachmedien Wiesbaden GmbH,   15
part of Springer Nature 2021
Z. He, *Future Sustainable Urban Freight Network Design in the Large Cities and Megacities*, Sustainable Management, Wertschöpfung und Effizienz,
https://doi.org/10.1007/978-3-658-34203-6_2

- What is the relevance of the main topics on freight network design and distribution innovations?
- How to further promote the sustainable urban freight network in future research?

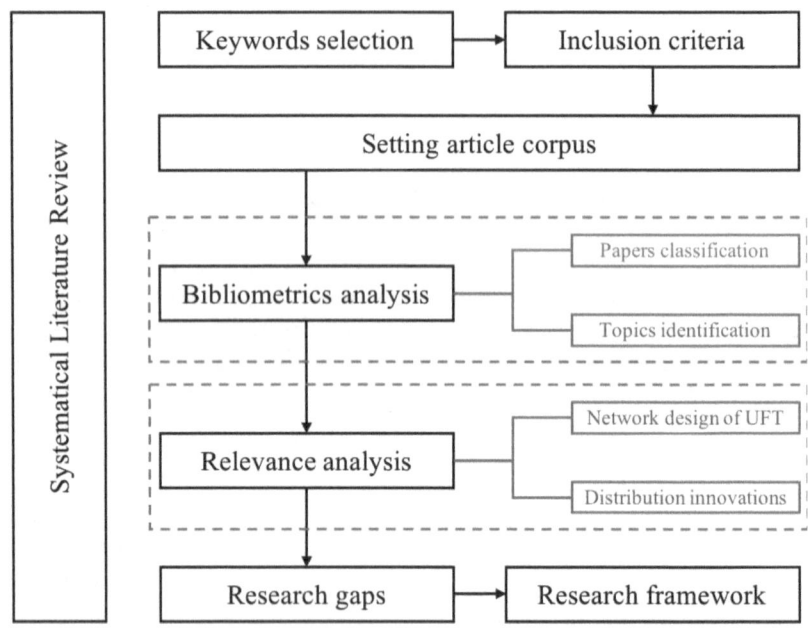

Figure 2.1 Structure of Chapter 2

This chapter presents the core content of the published paper. this chapter is organized as below: Section 2.2 introduces the research background and motivations of this chapter. Section 2.3 is the research question of this chapter, and the methodology is based on the general framework of SLR. Section 2.4 followed the approach of SLR to classified the article corpus to the two groups: urban freight network design and urban distribution innovations. Meanwhile, the main topics of these two groups are distinguished separately. Subsequently, the relevance analysis is conducted between the main topics of these two article groups through cross-recognition. Section 2.5 exposed the main research gaps between these two article groups and developed the research framework for promoting the sustainability and flexibility of UFT. Section 2.6 is the conclusion of this chapter.

Freight network design and the distribution innovations' application are popular topics for sustainable urban logistics research. Nevertheless, consideration studies of freight network design have paid scant attention to the various distribution innovations. This observation reveals that sustainable urban freight research appears highly fragmented in these two topics: freight network design and distribution innovations. From a long-term view, this situation may limit further promotion of sustainability. This chapter aims to identify research gaps of literature to formulate the research framework of future sustainable urban logistics. To this end, a systematic literature review (SLR) method is used to analyze 164 papers and research works published in 2013–2018. The article corpus involved the innovative schemes of freight network design and the emerging delivery concepts in cities. According to the cross-relevance analysis of collected articles, the most significant research contributions on city logistics network design and the exploitation of distribution innovations are detected. Finally, four research gaps are identified, and the research framework of sustainable and flexible future urban freight planning (SFFUFP) is constructed through the integrated consideration of urban spatial development.

2.2   Introduction

The previous chapter mentions that the conventional urban freight system includes two types: single-tier and two-tier system (Benjelloun and Crainic 2009; Gragnani et al. 2004). The single-tier system is often used in small or medium-sized cities, and another one is more suitable for large or megacities (Dablanc 2007; Benjelloun and Crainic 2009). The relevant literature evidence demonstrates that considerable research focuses on the usage of urban distribution innovations to promote sustainability of urban freight transport. urban distribution innovation refers to adopting the emerging transport modes (e.g. delivery drones, freight tram.) to distribute goods within the urban areas, rather than only using conventional urban freight vehicles (i.e., fuel consumption truck/vans) (He and Haasis 2019). Meanwhile, a considerable body of studies focus on using these innovations in the one or two processes of the conventional urban freight network to reduce the negative environmental externalities (e.g., emission, congestions, and noise). Despite the fragmented application of these innovations that can improve sustainability in the short-term, from a long-term perspective, these innovations operate together as a system that challenged the network structure of conventional urban freight transport. An example is that the urban freight tram transforms the two-tier urban freight system into a partial three-tier system passively, as this innovation requires building/transforming the public transit station to integrate the passenger and freight flow in the urban logistics network. However, this requirement is possible to exacerbate the land-use conflicts and changes the stakeholders' structure.

Additionally, the future sustainable urban logistics system is impossible to implement only one or two emerging transport modes. The previous discussions reveal that the passive transformation of the urban freight network exacerbates the conflict with the cities from a long-term perspective, caused by the fragmented applications of various distribution innovations. Consequently, sustainable urban freight network design has to systematically consider the impacts of the integrated operation of various distribution innovations. Hence, it is essential to understand which distribution innovations are considered in the existing studies of urban freight network design and the relevant research gaps. Hence, it is essential to understand which distribution innovations are considered in the existing studies of urban freight network design and the relevant research gaps. This effort contributes to promoting the long-term planning of sustainable urban freight transport.

For understanding the relevant research gaps, a systematic literature review is an appropriate method. Concurrently, it is also the first step to investigate the long-term planning of SUFT. However, to the best of my knowledge, there is no such research to discussing the research gaps between the urban freight network design and distribution innovations. Although urban freight network design and distribution innovations have been addressed in a growing number of journal publications, an overview of research focusing on these two topics and systematic cross-analysis is lacking. Additionally, the existing literature review papers of city logistics did not systematically discuss these two topics simultaneously. For instance, Björklund and Johansson (2018) have discussed the papers related to urban consolidation center (UCC) and the future research directions; Rose et al. (2017) used the systematic literature review method to analyze the research gaps between urban research and city logistics studies; Lagorio et al. (2016) contributed a systematic analysis of the scientific articles that address urban logistics from a logistics and management perspective; Furthermore, the literature evidence demonstrates that a systematic cross-analysis is lacking between the research topics of urban freight network design and distribution innovations. Therefore, this chapter uses the systematical literature review (SLR) method to understand the relevant research gaps.

With this in view, this chapter employs the method of systematical literature review (SLR) to address this gap. Collecting information is from 164 papers published in the period 2013 to 2018. This chapter provides an overview of the main topics regarding network design and distribution innovations.

2.3   Research Questions & Methodology

This chapter aims to investigate the existing research gaps between the research in urban freight network design and distribution innovations. The research questions includes:

- RQ.1. what are the main topics that have been considered in the different network structures, and which topic involves distribution innovations?
- RQ.2. what distribution innovations have been researched in transshipment transportation and last-mile delivery?
- RQ.3. What is the relevance of the main topics on freight network design and distribution innovations?
- RQ.4. How to further promote sustainable urban freight network in future research?

The systematic literature review (SLR) is used as the research method to judge trends and detect existing gaps in the scientific literature given the character of the research questions. Figure 2.2 is the research methodology of this chapter, which is use the experiences of Lagorio et al. (2016), Neghabadi et al. (2016), Khan et al. (2003), Denyer and Tranfield (2009); Kupiainen et al. (2015). The research methodology is consist of five steps:

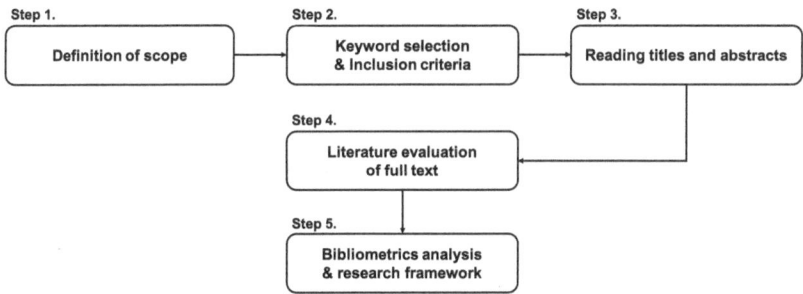

Figure 2.2 Research methodology. (Based on Lagorio et al. (2016) and Neghabadi et al. (2016))

Step 1. Definition of scope: First, this research has selected the Scopus database as the article source. The primary keywords consist principal research direction and diverse synonyms, e.g., urban freight transport, urban logistics, and city logistics. Additionally, selecting the papers and research works published in the field of logistics, transportation, and economics from 2013 to 2018.

Step 2. Keyword selection and inclusion criterion: the related keywords were identified and selected based on the Step 1, which comprise city logistics, urban logistics, network design, distribution innovations, last-mile delivery, and so on. Moreover, the keyword scope and the year of publication build the inclusion criteria. The literature is searched based on Table 2.1.

Table 2.1 Article selection

Items	Descripition
Main Keywords	Urban freight transport, city logistics, urban logistics, urban freight, urban delivery, distribution innovations, network design, transshipment transportation, line-haul transportation, last-mile delivery
Inclusion criteria	Transportation, Economic, Management
Language	English
Document types	Journal Articles & Conference Papers
Source	Scopus
Time interval	2013–2018

Step 3. Reading titles and abstract: followed the previous steps, more than 300 articles satisfy the inclusion criteria. Nevertheless, partial research are not related to the topic of urban freight network design or distribution innovations. Additionally, some articles have instead concentrated on the specific issues (e.g., health, social perspectives, and urban planning), which are also removed.

Step 4. Full text evaluation: after evaluating the full text of collected articles, 164 papers match the research purpose and requirements, constructing the article corpus. According to preliminary statistics, 58 articles are related to urban freight network design, and 106 papers have investigated urban distribution innovations.

Step 5. Bibliometrics analysis and gap identify: the main topics on the freight network design and distribution innovations are discussed separately. After the discussion, this study analyze the relevance of the main topics. Meanwhile, the intersection and gaps are discussed. According to the identified research gaps, the future research directions are discussed.

2.4 Bibliometrics Analysis

2.4.1 Descriptive Analysis and Classification of Papers

As mentioned previsouly, the article corpus is constructed by 164 papers. Figure 2.3 presents the distribution of the papers by year in the corpus. Despite the fluctuation in 2017, it is possible to appreciate the stable increase contributions related to urban freight network design and distribution innovations in 2013–2018. The peak in the number of papers was in 2018, when 45 articles covered network design and distribution innovations on urban freight transport. Based on the document types, the searched articles can be classified into two categories: 1) conference papers and 2) articles published in scientific journals. Figure 2.3 shows that the 24 conference papers are published in 2016 that is the peak of conference papers. In contrast, the published peak of journal articles was in 2018, which have 30 related papers.

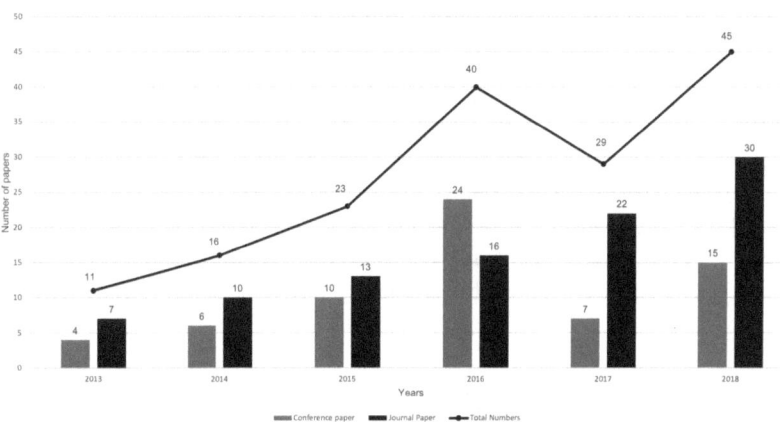

Figure 2.3 Classification of different articles by origin and by year

Additionally, the studies on network design and distribution innovation present a crossing trend. For example, some research has considered integrating the public transit system into the urban freight network design (e.g., Fatnassi et al. (2015); Masson et al. (2017); Liu et al. (2018)). In contrast, the several studies focused on using the public transit system in the transshipment transportation or last-mile delivery. This observation implies that the paper corpus can be classified into the two groups.

The research in freight network design focuses on the entire urban freight network structure, which is not just the one freight process. In fact, these studies mentioned or can be identified the the freight network structure, such as the two-echelon logistics (Li et al. 2018) and two-tier city logistics (Crainic and Sgalambro 2014). In contrast, partial research paid more attention to the last-mile delivery or transshipment transportation, or assessing the potential effectiveness of urban freight solutions in one process. The research perspective of these studies is not the entire urban logistics network structure. Meanwhile, it is challenging to identify the types of freight network structures in their research. Given that, this research defined the two literature groups: article group of distribution innovations is focusing on the application of emerging transport mode in transshipment transportation or last-mile delivery; the papers in group of network design can be identified the type of freight network structure.

Figure 2.4 shows the article's classification framework, which followed a two-stage approach. The first step is to determine whether the relevant literature considers the entire urban freight network structure. After reviewing the research problems of listed papers, the literature corpus can be classified into two article groups: network design and distribution innovations. Figure 2.5 depicts the statistical results of the topic identification. According to the classification, the groups of network design and distribution innovations have 58 articles and 106 papers separately. In the network design group, 60% of papers (35 articles) have paid attention to the two-tier system. In the distribution innovation group, 83% of papers (88 articles) have focused on last-mile delivery. This statistical result highlights that the two-tier system is currently a primary network structure in urban logistic planning, and considerable research has concentrated on the application of distribution innovations in last-mile delivery.

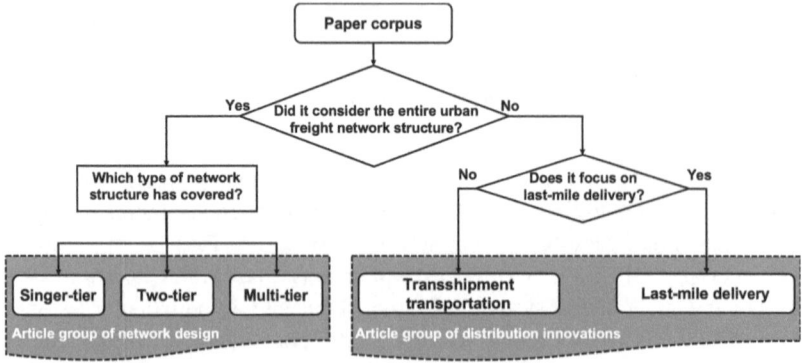

Figure 2.4 The framework of papers classification

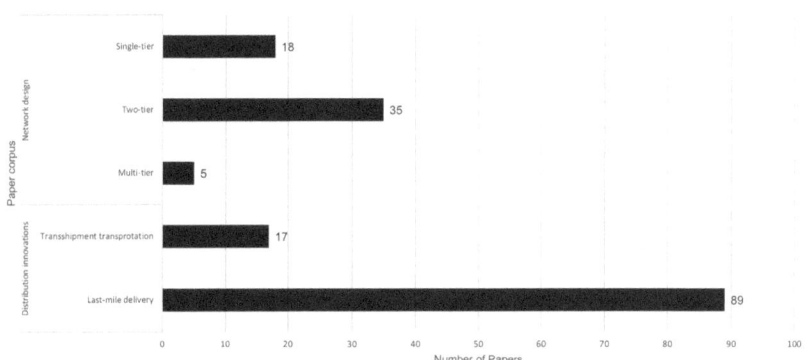

Figure 2.5 The numbers of papers on two groups

2.4.2 Analysis of Papers on Freight Network Design

To responding to RQ.1, the network design articles have performed a classification by the main addressed topics. The vertical dimension includes three kinds of urban freight network structure, and the horizontal dimension is involved in the main addressed topics of the related papers. Table 2.2 demonstrates the primary addressed topics in the article group of network design. It is noteworthy that several studies covered two topics. For example, Yang et al. (2016) analyzed the topics of vehicle-route problem and low emission. Given that, articles involving multiple topics were classified into the corresponding multiple horizontal topics.

The statistical result shows that the two high-frequency topics on network design group are UCC & collaboration and public transit logistics. In the topic of UCC & collaboration, 13 papers are associate with the single-tier system of urban logistics, and only 9 articles have discussed the two-tier system. Although UCC & collaboration are favorite topics in the research field of sustainable urban logistics, UCC strategy is appropriate for medium-sized or small cities (Dablanc 2013). In the article group of network design, related studies have focused on selecting the UCC's location and optimizing the distributed routes.

In recent years, public transit logistics has increasingly become a popular topic. In the literature on this topic, 3 articles involved the multi-tier urban logistics system. For the urban logistics providers, integrating the freight into the urban public transit system is a feasible solution for decreasing traffic congestion and emission. Nevertheless, the public transit logistic radically challenges the conventional urban freight network structure since it requires building/transforming the new public tran-

Table 2.2 Topics in the paper groups of freight network design

Topic	Description	Single-tier	Two-tier	Multi-tier
UCC & Con-solidation	Infrastructures/strategies that allow the consolidation of goods before urban delivery (e.g., urban consolidation center)	Estrada and Roca-Riu (2017); Lin et al. (2016); Asih et al. (2016); Saetta and Caldarelli (2016); Janjevic et al. (2016); Nguyen et al. (2015); Yang et al. (2015); Triantafyllou et al. (2014); Battaia et al. (2014); Daniela et al. (2014); Saragih et al. (2017); Muñoz-Villamizar et al. (2019); Wang et al. (2018)	Paddeu (2017); Wang et al. (2017); Ouhader and El Kyal (2017b,a); Manier et al. (2016); Faccio and Gamberi (2015); Olsson and Woxenius (2014); Lu (2014); Cepolina and Farina (2013)	
LRP solutions	The location routing problem solutions refer to selecting facilities location and optimizing the delivery path of vehicles	Boccia et al. (2018)	Crainic et al. (2015); Gianessi et al. (2015); Li et al. (2018)	Winkenbach et al. (2015)
VRP solutions	The vehicle routing problem refers to the optimization of the route of the individual or a fleet vehicles	Yang et al. (2016)	Nadarajah and Bookbinder (2013); Mancini (2013); Zhou et al. (2018); Anderluh et al. (2017)	
Low emission	Ways to reduce the emission of freight vehicle (i.e. CO_2, NOx and PMx, and acoustic)	Yang et al. (2016)	Browne et al. (2016); Navarro et al. (2016); Saeedi et al. (2018)	Yang and Gao (2015)

(Continued)

Table 2.2 (Continued)

Topic	Description	Single-tier	Two-tier	Multi-tier
Location selection model	Established the mathematical model for selecting the location of the infrastructure	Kuzmenko et al. (2017); Rao et al. (2015)	Pamučar et al. (2016); Lindawati and De Souza (2017)	
Transshipment platform	Infrastructure that shared urban logistic spaces to enable freight transfer between vehicles to access congested/restricted urban areas		De Oliveira et al. (2017); Merchan et al. (2016)	
Public transit logistics	Using bus/subway/tram to transport goods in cities		Shen et al. (2015); Fatnassi et al. (2015); Masson et al. (2017); Dampier and Marinov (2015); Stadkowski et al. (2014); He and Yang (2018); Liu et al. (2018); Pimentel and Alvelos (2018); Zhao et al. (2018)	Nuzzolo and Comi (2015); Behiri et al. (2016); Iannò et al. (2013)
Mobile depot	Mobile Depot is a trailer fitted with a loading dock, warehousing facilities and an office	Arvidsson and Pazirandeh (2017)	Ducret (2014)	
Autonomous vehicles	Usage of driverless vehicles to deliver goods		Scherr et al. (2018a)	

sit station to integrate passenger and freight flow. Additionally, this analysis did not find literature evidence regarding new network structure design.

2.4.3 Analysis of Papers on Urban Distribution Innovations

To respond to RQ.2, The articles of distribution innovations are divided depending on the primary addressed topics. According to Figure 2.4, this group is consists of two vertical dimensions: transshipment transportation and last-mile delivery. Table 2.3 presents the results of the identification of relevant topics. It is noteworthy that some topics have interrelated. An example is the mobile depot studies discussing joint operation with cargo bikes in last-mile delivery. Nevertheless, the literature evidence indicates the integrated operation of multiple distribution innovations (more than 2) lacks a systematic investigation and consideration.

The statistical result demonstrates that the electric vehicle is the highest-frequency topic in the article group of distribution innovations. Three other popular topics include cargo bike, ICT solutions, and public transit logistics. In this article group, almost 30% (32 papers) of papers discussed electric vehicles, 29 articles related to the usage of electric vehicles in the process of last-mile delivery. Moreover, the statistical result shows that the studies of cargo bikes and ICT solutions have focused on last-mile delivery. Concurrently, 12 papers on public transit logistics (92%) discussed its application in transshipment transportation. This observation reveals that partial innovations only can be used in a certain specific process of UFT. Furthermore, most topics in distribution innovations seem not covered in the literature group of network design.

2.4.4 Cross-relevance Analysis of the Topics

The previous discussion exposes that a cross-relevance analysis between the two article groups is necessary. To respond to RQ.3, this research defines the relevant symbols to perform this analysis, as depicted in Table 2.4. Furthermore, the horizontal and vertical topics in both Tables 2.2 and 2.3 are used to build the framework of cross-relevance analysis. After that, the cross-relevances of the two article groups are identified through the full-text evaluation, as indicated by Table 2.5.

The cross-relevance analysis shows that research in urban freight network design has covered five sub-topics of distribution innovations: electric vehicles, public transit logistics, mobile depot, autonomous vehicles, and cargo bikes. However, the

Table 2.3 Topics in the paper corpus of distribution innovations

Topic	Description	Transshipment transportation	Last-mile delivery
Electric vehicles	Applied the E-vehicles to transport the goods in urban areas	Rizet et al. (2016); Lebeau et al. (2015b); Giordano et al. (2018); Teoh et al. (2018); Koháni et al. (2017)	Cagliano et al. (2017); Franceschetti et al. (2017); Taefi et al. (2017); Wątróbski et al. (2017); Cossu (2016); Taefi (2016); Ahani et al. (2016); Lebeau et al. (2016); Schau et al. (2016b); Quak et al. (2016); Rizet et al. (2016); Taefi et al. (2016); Schau et al. (2016a); Liakos et al. (2016); Lebeau et al. (2015b); Lebeau et al. (2015c); Lebeau et al. (2015a); Schau et al. (2015); Taefi et al. (2015); Roumboutsos et al. (2014); Lebeau et al. (2013); Melo et al. (2014); Macharis et al. (2013); Van Duin et al. (2013); Giordano et al. (2018); Teoh et al. (2018); Pelletier et al. (2018); Morganti and Browne (2018); Mirhedayatian and Yan (2018); Muñoz-Villamizar et al. (2019); Lebeau et al. (2018); Koháni et al. (2017)
Modular E-vehicles	The special type of vehicles is used to deliver the goods to consumers by carrying one or multiple cabin modules		Rezgui et al. (2018); Rezgui et al. (2015); Andaloro et al. (2015); Aggoune-Mtalaa et al. (2015)
Public transit logistics	Integrated the passenger and freight activities (i.e., tram, subway, bus)	Kelly and Marinov (2017); De Langhe (2017); Gonzalez-Feliu (2016b); Strale (2014); Wang and Deng (2013); Regué and Bristow (2013); Behiri et al. (2018); Ozturk and Patrick (2018); Gonzalez-Feliu (2016a); Serafini et al. (2018); Dong et al. (2018)	Ewedairo et al. (2018)

(Continued)

Table 2.3 (Continued)

Topic	Description	Transshipment transportation	Last-mile delivery
Urban waterway logistics	Utilized a ship to transfer goods to the transit points by the inland waterway of the city	Labanauskas (2016); Janjevic and Ndiaye (2014); Seidlová et al. (2020)	Maes et al. (2015); Seidlová et al. (2020)
Taxi logistics	Applied the taxi to transport goods; the purpose is reduce traffic congestion		Chen and Pan (2016); Eidhammer et al. (2016); Li et al. (2014); Zhang and Wang (2018); Gao et al. (2018)
Cargo bike	Use of a cargo-bike for freight distribution in city centers		Rudolph and Gruber (2017); Melo and Baptista (2017); Koning and Conway (2016); Schier et al. (2016); Choubassi et al. (2016); Gruber and Kihm (2016); Gruber et al. (2015); Schliwa et al. (2015); Gruber et al. (2014); Lenz and Riehle (2013); Sárdi and Bóna (2018); Arnold et al. (2018); Lopez (2018)
Robotic vehicles	Use of autonomous (robotic) vehicles for freight distribution in city areas		Vleugel and Bal (2018); Haas and Friedrich (2017); Mitrea and Kyamakya (2017); Yu and Lam (2017); Molfino et al. (2014); Dinale et al. (2013); Muscolo et al. (2018); Beirigo et al. (2018)
Delivery drones	Use of drones for freight delivery in city areas		Kunze (2016); Mckinnon (2016); Mbiadou Saleu et al. (2018); Boysen et al. (2018)

(Continued)

Table 2.3 (Continued)

Topic	Description	Transshipment transportation	Last-mile delivery
Parcel lockers	The implementation of parcel lockers aims to reduce the traffic congestion in residential areas and enhance the efficiency of delivery		Lemke et al. (2016); Iwan et al. (2016); Deutsch and Golany (2018)
Mobile depot	A mobile depot is a trailer fitted with a loading dock, warehousing facilities, and an office		Verlinde and Macharis (2016); Verlinde et al. (2014); Marujo et al. (2018)
Units consolidation	Consolidated the goods between the various companies without in the UCC		Cepolina (2016); Lewandowski (2014); Moutaoukil et al. (2015); Asih et al. (2018)
ICT solutions	Application of internet communcation technology (ICT) are design new delivery strategies (i.e. human computer interaction)	Wang (2015)	De Marco et al. (2017); Bates et al. (2017); Dablanc et al. (2017); Cardenas et al. (2017); Pan et al. (2017); Perboli and Rosano (2018); Wang (2015); Rosano et al. (2018); Comi et al. (2018); Gayialis et al. (2018); Ali and Rahim (2018); Oppolzer et al. (2017); Tadei et al. (2016); Guerlain et al. (2016); Castillo et al. (2018)

Table 2.4 Symbols definition in the relevance analysis

Symbols	Definition
×	The one main topic of this corpus included this sub-topic
○	If literature of A[1] mentioned B[2]
●	If literature of B mentioned A
◐	If A and B mentioned each other in their corresponding literature

[1] **A indicates the sub-topic of network design**
[2] **B indicates the sub-topic of distribution innovations**

remaining six topics of distribution innovations lack a systematic consideration in research on urban freight network design. The details of crossed-topics is presented as follows.

(1) Electric vehicles
Applying electric vehicles are able to decrease the emission in urban freight transportation. A considerable body of studies on urban freight network design has focused on EVs' application. The article group of network design comprises three main themes presented as follow: The studies of UCC & collaboration discussed the application of EVs (e.g., Saetta and Caldarelli (2016); Estrada and Roca-Riu (2017); Lin et al. (2016); Janjevic et al. (2016)); Partial articles of LRP modeling analyzed urban freight network design by EVs (e.g., Gianessi et al. (2015); Li et al. (2018)); The research in low-carbon covered the joint operation of EVs and cargo bikes (e.g., (Navarro et al. 2016; Browne et al. 2016)). Another finding is that, in the distribution innovation group, the EVs' studies have mainly focused on last-mile delivery.

(2) Public transit logistics
Following the definition of public transit logistics, this crossed topic includes three themes: Buses are used to transship goods, and EVs or cargo bikes are responsible for last-mile delivery (Masson et al. 2017; Pimentel and Alvelos 2018) or by trucks (He and Yang 2018); Urban subways or metros are utilized tranship goods to the public transit station, then motorcycles and small pickup trucks are charge of last-mile delivery (Zhao et al. 2018). Urban trams are employed in transshipment transportation, then last-mile delivery is performed by EVs (Fatnassi et al. 2015) or cargo-bikes (Dampier and Marinov 2015).

(3) Cargo bikes
In fact, considerable research in network design has mentioned cargo bikes. For example, Dampier and Marinov (2015) discussed the usage of cargo bikes and EVs

Table 2.5 Cross-relevance analysis between each topic of network design and distribution innovations

Transshipment transportation	Last-mile delivery		UCC & Collaboration	LRP soulutions	VRP solutions	Low emission	Location selection model	Transshipment platform	Public transit logistic	Mobile depot	Autonomous vehicle
		Single tier	✕	✕	✕	✕	✕			✕	✕
		Two tier	✕	✕	✕	✕	✕	✕	✕	✕	✕
		Multi tier		✕	✕	✕		✕	✕		
✕	✕	Electric vehicle	◐	◐	●	◐	●		○	○	
	✕	Modular E-vehicle			●						
✕	✕	Public transit logistics	●				●	●	◐		
✕	✕	Urban waterway logistics									
	✕	Taxi logistics			●						
	✕	Cargo bike	○		●	◐			○	○	
	✕	Autonomous vehicle			●						◐
	✕	Delivery drones			●						●
	✕	Parcel lockers					●				
	✕	Mobile depot			●	●				◐	
	✕	Units consolidation	○								
✕	✕	ICT solutions	●								

in the public transit logistics system; Arvidsson and Pazirandeh (2017) analyzed the joint operation of mobile depot and cargo bikes; Anderluh et al. (2017) investigated the two-tier urban freight system based on vans and cargo-bikes. This evidence exposes that partial network design studies have comprehensively considered the joint operation of cargo bikes with other innovations. In contrast, the relevant research in distribution innovation has paid more attention to three themes: Impacts evaluation and potential effectiveness analysis of cargo-bikes in last-mile delivery (e.g., Melo and Baptista (2017); Rudolph and Gruber (2017)); Cost assessment of cargo bike (Choubassi et al. 2016; Arnold et al. 2018); Evaluating the collaborated operation of cargo bikes and EVs based on case studies (Sárdi and Bóna 2018).

(4) Autonomous vehicles
In the article group of network design, Scherr et al. (2018a) used AVs to optimize two-tier city logistics, which discussed the mixed autonomous fleets in transshipment transportation. The related papers in distribution innovations have focused on three themes: Optimization of delivery routes and charging stations' locations in the last-mile delivery (Yu and Lam 2017; Beirigo et al. 2018); The potential effectiveness assessment of AVs in last-mile delivery (Mitrea and Kyamakya 2017); Design the operational model for AVs in last-mile delivery (Molfino et al. 2014; Dinale et al. 2013).

(5) Mobile depots
In the group of network design, the related articles have discussed the collaborated transportation of mobile depot and cargo bike/EVs (Arvidsson and Pazirandeh 2017; Ducret 2014). In contrast, the relevant papers in distribution innovations have paid more attention to potential effectiveness assessment of moblie depot in transshipment transportation (Verlinde et al. 2014; Marujo et al. 2018)

According to the above analysis, this work determines that the network design studies have not covered five distribution innovations. This finding reveals that network design research lacks an integrated consideration of all urban distribution innovations, and the research in both article groups appeared highly fragmented. The literature evidence also demonstrates that the network design studies only covered several specific combinations of distribution innovations. These combinations comprise comprise the combination of EVs and cargo-bikes (Navarro et al. 2016; Browne et al. 2016); the combination of the public transit system and EVs/cargo-bikes (Masson et al. 2017; Pimentel and Alvelos 2018) or trucks (He and Yang 2018); the combination of the mobile depot and cargo-bikes (Verlinde et al. 2014; Marujo et al. 2018). Nevertheless, the research in distribution innovations has discussed more feasible combinations, such as, the combination of the delivery drones and trucks (Boysen et al. 2018). These findings highlight that the research in network design rarely considered the various combinations of distribution innovations. Moreover, the cross-relevance analysis did not find the literature evidence regarding the integration of distribution innovations.

The literature evidence also indicates that considerable studies have paid more attention to address the short-term problem by mathematical modeling, and the long-term planning of urban logistics has been rarely considered. Meanwhile, the influences of urban spatial development on urban freight networks have received less attention. The above findings expos that urban freight network design lacks a methodology framework of foresight research.

2.5   Main Research Gaps and Future Research Framework

2.5.1   Main Research Gaps

The previous discussions contribute to identifying some research gaps that merit further study by academics and practitioners. This work determines the four research gaps presented as follow:

Gap 1: It lacks a systematic consideration of integrating all distribution innovations into urban freight network design. In fact, future urban freight network is impossible to composed by one or two transport modes. Consequently, this gap possibly leads to the inconsistent with reality the studies of urban freight network planning. From a long-term view, this gap may exacerbate the land-use conflicts between the city and freight. Without this systematic consideration, the application of distribution innovations reduces the long-term cost-benefit for urban logistics providers. It also affects the formulation of urban freight policy to a degree. The filling of this gap is conducive to the long-term planning of SUFT. The previous discussion exhibits that this gap is caused by Gap 2 and Gap 3 described as follows.

Gap 2: Considerable studies have paid scant attention to the feasibility analysis and risk evaluation on the integration of distribution innovations, particularly on operations as a system. The result of the cross-relevance analysis indicates that several papers have discussed some combinations of distribution innovations. However, the relevant research has rarely considered the integration of various distribution innovations. For the logistics providers, the feasibility analysis and risk evaluation contribute to constructing the appropriate solutions associated with integrating distribution innovations.

Gap 3: Much less research has focused on design an innovative and flexible freight network structure to accommodate various distribution innovations and the challenges of urban spatial development. The literature evidence exposes that the studies have commonly concentrated on the conventional urban freight network. Notwithstanding, the integrations of distribution innovations are radically changing the conventional urban freight network structure. From a long-term view, this change is maybe a barrier to promoting sustainable and flexible urban logistics in future cities. Hence, designing a flexible network structure is conducive to the integration of distribution innovations and is a critical component of the long-term planning of SUFT.

Gap 4: The foresight research on combining urban development with long-term planning of SUFT is lacking. The existence of an urban freight transport strategy should be embedded in an overall sustainable development strategy with a long-term perspective (Approximately 20–30 years) (Wolfram 2004). Nevertheless, considerable research has focused on the short-term problem of sustainable urban logistics, and long-term planning is rarely considered. Meanwhile, the impacts of urban spatial development on urban logistics planning have received limited attention. Additionally, the operational integration of distribution innovation is a long-term sustainable transition process based on urban spatial development. Consequently, the foresight research of SUFT needs to systematically consider the urban spatial development from a long-term perspective.

2.5.2 Future Research Framework

To respond to the above gaps, this work formulates a research framework of sustainable and flexible future urban freight planning (SFFUFP), as presented in Figure 2.6. This framework comprises two primary aspects: the network structure of SUFT and operational strategies of SUFT. First, the network structure of future SUFT must comprehensively estimate the future trends of urban spatial development from a long-term view and its impacts on urban logistics. Hence, it is essential to evaluating the interaction of urban spatial development and city logistics. Given this evaluation focuses on long-term planning (Approximately 20–30 years), it is significant to perform the foresight research of urban development and SUFT (Addressing Gap 4). The foresight research is future-oriented that needs a long-term (next 10 to 25 years or more) perspective (Glenn 1994; Mozuni and Jonas 2016; Conway and Voros 2003).

For addressing Gap 3, designing an innovative & flexible network of future SUFT must systematically consider the integration of distribution innovations. Meanwhile, the operational strategies of future SUFT are based on the innovative network structure and integration of distribution innovations. The integrations of distribution

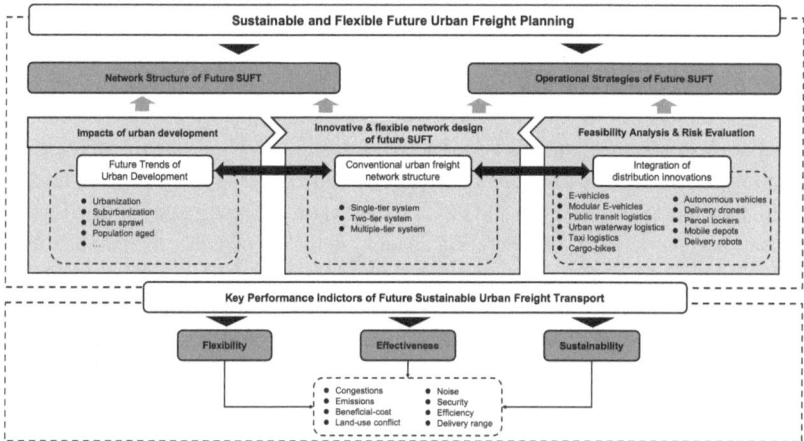

Figure 2.6 Research framework of sustainable and flexible future urban freight system. (Source: Author's own elaboration)

innovations need feasibility analysis and risk evaluation to formulate feasible solutions (Addressing Gap 2). Owing to the single-tier or two-tier network structure being inflexible and unsustainable for future cities, the current network structure of urban freight should be optimized and improved based on the integration of distribution innovations. The literature evidence exhibits that the integrations of distribution innovations challenged the conventional urban freight network. Therefore, future research must consider the integration solutions of distribution innovations to design a suitable network structure (Addressing Gap 1). The key performance indicators of future urban freight transport need to add flexibility and sustainability criteria to accommodate the challenges caused by urban spatial development.

2.6   Conclusion of This Chapter

This chapter aims to provide a systematic analysis of the scientific literature to identify the research gaps between the urban freight network design and urban distribution innovations. To the best of my knowledge, such a study is absent. Despite the transport mode playing a critical role in composing urban freight networks, network design studies only mentioned partial distribution innovations. Moreover, the high fragmentation of these two topics serves as a barrier to further promoting sustainable city logistics within long-term planning. Therefore, a systematic literature review is essential for subsequent research.

As expected, the first result is that the research in network design lacks a systematic consideration of all distribution innovations. Although there are 12 topics of distribution innovations, the studies of network design have only covered five topics. With further discussion, this gap is proved to be caused by the following two results. (1) It lacks feasibility analysis and risk evaluation on the integration of distribution innovations, particularly on operations as a system. (2) considerable studies have paid less attention to design an innovative and flexible freight network structure to respond to the integrations of distribution innovations and the challenges of urban spatial development. Furthermore, the literature evidence reveals that the research in these two topics has concentrated on solving short-term specific problems based on the data collection or experience analysis from the real-world setting. However, the existence of an urban freight transport strategy should be embedded in an overall sustainable development strategy with a long-term perspective (Approximately 20–30 years). Therefore, it is essential to integrate urban spatial development trends into the long-term planning of sustainable city logistics.

According to the identified research gaps, this chapter develops the research framework of SFFUFP from a long-term planning perspective that comprises three main dimensions: integration of distribution innovation, flexible and sustainable urban freight network, and the trends of urban development. This framework provides systematic thinking to resolve long-term planning of sustainable urban freight transport. It also contributes to urban logistics providers in enhancing the benefit-cost and performance of future sustainable city logistics. Meanwhile, this framework can alleviate future contradictions between the city and the freight caused by the application of distribution innovations and urban development. This chapter's limitation is that the appropriate research methodologies that can be used in the framework are not further discussed. The proposed framework has integrated the trends of urban development and integration of distribution innovations, which caused the long-term planning of SUFT to become more complex. Despite the method mix is an efficient solution, it needs further discussion. Consequently, the next chapter discusses the appropriate research methods based on the proposed framework.

Theoretical Framework of Future SUFT 3

3.1 Logical Arrangement of the Chapter

This chapter presents the theoretical framework of foresight research on sustainable urban freight transport. As mentioned in chapter 2, considerable research focuses on the short-term planning of SUFT. This finding reveals that the theoretical framework for the long-term planning of SUFT remains lacking (Gap 4 as mentioned in Chapter 2). Before the systematic discussion of the future urban freight system, it is essential to develop the theoretical framework of the foresight research based on the proposed research framework in chapter 2. This framework is intended to select appropriate methods of foresight research for SUFT, as well as the to guide to followed research steps. Figure 3.1 shows the logical structure of this chapter.

This chapter was published as a article[1] in the *Sustainability*. The content exposed in this chapter aims to resolve four sub-questions of this work as below:

- What is the stat of the art on foresight research, and which methods are suitable for the research of future sustainable urban freight transport?
- Given the exogenous and endogenous trends of UFT, how to use the general framework of foresight research to design the future sustainable urban freight transport?
- How to select appropriate methods of foresight research for long-term planning of SUFT?

---

[1]He, Z and Haasis, H.D (2020). A Theoretical Research Framework of Future Sustainable Urban Freight Transport for Smart Cities. *Sustainability 12*(5), 1975

© The Author(s), under exclusive license to Springer Fachmedien Wiesbaden GmbH, part of Springer Nature 2021
Z. He, *Future Sustainable Urban Freight Network Design in the Large Cities and Megacities*, Sustainable Management, Wertschöpfung und Effizienz, https://doi.org/10.1007/978-3-658-34203-6_3

- How to combine the selected methods to design the theoretical framework of foresight research?

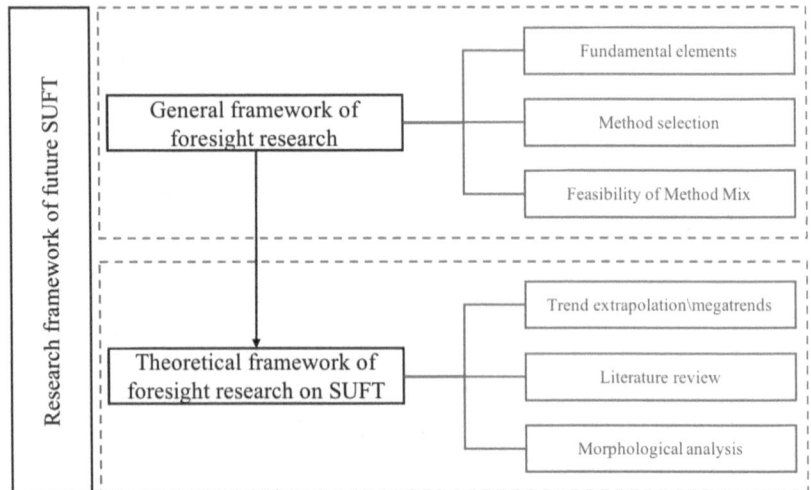

Figure 3.1 Structure of Chapter 3

As published paper, this chapter is organized as below: Section 3.2 introduces the research background and motivations of this chapter. Section 3.3 is the research question and methodology in the published paper. Section 3.4 is a systematic literature review of foresight research that is to identify popular research methods. Subsequently, exogenous and endogenous trends of future urban logistics are discussed in Section 3.5. Combined with the above steps, the appropriate research methods are selected and discussed in Section 3.6. Meanwhile, the feasibility of the chosen method mix is further discussed and analyzed. After that, Section 3.7 indicates the theoretical research framework of foresight research on future sustainable urban logistics. In Section 3.8, the sustainability of future urban logistics is discussed further. Lastly, the conclusion of this chapter is in Section 3.9.

This chapter aims to construct a theoretical research framework for sustainable urban freight transport (SUFT) from the perspectives of future urban development and distribution innovations, which discusses the appropriate research methods as well. Urban freight transport plays a critical role in the promotion of sustainable and liveable cities. According to the literature review, considerable research on SUFT focuses on resolving some specific problems with a short-term perspective. It is noted that the existence of an urban freight transport strategy, which should be embedded in an overall sustainable development strategy with a long term perspective (Approximately 20–30 years). Nevertheless, considerable research has paid scant attention to the long-term planning of SUFT. Given this, this chapter contributes to fulfilling this gap. First, this chapter employs the systematical literature review (SLR) to detect the published paper of foresight research in the past sixteen years (2003–2018). This step contributes to understanding the research methods that can be used in foresight research. Subsequently, this chapter discusses both the impacts of urban development and distribution innovations on future SUFT, which are used to select the appropriate methods to construct the theoretical research framework. In the end, the theoretical research framework of long-term planning on SUFT is developed based on the two future perspectives: the trends of urban development and the application of urban distribution innovations. This framework is intended to discuss the way to design sustainable urban logistics taking into account urban development and distribution innovations.

3.2   Introduction

Economic growth necessitates flexible transportation to eases access to resources and trade markets (Rassafi and Vaziri 2005). Transportation is a main concept to promote social intelligent approaches and economic development (Bamwesigye and Hlavackova 2019). Urban freight transport (UFT) has been defined as a process and a system to collect, transport, and distribute goods within urban areas. Although the fact that urban freight activities have continually contributed to the economic growth of cities, it has caused a majority of environmental externalities within urban areas. These negative externalities primarily consist of air pollution, congestion, noise, etc. (Anderson et al. 2005; Wittlöv 2012). Therefore, considerable research focuses on promoting sustainable urban freight transport (SUFT), which is commonly based on the conventional urban freight network. The dimensions of sustainability primarily include economic (e.g., economic performance), environmental (e.g., emissions, transport), and social (e.g., public policy, customer privacy) (Global Reporting Initiative 2013). Conventional urban freight network generally consists of two types: single-tier and two-tier. The former system is commonly used in small or medium-sized cities, and the two-tier system is more suitable for large/megacity (Dablanc 2007; Benjelloun and Crainic 2009). However, city development has brought challenges for the conventional network structure of UFT, particularly for the large/megacities around the world. It is noted that considerable research has paid less attention to the connections between freight transport and urban development (Cui et al. 2015). This result reveals that the research on SUFT lacks a systematic consideration of city development in a long-term view. Indeed, the existence of an urban freight transport strategy, which should be embedded in an overall sustainable development strategy with a long term perspective (Approximately 20–30 years) (Wolfram 2004). Therefore, it is critical to a comprehensive consideration between city development and sustainable urban freight planning from a long-term view.

In recent years, the concept of 'smart city' has increasingly become a popular topic in the academic field. This concept has arisen as a solution to improve the sustainability and liveability of cities, which is based on the effective urban management of governance, energy, and transportation (Hammad et al. 2019; Ferraris et al. 2018). Since 2018, some research has focused on the topic of sustainable transport for smart cities, which primarily around the smart mobilities. For example, Al-Thani et al. (2018) adopted the Delphi approach to investigate the influences of both advanced transport and communication technologies on the future sustainability of the city of Doha and its neighborhoods. Freudendal-Pedersen et al. (2019) discussed around the impacts of mobilities on smart cities, particularly on the aspects of automation and sustainability. Tobey et al. (2019) demonstrated a conceptual framework for planning smart communities to take account of the sustainable transport, which was employed an iterative three-phase development loop. Hammad et al. (2019) proposed the mathematical optimization framework to optimize the zoning, land-use allocation, location of novel constructions, and the investment decision-making related to infrastructure projects in smart cities. This framework is able to connect to other platforms in the city setting. Bamwesigye and Hlavackova (2019) has discussed the global heterogeneous characteristics of both sustainable transport and smart cities. Behrendt (2019) indicated that the vast majority of European policy discussions on the topic of smart cities revolve around cars (including autonomous cars and smart vehicles), while cycling is scantly considered. Based on this result, he made policy suggestions for addressing these issues and for future research. These works have widely discussed the application of innovative sustainable transport modes in future smart cities. Notwithstanding, much less research has paid attention to the impacts of these innovative transport modes on the future sustainable urban freight transport. Additionally, these papers have a specific focus on the notion of smart cities based on ICT or IoT, the physical perspective of urban development has scantly considered. An example is that urban population growth causes urban sprawl to increase the distribution range and delivery frequency. Although the application of these innovative transport modes can reduce the negative environmental impacts by freight movements, this gap is to restrict the sustainability of future SUFT in aspects of economics and socials. Given that, this chapter specifically focuses on the physical perspective of urban development and the distribution innovations with smart cities.

The trends of urban development are the exogenous trends that have exacerbated the challenges of the urban freight system. For responding to these challenges, the urban logistics providers have devoted to finding the appropriate endogenous solutions to promote sustainability, effectiveness, and security. The usage of emerging transport modes is an efficient solution for logistics providers. An example is utilizing electric vehicles (EVs) to deliver goods to customers within urban areas, which can reduce air pollution. Notwithstanding, various distribution innovations operate together as a system that radically influences the conventional urban freight network (He and Haasis 2019). An example is using urban freight tram need to build serval transit stations that integration of passenger and freight. Although the fact that considerable research has paid more attention to the usage of one or two distribution innovations in the urban freight system, they focus on short-term planning (Approximately 5–10 years). This observation implies that comprehensive consideration of the integration of urban distribution innovations and their impacts on the conventional urban freight network is lacking. Additionally, several technology companies have launched some projects of future urban freight vehicles. An example is a concept of "Future urban freight mobility" proposed by the Volkswagen (Germany) in 2018, this vehicle is integrated the mobile depot, robotic vehicle, and delivery robots together. From sustainable transition perspectives, these projects are "new technologies typically link to the old technology in the form of an auxiliary add-on, often to improve its functioning" (Arvidsson and Pazirandeh 2017). From a view of futurology, this finding reveals that using urban distribution innovations on the conventional urban freight system is possible for a barrier to flexibility and sustainability of UFT. Therefore, foresight research between urban distribution innovations and urban freight network planning is also necessary.

To sum up, both exogenous (city development) and endogenous (distribution innovations) trends of UFT have exacerbated the challenges of the conventional urban freight network from a long-term perspective. Therefore, the foresight research of SUFT contributes to the sustainable transition of city logistics, thereby promoting the sustainable & liveable cities in the future. After review the published paper of city logistics, considerable research focuses on addressing the specific problems in the short-term. This finding reveals that much research has less employed foresight methods to investigate future sustainable urban freight transport. Applying foresight research methods is an efficient solution for researching sustainable urban logistics from exogenous and endogenous tendencies. To this end, the SLR of foresight research contributes to the understanding state of the art on the foresight research and selecting appropriate methodologies for future sustainable urban freight transport. For fulfilling these gaps, this chapter adopts the SLR approach to detect the foresight research articles, which are published in 2003–2018. Based on the findings in the previous step, this chapter use the overview approach to discuss the impacts of urban development and distribution innovations on the future sustainable urban freight system, which are used to select the appropriate methodologies of foresight research to construct the theoretical framework. Meanwhile, The general framework of foresight research is used to improve the theoretical framework that is proposed in this chapter.

3.3   Research Questions & Methodology

The previous chapter identifies that the long-term planning of sustainable urban freight transport or relevant foresight research is lacking. Additionally, the research on urban freight network design paid scant attention to both trends of urban development and the integrated application of distribution innovations. This result highlights that considerable research has paid scant attention to the long-term planning of sustainable urban logistics as well as the impacts of these two trends for the UFT. At present, to the best of our knowledge, such a study is absent. Unmistakably, comprehensive consideration of these two trends to design urban freight network is capable of further promoting sustainability and flexibility of future urban freight system. To this end, this chapter aims to develop a theoretical framework of foresight research on SUFT to resolve this gap. Consequently, the research questions (RQ) of this chapter were presented as follows:

RQ 1. What is the stat of the art on foresight research, and which methods are suitable for the research of future sustainable urban freight transport?
RQ 2. What are the exogenous and endogenous trends of SUFT?
RQ 3. How to select appropriate methods for the long-term planning of SUFT?
RQ 4. How to conduct the long-term planning of sustainable urban freight transport from future perspectives?

For responding to the above research questions, this chapter formulate the research methodology as depicted by Figure 3.2. First, the SLR method is used to detect foresight research articles published from 2003 to 2018 on Scopus. This step is intended to understand the state of art of foresight research and determine research methods in the articles. Subsequently, both impacts of urban development and distribution innovations on urban freight transport have discussed. Based on this discussion, the appropriate research methods is selected for the long-term planning of SUFT. In the end, the theoretical research framework is developed based on previous steps.

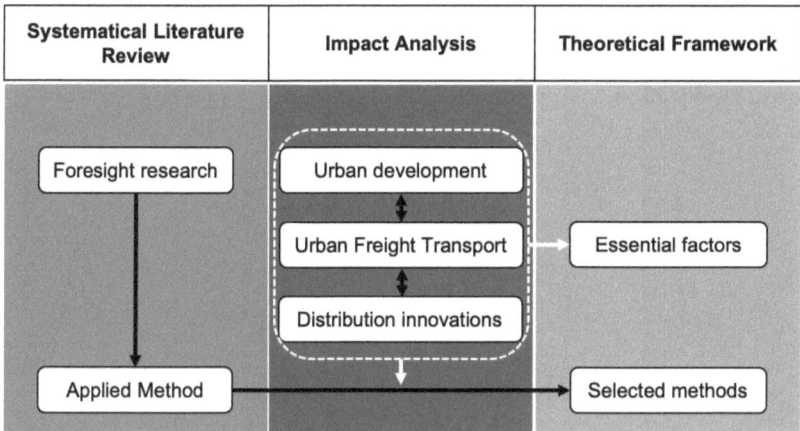

Figure 3.2 Research methodology. (Source: Author's own elaboration)

3.4   Literature Review of Foresight Research

For responding to RQ.1, this chapter employs the systematic literature review (SLR) to detect the research articles published in 2003–2018. This review aims to understand which academic field has used the approach of foresight research and the applied methods in these articles, and the search is launched through the first set of criteria similar to that described in Table 3.1. In the end, 58 papers have matched this objective (Table 3.1).

Table 3.1 Paper selection

Items	Description
Main Keywords	Foresight research
Language	English
Document types	Journal Articles, Conference Papers, Books Chapters
Source	Scopus
Time interval	2003–2018

3.4.1   Descriptive Analysis of Papers

As presented by Figure 3.3, the peak in the number of papers was in 2017 when 14 articles are covered foresight research on the distinct academical field. Despite the fluctuation in 2018, it is possible to appreciate the stable increase in contributions related to foresight research in the last sixteen years. Of these 58 articles, eleven papers were published in the journal of *Foresight*.

Figure 3.3 Number of academic publications on foresight research

To respond to the research objective, this chapter classifies this corpus through the subject area of these 58 papers and employed the Scopus analysis system of search results. The literature has mainly covered 11 subject areas. In which of these subject areas, *Others* is consist of *Biochemistry, Genetics & Molecular Biology, Earth & Planetary Sciences, Environmental Science, as well as Materials Science*.

As presented by Figure 3.4, the subject area of *Business, Management and Accounting* was accounted for the 26.7% of the article corpus. There are 28 papers in this field. Both subject of the *Engineering, Economics, Econometrics and Finance*, and *Social Science*, have accounted for 10.5% respectively. This finding highlights that foresight research has received more attention in these subject areas, particularly on the *Business, Management and Accounting*.

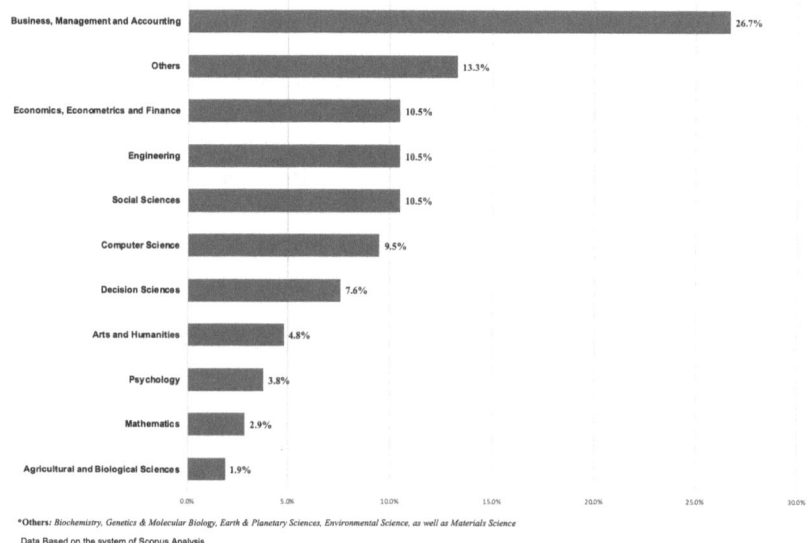

Figure 3.4 Subject areas of academic publications on foresight research

3.4.2 Analysis of Papers on Foresight Research

Followed the classification of the subject area, the keywords of the article corpus are detected and discussed. As indicated by Table 3.2, the topic "Technological innovations" covers the ten subject areas. An example is that the research paper of Shostak et al. (2017) has covered six subject areas. The high rate of covering implies that this topic is a popular field in foresight research. This finding also reveals that distribution innovations need to be systematically estimated in the foresight research of SUFT. Additionally, 22 articles are related to the topic of "Technological innovations". Nevertheless, only 3 articles involve the topic "Transport & Supply chains". In these three research papers, Fiorini and Lin (2015) have analyzed the application of foresight studies in the transport sector, they aim to present good practices and potential benefits of using foresight studies in the transport sector. Furthermore, Strzelczak (2015) has discussed possible novel ontology-aided solutions for managing manufacturing and logistics operations, which result from foresight research of industries. Strzelczak (2017) has investigated the feasibly functional arrangements of production internet throughout reflection on the state-of-art as well as supplemented by foresight research. This finding reveals that, thus far, the foresight research on urban freight planning is lacking, as this analysis in not locate evidence of literature review regarding the foresight research of urban logistics.

Owing to urban development and distribution innovations radically exacerbating the challenges of urban logistics, long-term planning of urban freight transport can further promote sustainable and liveable cities. Before the discussion of critical factors on future urban logistics planning, it needs to determine the foresight research methodologies. Given this, the applied methods of article corpus have been detected and discussed.

3.4.3 Main Research Methodologies Applied in the Article Corpus

According to the full paper reading, the main applied methodologies of the article corpus have been identified. These research approaches are consist of literature review/overview, survey/interview, roadmapping/technology roadmapping, Delphi, scenario, trends exploration, workshops/brainstorming, bibliometrics, and SWOT. The definition of these nine methods are presented as follows:

- **Literature review/Overview** is a general method. The papers are commonly structured around related topics and use a discursive writing style.
- **Survey/Interview** refer to investigate the specific people groups based on the Pre-set questions. The purpose is to gather knowledge of interviewees.
- **Roadmapping/Technology roadmapping** is a method that outlines the future field and generating a timeline. Related factors include technologies, regulatory, and market structures, etc.
- **Delphi** is a method that involves surveying/interviewing a panel of experts to arrive at a group opinion or decision.
- **Scenario** is constructing a systematic and internally consistent vision associated with the future.
- **Trends exploration** is a method of forecasting future trends based on the assumption of the future is a continuation of the past.
- **Workshops/Brainstorming** is commonly employed in face-to-face or online group working sessions, which can generate new ideas around a specific field of interest.
- **Bibliometrics** is a method based on a quantitative and statistical analysis of publications.

Table 3.2 Topics in the paper groups of foresight research and their subject areas

Topic	Description	Papers	Subject Area Business, Management & Accounting	Engineering	Economics, Econometrics & Finance	Social Sciences	Computer Science	Decision Sciences	Psychology	Arts & Humanities	Mathematics	Agricultural & Biological Sciences	Other
Technological innovations	The foresight research of emerging technologies (e.g., information and communications technology, digitalization) and their impact analysis	Mazurkiewicz and Poteralska (2018); Kaivo-oja (2017); Gudanowska et al. (2016); Gudanowska (2014); Zolkifly and Hussin (2017); Shcherbinin and Prokhorov (2018); Shostak et al. (2017); Lee et al. (2015); Voronina and Moroz (2017); Stahl (2013); Cho and Kim (2014); Aniskin et al. (2017b); Ramos et al. (2012); Chan and Daim (2012); Dobrzańska-Danikiewicz et al. (2011); Carsten Stahl (2011); Magruk et al. (2011); Dobrzańska-Danikiewicz and Lukaszkowicz (2010); Dobrzańska-Danikiewicz (2010); Yuan et al. (2010); Damrongchai and Michelson (2009); Santonen et al. (2008)	✓	✓	✓	✓	✓	✓		✓	✓	✓	✓
Company development	The foresight research of company development, and applied framework	Kononiuk et al. (2017); Kováříková et al. (2017); Dudin et al. (2017); Rohrbeck et al. (2015); Kaivo-Oja (2014)	✓	✓	✓				✓				
Uncertainty analysis	Integrating the concept of uncertainty to the foresight research	Magruk (2017); Mendonça et al. (2009)	✓	✓	✓	✓							
Strategic/Policy making	Using the theory of foresight research to develop future strategies/policy	Iden et al. (2017); Vervoort and Gupta (2018); Lee and Chuang (2012); Amsteus (2011); Dobrzańska-Danikiewicz et al. (2010); Amanatidou (2008)	✓		✓	✓		✓					✓

(Continued)

Table 3.2 (Continued)

Topic	Description	Papers	Business, Management & Accounting	Engineering	Economics, Econometrics & Finance	Social Sciences	Computer Science	Decision Sciences	Psychology	Arts & Humanities	Mathematics	Agricultural & Biological Sciences	Other
Management innovation	Using the theory of foresight research to develop innovative measures of management	Aniskin et al. (2017a); Ejdys and Szpilko (2013); Jari and Theresa (2017)	✓	✓			✓				✓		
Methodological research	Developing the foresight research methods	Spickermann et al. (2014); Birko et al. (2015)	✓						✓			✓	✓
Energy	The foresight research of energy (marketing)	Paananen and J. Mäkinen (2013); Pysar et al. (2018)	✓	✓								✓	✓
Transport & Supply chains	The foresight research in the field of transport, logistics and supply chain management	Fiorini and Lin (2015); Strzelczak (2015); Strzelczak (2017)		✓				✓					
Financial systems	The foresight research of financial and economic system	Mikolajewicz-Woz'Niak and Scheibe (2015)			✓			✓					
Marketing management	The foresight research of marketing management in different size enterprises	Danko et al. (2018); Malanowski and Zweck (2007)	✓	✓			✓						
Psychological Science	The foresight research of psychology knowledge and practice	Erik Karlsen et al. (2010); Hayward (2003)	✓		✓			✓	✓				
Demographic change	The foresight research of demographic change	Farrelly (2014)		✓						✓			
Others	It includes the social network analysis, methods of foresight research, agriculture, and knowledge management	Schartinger et al. (2012); Barker et al. (2011); Su and Lee (2010); Nugroho and Saritas (2009); Lee et al. (2008); Puga (2007)	✓			✓	✓						

- **SWOT** is a strategic planning approach that can help a personality or organization identify strengths, weaknesses, opportunities, and threats regarding the business competition or project planning.

The resulting classification of article corpus is reported in Figure 3.5, where each paper can employ more than one research method. As expected, the literature review/overview is the primary applied methodology in the article corpus. Only one paper was adopting the SWOT analysis. In these studies, the maximum number of methods per paper is two. For example, the research of Fiorini and Lin (2015) has employed the literature review/overview and scenario approaches; Lee et al. (2008) has adopted the methods of literature review/overview and trends exploration. This finding highlights that the method mix is a general methodology for foresight research. Finally, the applied methods of the article corpus are needs to further classification and discussion.

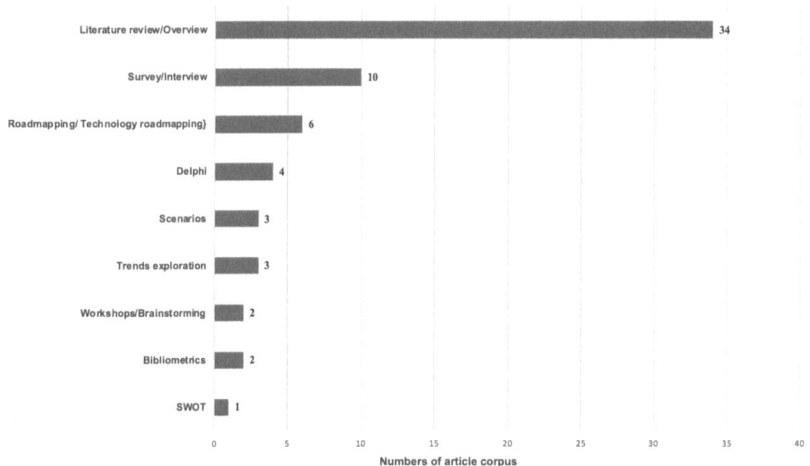

Figure 3.5 Types of research methods in the corpus

Connecting the research methods with the topics covered in each paper, the results are presented in Table 3.3. The approach of the literature review/overview is widely used in the method mix. Although most papers are not mentioned the literature review/overview method, this approach is commonly used for fundamental descriptions (e.g., Lee et al. (2015); Dobrzañska-Danikiewicz (2010); Cho and Kim

Table 3.3 Topics and applied methods in the corpus

	Literature review/Overview	Survey/Interview	Delphi	Scenarios	Trends exploration	Workshops/Brainstorming	Roadmapping/Technology roadmapping	SWOT	Bibliometrics
Technology innovations	Kaivo-oja (2017); Gudanowska et al. (2016); Gudanowska (2014); Stahl (2013); Zolkifly and Hussin (2017); Shcherbinin and Prokhorov (2018); Voronina and Moroz (2017); Ramos et al. (2012); Chan and Daim (2012); Dobrzańska-Danikiewicz et al. (2011); Carsten Stahl (2011); Magruk et al. (2011); Yuan et al. (2010); Damrongchai and Michelson (2009); Santonen et al. (2008)	Lee et al. (2015); Dobrzańska-Danikiewicz (2010)	–	–	–	Voronina and Moroz (2017)	Aniskin et al. (2017b); Dobrzańska-Danikiewicz and Lukaszkow-icz (2010); Mazurkiewicz and Poteralska (2018)	–	Shostak et al. (2017); Cho and Kim (2014)
Company development	Kononiuk et al. (2017); Dudin et al. (2017); Rohrbeck et al. (2015); Kaivo-Oja (2014)	Kováříková et al. (2017)	–	–	–	–	–	–	–

(Continued)

Table 3.3 (Continued)

	Literature review/Overview	Survey/Interview	Delphi	Scenarios	Trends exploration	Workshops/Brainstorming	Roadmapping/Technology roadmapping	SWOT	Bibliometrics
Uncertainty analysis	Magruk (2017)	–	Mendonça et al. (2009)	Mendonça et al. (2009)	–	–	–	–	–
Strategic/Policy making	Iden et al. (2017); Vervoort and Gupta (2018); Amanatidou (2008)	Amsteus (2011)	Lee and Chuang (2012)	–	–	–	Dobrzańska-Danikiewicz et al. (2010)	–	–
Management innovation	Ejdys and Szpilko (2013); Jari and Theresa (2017)	–	–	–	–	–	Aniskin et al. (2017a)	–	–
Methodological research		Spickermann et al. (2014)	Birko et al. (2015). Spickermann et al. (2014)	–	–	–	–	–	–
Energy	–	–	–	–	Paananen and J. Mäkinen (2013); Pysar et al. (2018)	–	–	–	Paananen and J. Mäkinen (2013)
Transport & Supply chains	Fiorini and Lin (2015); Strzelczak (2017)	Strzelczak (2015); Strzelczak (2017)	–	Fiorini and Lin (2015)	–		Strzelczak (2015)	–	
Financial systems	Mikołajewicz-Woz'Niak and Scheibe (2015)	–	–	–		–	–	–	–

(Continued)

Table 3.3 (Continued)

	Literature review/Overview	Survey/Interview	Delphi	Scenarios	Trends exploration	Workshops/Brainstorming	Roadmapping/Technology roadmapping	SWOT	Bibliometrics
Marketing management	–	Danko et al. (2018)	–	–	–	–	–	Malanowski and Zweck (2007)	–
Psychological Science	Erik Karlsen et al. (2010), Hayward (2003)	–	–	–	–	–	–	–	–
Demographic change	–	–	–	Farrelly (2014)	–	–	–	–	–
Others	Barker et al. (2011); Su and Lee (2010); Lee et al. (2008); Puga (2007)	Schartinger et al. (2012); Nugroho and Saritas (2009)	–	–	Lee et al. (2008)	Schartinger et al. (2012)	–	–	–

(2014)). In addition, the other method mix is also involved in the article corpus. An example is that Mendonça et al. (2009) have adopted the methodologies of the Delphi and scenario analysis. This finding reveals that the method mix is an efficient solution for foresight research. Hence, the foresight research of sustainable urban freight transport also needs to consider the feasibility of the distinct method mix comprehensively.

According to the preliminary discussion, these nine methods are unable to develop a foresight research framework for the future sustainable urban freight transport based on the dimensions of urban development and distribution innovations. Although the methods of literature review and trend exploration seem to be suitable methodologies, it is a lack of a method to develop the operational strategy and network structure for future sustainable urban freight transport. Given this, it essential to integrated the other methodologies of foresight research into further discussion. Besides the above nine methods that can be used in foresight research, indeed, 25 methods are commonly employed in this field. The research of Popper (2008) has systematically discussed the method selection for foresight research. In order to select the appropriate methods for developing the foresight research framework of sustainable urban freight transport, it is vital to systematically discuss the critical impact-factors of future sustainable urban freight transport. The first step is to understand the applied frequency of 25 foresight methods and the feasibility of their method mix.

3.5   Exogenous & Endogenous Trends of SUFT

The above section demonstrates that considerable research has paid attention to the long-term planning of sustainable urban freight transport. For responding to RQ 2, it is essential to understanding the future trends of sustainable urban freight transport. As mentioned previously, city and freight maintain a set of core relations (Rodrigue et al. 2016). However, a considerable body of research has paid scant attention to the links between urban development and city logistics planning (Cui et al. 2015). Therefore, the future trends of urban development is an external factor of sustainable urban freight transport, which is defined as the exogenous trends of SUFT. Exogenous trends have exacerbated the challenges of sustainable city logistics. An example is that urban population growth has motivated the logistics providers to increase the delivery frequency within urban areas, which has caused traffic congestions and exacerbated the land-use conflict. To this end, urban logistics providers have employed or launched emerging transport modes to decrease environmental externalities to promote the sustainability of urban logistics. For example, electric vehicles, delivery drones, and parcel lockers. This observation highlights that conventional urban freight transport has increasingly transformed into a brand-new system of urban freight transport based on urban distribution innovations. From a view of physical distribution, urban distribution innovations can be defined as the endogenous trends of sustainable urban freight transport. According to the above discussion, this chapter adopts the approach of literature overview to discuss the exogenous and endogenous trends of sustainable urban freight transport.

3.5.1 Exogenous Trends: Urban Spatial Development

Urban population growth is a critical element for generating urban issues. Figure 3.6 shows that the world's urban population and the average annual rate of changes in the period of 1995–2018, while it includes the prediction until the year 2030. By 2030, the world's urban population will reach more than 5 billion, 68% of the world's population is projected to be living in the city by 2050 (UN DESA 2018). This growt implies that the city needs to construct lots of new residential areas and commercial areas. Housing accounts for more than 70% of land use in most cities and determines urban form and densities, one billion new homes are needed worldwide by 2025 (UN-Habitat 2016). The urban sprawl leads to increases the numbers of large and megacities around the world. By 2015, there were 44 large cities and 29 megacities (UN-Habitat 2016). By 2030, the world is projected to have 43 megacities with more than 10 million inhabitants (UN DESA 2018) and approximately 67 large cities. From a long-term perspective, the urban range growth has motivated the logistics providers to employ the two solutions: usage of infrastructure expansion to increase the delivery range and freight capacity; or using more freight fleets to increase the delivery frequency within urban areas. These two solutions exacerbate the conflicts between the city and freight from future perspectives. The infrastructure expansion deteriorates the land-use conflicts and requires the logistics provider to increase the cost of construction, operation, and labor. In cities, the new building's locations create traffic demand in the existing network structure (Hammad et al. 2017). This causes external traffic loadings on the existing network, and it leads to major transportation delays to network users if not have excellent planning (Hammad et al. 2019). In consequence, this solution restricts the sustainability of urban freight transport in aspects of economic and social dimensions. For another response solution, despite freight fleets increase is able to enhance the efficiency of the urban logistics, it is in the degree to exacerbate the congestions and parking land conflict within urban areas. Although the logistics providers can employ the clean-energy mobilities (e.g., cargo-bikes and EVs) to reduce the emissions, this solution is a barrier for the sustainability in dimensions of social and environmental.

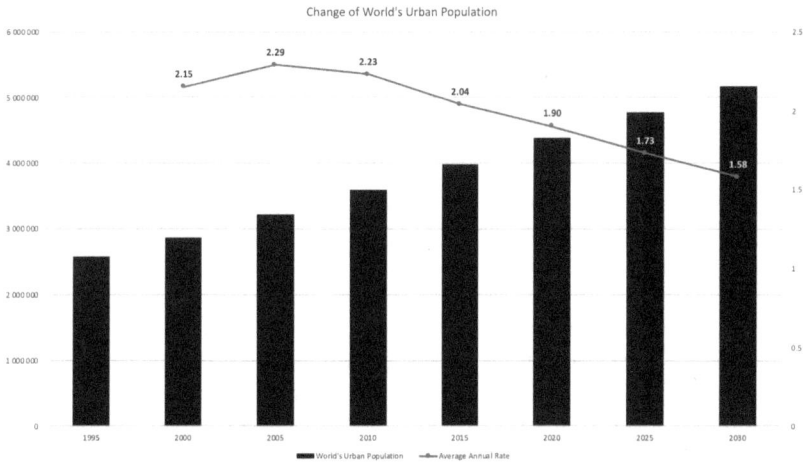

Figure 3.6 The change of world's urban population. (Adapted from UN DESA (2018))

Additionally, urban demographic expansion and disorganized growth have engendered the persistent issues and emerging urban challenges (UN-Habitat 2016). In which of these challenges, climate change by urban emission has become a core issue for sustainable development. Cities are responsible for more than 70% of global carbon dioxide emissions (UN-Habitat 2016), almost 5.5% of the total annual greenhouse gas emissions are generated by the logistics and transport sectors, around 57% of which are caused by road freight transport (Doherty and Hoyle 2009). However, a wide range of research shows that transportation systems in most of the cities and urban areas are unsustainable (Bamwesigye and Hlavackova 2019). Although some research on sustainable transport for smart cities has discussed the transport emission reduction in future urban planning agenda (e.g., (Freudendal-Pedersen et al. 2019; Behrendt 2019)), urban freight is still not specific integrated into the future sustainable urban planning system. Due to urban planning is focused principally on passenger transport, sustainable development measures mainly focus on passenger transport (Behrends et al. 2008). It led to that the freight transport issues at the city level are still not well understood, not quantified, and there is no methodology aimed explicitly at the analysis and planning of freight movements (Crainic et al. 2004; Behrends et al. 2008). In recent years, the sustainable urban planning system has integrated the transport emission reduction into the future planning agenda. This trend implies that logistics providers need to connect the sustainable urban freight strategies to the other modules of the future urban planning agenda, which is at the city level. Despite the application of clean-energy freight mobility is an efficient solution for promoting sustainability, sustainable urban freight strategies need to comprehensively consider the whole urban planning schemes from a view of the city level.

As mentioned previously, the technology development motivated the notion formulation of smart cities. Although the fact that this concept is based on the development of information and communications technology (ICT) and the internet of things (IoT), it also influences the physical perspective of urban development. For example, the zones, infrastructure allocations, and urban transport networks (Hammad et al. 2019; Tobey et al. 2019). It is noted that the universal agreement on a specific definition of a "smart city" still lacks, at present, its primary field is in the usage of ICT and IoT in the sectors of infrastructure, buildings, and energy (Kramers et al. 2014). This finding highlights that academia appears no consensus in the physical changes of urban development by the smart city trend. However, it is vital to systematically consider the impacts of the smart city concept on urban development and overall arrangement from physical perspectives.

Besides these, the age changed of the urban population also challenges the future sustainable urban logistics. Globally, the population aged 60 or over is the fastest growing at 3.26% per year; by 2050, 25% of the population in all regions except Africa will be aged 60 or over (UN DESA 2015a). Compared with this, the youth population (aged 15 to 24) accounting for a further 17% (UN DESA 2015b). The high proportion of these two groups possibly causes commodity demand polarization. Owing to body reason for the aged population, they focus on health care, medication, daily necessities, and convenient pick-up goods, which is provided by urban logistics. In contrast, youth people pay more attention to digital products, clothes, delivery security, and transport duration, etc. This finding highlights that urban logistics providers need to balance commodity demand polarization for providing differentiation delivery service within future urban areas.

Moreover, suburbanization plays a critical role in the exogenous trends of SUFT. Both economic factors and quality of life have contributed to the urban resident to move outside the congestion urban core areas. The reason for that land and housing in the suburbs is cheaper than city core areas, with low-density living, often resulting in a better quality of life and improved access to amenities (UN-Habitat 2016). It is noted that the ensuing pattern of urban development is consists of the displacement of population, industries and services from the city center to the periphery, and the creation of new centers with their own economic and social dynamics (UN-Habitat

2016). This finding implies that the distribution changed of urban areas aggravates the negative environmental externalities caused by delivery frequency growth and freight range extension.

To sum up, the exogenous trends have radically influenced the conventional urban freight system. Although the fact is that the usage of clean energy mobility contributes to decreasing the emission for promoting sustainability of urban freight transport, both urban development trends and urban population growth are possible to restrict the other components of dimensions on sustainability (i.e., Social and Economic). For example, the traffic congestions caused by delivery frequency arise, and the infrastructure expansion exacerbates the land-use conflict. Therefore, the long-term planning of sustainable urban freight transport needs to systematically consider these exogenous trends. The objective is designing a flexible and sustainable urban freight system for responding to the future challenges of urban development. For responding RQ.3, this chapter is to discuss further the appropriate methodologies, which can analyze these exogenous trends to connect with the research on the long-term planning of SUFT.

3.5.2 Endogenous Trends: Urban Distribution Innovations

As mentioned previously, the notion of smart cities has motivated the application of innovative transport mobilities in the urban transport system. An example is the autonomous vehicles (Freudendal-Pedersen et al. 2019). The usage of urban distribution innovations is an efficient solution for promoting sustainable urban freight transport. The definition of urban distribution innovations is applying emerging transport modes to reduce the negative impacts of urban freight movements, thereby promoting sustainability of the city logistics (He and Haasis 2019). According to the literature review, there are eleven urban distribution innovations: electric vehicles (EVs), public transit logistics, taxi logistics, cargo-bikes, parcel lockers, delivery drones, robotic vehicles, delivery robots, modular vehicles, mobile depots, and urban freight ships.

Table 3.4 indicates the definition of these eleven distribution innovations and the applicative implementation process in urban freight transport. According to the literature retrieval and filtering, this work determines that considerable research has paid scant attention to the integration of urban distribution innovations that operate together as a system. At present, there is very little research work and systematically prepared findings in this area. The integration of urban distribution innovations is an efficient solution for further promoting sustainable urban freight transport (He and Haasis 2019). Lots of logistics providers and technology companies indeed

Table 3.4 Distribution of the eleven topics in distribution innovations. (Adapted from He and Haasis (2019))

Topic	Describing	Transshipment transportation	Last-mile delivery
Electric vehicles	Applied the E-vehicles to transport the goods in urban areas	×	×
Modular E-vehicles	The special type of vehicles is used to deliver the goods to consumers by carrying one or multiple cabin modules		×
Public transit logistics	Integrated the passenger and freight activities (i.e., tram, subway, bus)	×	×
urban freight ships	Utilized a ship to transfer goods to the transit points by the inland waterway of the city	×	×
Taxi logistics	Applied the taxi to transport goods; the purpose is reduce traffic congestion	×	
Cargo bike	Use of a cargo-bike for freight distribution in city centers		×
Robotic vehicles	Use of autonomous (robotic) vehicles for freight distribution in city areas		×
Delivery drones	Use of drones for freight delivery in city areas		×
Delivery robots	use of small robots to delivery goods to the destination		×
Parcel lockers	The implementation of parcel lockers aims to reduce the traffic congestion in residential areas and enhance the efficiency of delivery		×
Mobile depot	A mobile depot is a trailer fitted with a loading dock, warehousing facilities, and an office		×

have launched similar concepts for future SUFT. For example, *DHL Express* (2017) has piloted the City Hub concept in Frankfurt, Germany, and Utrecht, Netherlands; the vehicles combine with a customized trailer carrying up to four small containers and then use of DHL Cubicycles (a cargo bike that is able to carry a container) to complete last-mile delivery (Deutsche Post DHL Group 2017); *Workhorse Group* have developed the *HorseFly UAV Delivery* system that is fully integrating with the electric/hybrid delivery trucks, while UPS has tested residential delivery with Drone launched from Atop Package Car (Workhorse Group 2016). These projects demonstrated that operational integration of the different urban distribution innovations is an irreversible trend for future sustainable urban freight transport.

Additionally, some research has mentioned the operational integration based on partial distribution innovations. For example, Kikuta et al. (2012) have discussed that *Yamato Transport Co.* (Japan) has been adopting a tram system for transhipping goods to Arashiyama in Kyoto, then using cargo-bikes to conduct the last-mile delivery within urban areas. He and Haasis (2019) has proposed the concept of sustainable inner-urban intermodal transportation, which is integrating these eleven distribution innovations by small standardized containers. Nevertheless, much less research focuses on systematically selecting these different innovations to construct delivery strategies for future sustainable urban freight transport. It is noted that a systematic selection method contributes to logistics providers to construct efficient sustainable freight strategies for future cities. This finding also highlights that systematic consideration of operational integrations on distribution innovations is necessary for future SUFT.

To sum up, both exogenous and endogenous trends have radically influenced the short-term planning of sustainable urban freight transport. The result of section 3 has indicated that, thus far, there is very little research work and fewer systematically prepared findings for the long-term planning of SUFT. The previous analysis demonstrates that the long-term planning of SUFT needs to systematically discuss and integrated consider these two trends. Therefore, the selection of the appropriate research methods plays a critical role in developing a theoretical framework of future sustainable urban freight transport. Furthermore, exogenous and endogenous trends maintain a set of relations that influences each other. The operational integration of distribution innovations needs to consider the future trends of urban development. Meanwhile, sustainable strategies of urban planning have to integrate urban freight transport into the urban development agenda. Owing to the exogenous and endogenous trends is interlocking and complex components on urban freight planning, selecting the appropriate research methods is a critical step for constructing the framework. In view of this, this chapter discusses the foresight research methods, which are suitable for investigating both exogenous and endogenous trends.

3.6   Appropriate Methodology Selection

Despite the nine approaches have been employed in the article corpus, these methodologies are not enough to construct a feasible framework for future sustainable urban freight transport. Concurrently, the feasibility of the distinct method mix is also necessary to be further discussed after determining the appropriate methods. Therefore, this section analyzes the impacts of urban development and distribution innovations on future urban freight transport. Meanwhile, this chapter followed the general framework of foresight research to discuss the method selections and feasibility of methods mix systematically.

3.6.1   Fundamental Elements of Foresight Research Framework

In academic discourse, the term *Foresight* is used to delineate from forecasting and emphasize the explorative nature of the processes involved (Schatzmann et al. 2013), while is also a capacity to systematically think about the future to inform decision making today (Conway 2015). Furthermore, considerable scholars suggest that foresight research is future-oriented, which needs from a long-term (next 10 to 25 years or more) view (i.e. Glenn (1994); Mozuni and Jonas (2016); Conway and Voros (2003)). Therefore, the approach of foresight (future) research is "the tools, methods and thinking styles used to build an organizational foresight capacity, usually interdisciplinary and inclusive rather than restricted to a particular philosophy, discipline or method" (Conway 2015). Additionally, the approaches use a longer-term (10 to 20 or more year time) frame to facilitate thinking that moves beyond the boundaries of convention and the status-quo (Conway 2015).

Following the understanding of the relevant concept of foresight research, the general framework of foresight research needs to discuss further. Popper (2008) has demonstrated the general framework of foresight research that as depicted by figure 3.7. His research exhibited that foresight research is a systematic process with five interconnected and complementary phases: (1) Pre-foresight phase, (2) Recruitment phase, (3) Generation phase, (4) Action phase, and (5) Renewal phase. In the general framework of the foresight process, the "methods mix" refers to the combination of foresight methods which 25 approaches are used in 886 cases (Popper 2008). In his research, these sets of data are cited from *European Foresight Monitoring Network* (EFMN)[2] and *Strategic Euro-Latin Foresight Research and University Learning Exchange* (SELF-RULE) [3]. Figure 3.8 shows these 25 approaches as well as their used frequency in the 886 cases. The usage of the literature review (LR) accounts for almost 54%, which is the most extensive method in these cases. Besides on the LR, the foresight methods also include the future workshop, key technologies, interviews, technology road mapping, cross-impact/structural anal-

---

[2]EFMN, https://www.efmn.eu
[3]SELF-RULE, www.self-rule.org

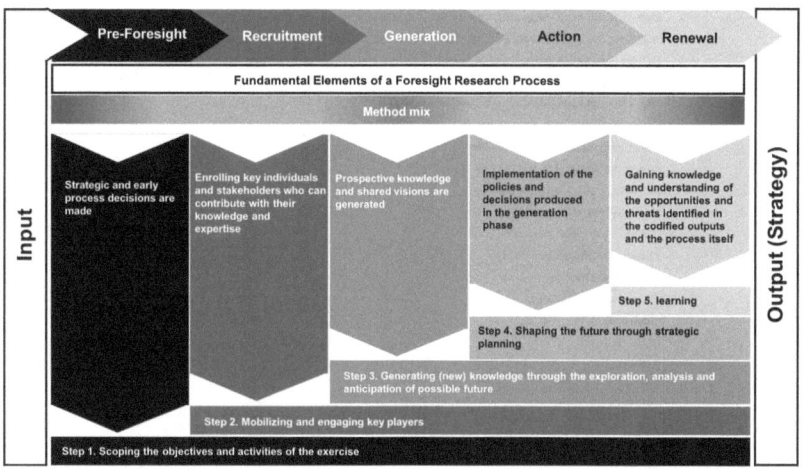

Figure 3.7 General framework of foresight research. (Adapted from Popper (2008))

ysis, morphological analysis, etc. Due to owning 25 foresight research methods, selecting the appropriate method is a critical success element for long-term planning of sustainable urban freight transport.

For responding to RQ.4, selecting the appropriate foresight research methods play a critical role in this chapter. In these 25 methods, the qualitative methods are more widely used than quantitative and semi-quantitative ones (Popper 2008), such as the LR, expert panels, trends extrapolation/megatrends, morphological analysis, etc. Because the research in futurology is inescapably identified by subjective and creative descriptions of the changes creating or shaping the future (Popper 2008). For responding to RQ.3, this chapter discusses and selects the appropriate foresight research methods by the general framework of foresight research.

3.6.2   Method Selection of Foresight Research on Future Sustainable Urban Logistics

Based on the previous discussion, 25 methods can be used in foresight research. Combined with the issues of city logistics, this work selects 3 methods that presented as followed.

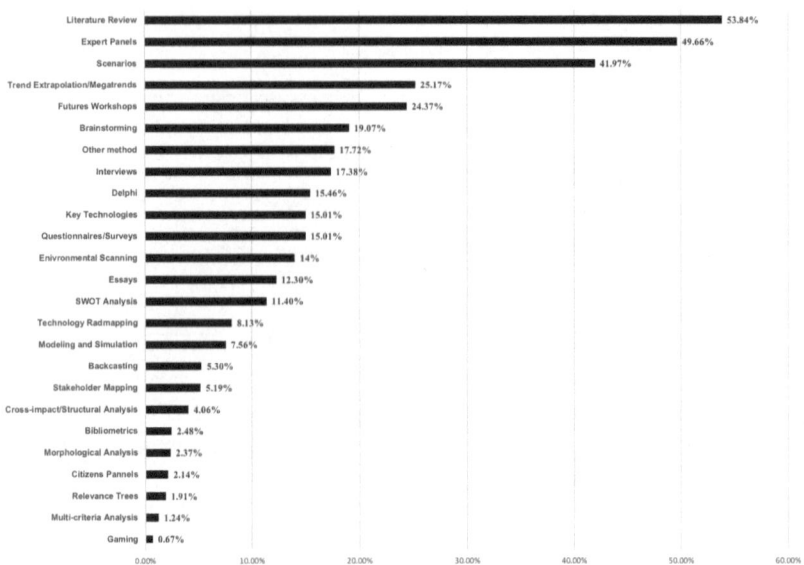

Figure 3.8 Use frequency of 25 foresight research methods. (Adapted from Popper (2008) who is based on EMFN and SELF-RULE)

(1) The Method of Trend Extrapolation/Megatrends

This method assumes the future is a continuation of the past, which can provide a rough idea about the present and past developments in the future (Popper 2008). City logistics is a complex system that involved the stakeholders, environmental externalities, benefit-cost balance, and other issues. The sustainable urban freight system is a popular topic in this field due to it plays a crucial role in the sustainable and liveable city in the future. Nevertheless, considerable research has paid scant attention to the links between urban freight planning and the trends of city development (Cui et al. 2015). Concurrently, the city development as the exogenous trends that has radically influenced the urban freight system. For example, urbanization has increased the delivery range of city logistics; the urban population growth has exacerbated both congestions and emissions created by freight demands increased.

For responding to these trends, the urban logistics providers aims to find the appropriate endogenous solutions to promote the sustainability of urban freight. In fact, many issues of city logistics are around transport modes. An example is that environmental externalities created by freight activities, which include emissions, congestions, and noise, etc. (Anderson et al. 2005; Wittlöv 2012). In consequence, a majority of technology enterprises have launched/produced the project of emerging transport modes for urban freight transport. An example is the Velove Armadillo cargo bike produced by the Swedish company Velove (Velove Cororpation nd). Moreover, the logistics provider has developed emerging operational strategies based on urban distribution innovations. For instance, the DHL Express piloted the *City Hub* concept (2017) that is the vehicles combined with a customized trailer carrying up to four containers, then the use of DHL Cubicycles (a cargo-bike able to carry a container) to complete last-mile delivery (Deutsche Post DHL Group 2017). Therefore, the use of distribution innovations is an efficient solution for future urban freight system (He and Haasis 2019), such as the implementation of electric vehicles can reduce the emission created by freight activities.

Understanding the future trends of urban development and city logistics plays a critical role in foresight research on sustainable urban freight planning. Furthermore, it is critical to analyze both interactions and impacts between them. The next problem is how to understand the future trends of city and freight. According to the used frequency of the foresight method, this research selects the method of LR to discuss the specific content of both trends.

(2) The Method of Literature Review
The method of LR is an environmental scanning process, which is constructed by around the themes and related theories of the relevant articles (Popper 2008). The systematical literature review (SLR) as a specific method is extensively used. As mentioned previously, foresight research of sustainable urban freight planning needs to understand the exogenous and endogenous trends of urban freight transport, namely the trends of urban development and the trends of urban distribution innovations. To respond to these problems, the method of LR is a suitable approach to understanding both trends. It is noted that, from a long-term perspective, the application of emerging transport mobility has changed the conventional urban freight network (He and Haasis 2019). An example is that the urban freight tram/metro system uses the integrated transit station, which changes the freight network structure into the multi-tier (three/four tier) structure (e.g., Shen et al. (2015); Fatnassi et al. (2015); Masson et al. (2017)). It is foreseeable that the various distribution innovations will be operated together as a system in the future. The collaboration and integration of distinct distribution innovations have increasingly become the future trends of sustainable urban logistics. From a view of long-term planning, this finding implies that the application of various distribution innovations in the future possibly exacerbate the inflexibility of the conventional urban freight network. To this end, the first question of LR is the research status regarding urban freight network design and the urban distribution innovations, which need to analyze and discuss further.

Meanwhile, the interaction and impacts of both topics also have to further analyze and discuss from a futurology perspective.

In recent decades, urban development has exacerbated the challenges of city logistics. The urban population growth is the primary element that caused persistent issues and emerging urban challenges (UN-Habitat 2016). In this end, the impacts of these issues and challenges on the urban freight system need an in-depth discussion and further analysis. The usage of literature review contributes to understanding the specific content of future trends on urban development. Therefore, the LR method is an efficient and appropriate approach for understanding the future trends of both city development and urban distribution innovations. Additionally, the dimensions of design future sustainable urban freight systems include urban freight network structure and emerging operation strategies. The objective of the future sustainable urban freight system design is further promoting the sustainability from the perspectives of environmental, social, and economic dimensions. It aims to increase the flexibility of conventional urban freight network structure. The next step is to select an appropriate foresight method to design future urban freight system.

(3) The Method of Morphological Analysis
The method of morphological analysis is systematically structuring and comprehensively studying the total set of relationships contained in multi-dimensional, non-quantifiable, problem complexes (Zwicky 1969; Ritchey 1998). This method enables us to systematically predicting possible future technologies and feasible solutions. As mentioned previously, the foresight research of city logistics needs to comprehensively consider three dimensions: the trends of city development, the application of urban distribution innovations, as well as the network structure of the urban freight system. Meanwhile, the interactions and impacts between each dimension need to further studies that are from a view of multi-dimensional.

Moreover, the future trends of applied urban distribution innovations are used integration approach to compose the emerging operational strategies, such as the concept of "sustainable inner-urban intermodal transportation" (He and Haasis 2019), and the "city logistics hubs" is launched by DHL (Germany). Given that multiple distribution innovations are presumably used in the future urban freight system, the selection of these innovations and combination is also an investigate topic for the foresight research of urban logistics. It is noted that this topic also belongs to the issue of multi-dimensional and non-quantifiable. Besides the operational integration of urban distribution innovations, considerable technology enterprises have launched several specific projects of developing emerging transport mobility. An example is ZF Friedrichshafen AG (Germany) has proposed *Autonomous Depot* that is a robotic vehicle equipped with the parcel lockers (as depicted by Figure 3.9). From a

view of technology companies, integrated technologies of various distribution innovations are able to develop the brand new transport modes for future city logistics.
Forecasting the possible future transport modes is also a crucial component for the
long-term planning of sustainable urban freight transport. Due to the applications
of different transport modes that have influenced the freight network structure, the
prediction of future technologies contributes to design a flexible network structure
from a long-term view, which thereby further promoting sustainability. These findings, as discussed previously, highlight that the method of morphological analysis
is one of the efficient solutions for the foresight research of future urban logistics.

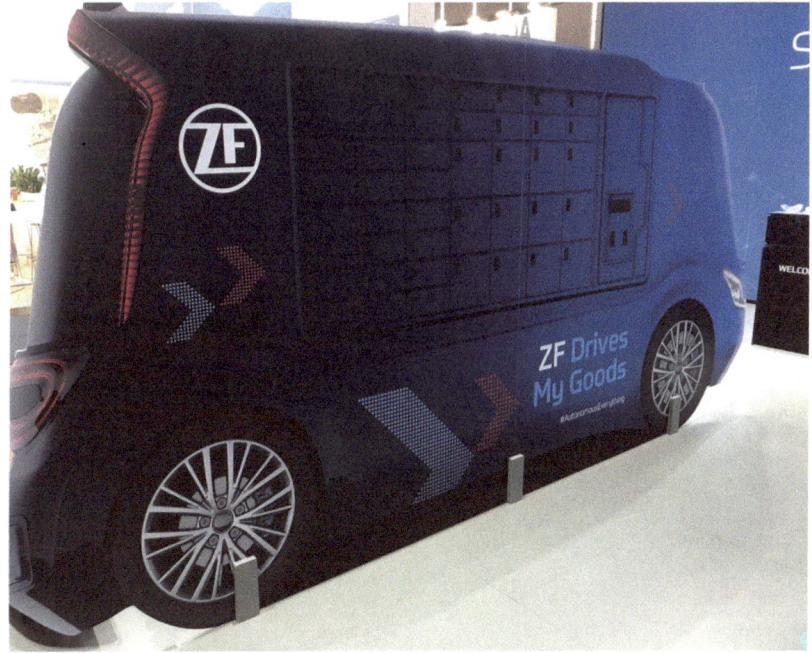

Figure 3.9 Autonomous Depot. (Photo by Author, Hannover Messe 2019, Germany)

After determining the possible future distribution models in city logistics, the
next step is to design a flexible and sustainable urban freight network structure.
Indeed, considerable research on city logistics planning is mainly based on the conventional urban freight network structure, namely single-tier or two-tier system.
The research perspective of these articles is also from a view of short-term plan-

ning. As mentioned previously, foresight research focuses on long-term planning. The method of morphological analysis contributed to the understanding of future urban logistics. The morphological analysis contributes to design a flexible urban freight network structure due to it is a qualitative methodology for systematic consideration of all external factors. This finding reveals that the usage of morphological analysis is a suitable method to design future urban freight system, particularly after understanding the mega-trends of city and freight.

3.6.3 The Feasibility of Method Mix

Based on the previous discussion, this chapter identified the appropriate methods for the foresight research of the future sustainable urban freight system. These methods are consist of trend extrapolation/megatrends, literature review, and morphological analysis. Followed the general framework of foresight research (Figure 3.7), the next step is further analyzing the feasibility of the method mix. This process is to understand the relationships and influence of methods among themselves by creating a methods combination matrix (MCM). MCM shows the total frequency of a method employed in a sample of 886 cases (Popper 2008). Given this, this chapter discusses the feasibility of the method mix between the trend extrapolation/megatrends, literature review, and morphological analysis.

Table 3.5 Frequency of using method mix. (Adapted from Popper (2008) who is based on EMFN and SELF-RULE)

	Trend Extrapolation /Megatrends	Literature Review	Morphological Analysis
Trend Extrapolation /Megatrends	–	Very high	High
Literature Review	Very high	–	Very high
Morphological Analysis	High	Very high	–

Table 3.5 exhibits that the method combination of LR and trend extrapolation/megatrends is a "high combination" that accounts for almost 40–59% in the 886 cases. Furthermore, the method combination of LR and morphological analysis is a "very high combination" that accounts for approximately above 60%. In the end, the method combination of trend extrapolation/megatrends and morphological analysis is also a "high combination". This finding reveals that the combinations between

these three methods were widely used in foresight research. In the previous section, the suitabilities of these three methods have separately discussed for the foresight research of city logistics. Combined with the feasibility of the method mix, these three methods have identified eventually that are used to develop the theoretical framework of foresight research on sustainable urban freight transport.

3.7 Theoretical Research Framework of Future SUFT

For responding to RQ.4, this chapter defines the research method as the vertical dimension of the framework and research elements as its horizontal dimension. The three methods of foresight research are selected: trend extrapolation/megatrends, literature review, and morphological analysis. Followed the general framework of foresight research, the research elements include the three dimensions: urban development, distribution innovations, and urban network structure. Moreover, the urban freight network is primarily composed of the transport fleets, infrastructures, and destination locations from a view of physical transport. It is noted that, besides the vertical and horizontal dimensions of the framework, the sustainable transition is also a critical role for city logistics. Based on these discussions, the components of the framework are identified.

Although the logistics providers and technology enterprises have promoted innovative transport modes to achieve sustainability, currently, these emerging strategies unable to entirely replace the original system. Owing to relevant companies need to comprehensively consider the cost of emerging transport strategies as well as the urban land-use conflict of constructing new infrastructure. Therefore, the logistics providers commonly used transition perspective to develop the appropriate operation measures. According to the literature review, the *transition perspective* can be understood as that is based on the co-evolution of the different actors on the different levels (Geels and Schot 2007), and a significant component of innovation is the new combinations of existing elements (Geels 2011). In fact, both logistics providers and technology enterprises have promoted a sustainable transition process is involved in the combination of existed and emerging elements. This combination includes the infrastructure, transport modes, as well as strategy/policy, etc. The sustainable transition process is a nonlinear, complex, and long-term process that results from the interplay of development (Arvidsson and Pazirandeh 2017). In consequence, from a view of the long-term planning, the logistics providers commonly used the new technologies/infrastructures/strategies to connect to the old technologies in the form of an auxiliary add-on, thereby improving its functioning (Arvidsson and Pazirandeh 2017). This process likewise for the new infrastructure of supporting the application of emerging transport modes. Moreover, the sustainable transition can promote the sustainability of urban freight system from the perspectives of the cost-saving, and decreasing the environmental externalities, etc.

Figure 3.10 shows the theoretical research framework of future sustainable urban freight Transport. This framework contributes a research model to the urban logistics providers can make the transition to the flexible and sustainable system of urban freight. It also helps the logistics providers to better accommodate to the exogenous and endogenous trends of urban freight transport from a long-term view. First, using the method mix of the trends extrapolation/megatrends and Literature review to discuss the exogenous and endogenous trends of sustainable urban logistics. After that, the impacts of urban distribution innovations on the conventional urban freight network need to further analysis, while detecting the research gaps between these two topics based on the systematic literature review. Based on the previous discussions, the next step is using the method of morphology analysis to study the future strategy of urban freight distribution. Subsequently, analyzing the implication of exogenous trends on conventional urban freight network is necessary. In the end, integrated the previous two steps to discuss the future urban freight network structure, thereby further promoting its sustainability and flexibility.

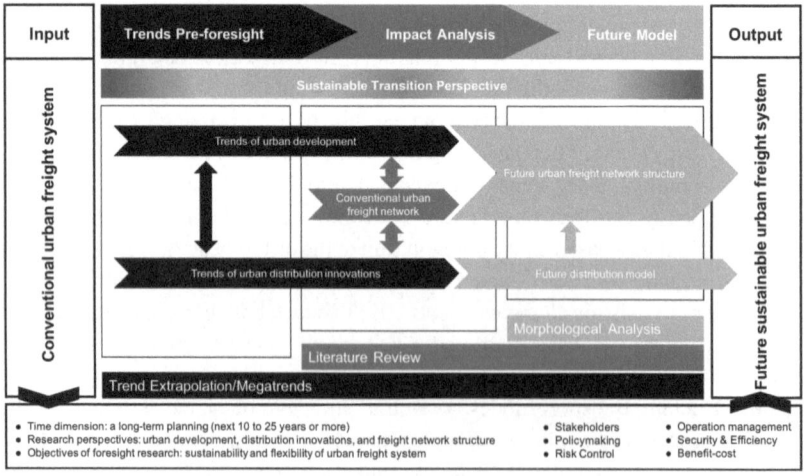

Figure 3.10 Theoretical research framework of future SUFT. (Source: Author's own elaboration)

Figure 3.11 demonstrates more details related to this research framework. In first, the method mix of literature review and trend extrapolation is used to understand the exogenous and endogenous trends of future sustainable urban freight transport. Furthermore, cross-impact analysis is intended to determine the impacts factors of both trends on sustainable urban freight transport, which are the parameters in the morphological matrix. After that, the approach of morphological analysis is employed to construct the appropriate strategies of sustainable urban freight transport with a long-term perspective. In the end, the network structure of the future sustainable urban freight transport needs further discussion based on innovative sustainable urban freight strategies. The evaluation& assessment system is consists of sustainability, flexibility, and external criteria. Sustainability includes three dimensions: environment, economy, and society. The flexibility evaluation is based on three aspects: passive expansion of logistics infrastructure, passive increase freight fleets, and addressing short-term issues or not. Besides these, there are three external criteria: benefit-cost analysis, efficiency assessment, and security evaluation. From a long-term view, endogenous trends are possible to change the stakeholders. An example is the usage of public transit logistics, which is to integrate the passenger and freight within urban areas. Additionally, the research on future sustainable urban freight transport needs to consider decision support and the formulation of urban freight policy. Moreover, the application of distribution innovations has to be supported by the information and communications technology (e.g., the control platform for the delivery robots and drones). Although the current urban planning agenda focuses on the passenger, integrating sustainable freight into the urban planning agenda contributes to the formulation of long-term sustainable strategies for the cities. Furthermore, consumers' behavior change and technology innovations (e.g., 3D-printer) are critical components for the long-term planning of SUFT. Meanwhile, the replacement strategies of freight vehicles need to further discuss from a transition perspective.

This framework aims to handle the challenges of city logistics created by the exogenous and endogenous trends of urban freight. Notwithstanding, some external factors also need to consider systematically. Indeed, research of urban freight system needs to systematically consider many elements due to the city logistics is a complex system that involved multiple dimensions (i.e., stakeholders, infrastructures, and policymaking, etc.). The foresight research of sustainable city logistics also needs to consider these dimensions. The interplay of stakeholders is a critical factor for the policymaking of city logistics. This sustainable transition process is possible to change the relations of stakeholders. It is noted that the application of emerging

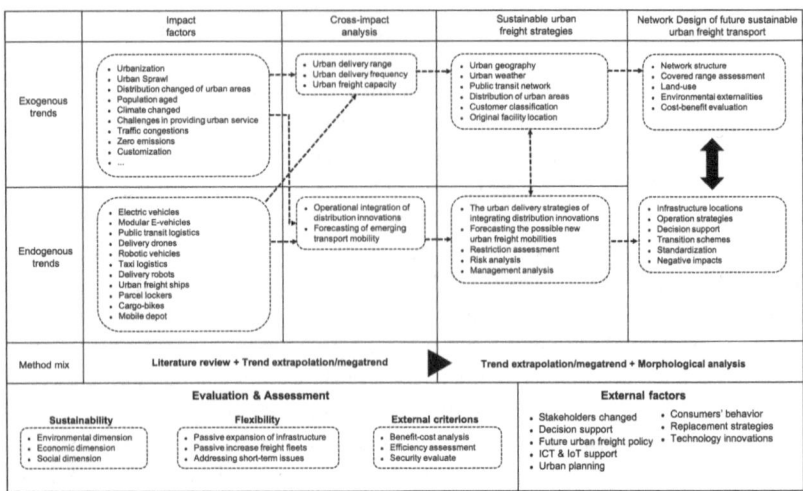

Figure 3.11 Description of theoretical research framework on future sustainable urban freight transport. (Source: Author's own elaboration)

transport modes also needs support from the urban freight policy. For example, constructing the tram transit station that integrated the passenger and freight, and the using delivery drones within urban areas. Hence, both research on urban freight policymaking and stakeholders' impacts are critical components of the future urban freight system in long-term planning.

Additionally, the logistics providers are primarily concerned with the risk evaluation and operation management under this sustainable transition. The possible risks include laws, costs, as well as the security and effectiveness of urban delivery, etc. Due to the real situation of each city exist gaps, the risk evaluation contributes to the logistics providers to better achieve the goals of the transition, namely sustainability and flexibility. From a view of operation management, integration of various distribution innovations that operate together as a system is an emerging challenge for the logistics providers. Likewise, these challenges exacerbate the possible risks, which also need to prediction and control through foresight research. In conclusion, future research directions need to comprehensively consider these elements based on the foresight research of urban freight system.

3.8   The Sustainability of Future SUFT

The definition of sustainable development is "a development that meets the needs of the present without compromising the ability of future generations to meet their own needs" (Brundtland et al. 1987). The principles of sustainable urban transport include three dimensions: Social equity, economic growth, and environmental protection. As demonstrated by Behrends et al. (2008), a SUFT system needs to fulfill all the following objectives:

- "to ensure the accessibility offered by the transport system to all categories of freight transport;
- to reduce air pollution, greenhouse gas emissions, waste and noise to levels without negative impacts on the health of the citizens or nature;
- to improve the resource- and energy-efficiency and cost-effectiveness of the transportation of goods, taking into account the external costs and;
- to contribute to the enhancement of the attractiveness and quality of the urban environment, by avoiding accidents, minimizing the use of land and without compromising the mobility of citizens."

Based on the previous discussion, it is vital to systematically consider the exogenous and endogenous trends to design future sustainable urban freight transport. Admittedly, applying the distribution innovations is in a degree to reduce the negative environmental externalities, which can promote sustainability from the dimension of environmental protection. Nevertheless, the fragmented application of distribution innovations is to increase the total costs of logistics providers, exacerbate the urban space conflicts, and challenges the capacity of existing transport networks. From the dimensions of economic and social, it restricts the further promotion of sustainability. The sustainability of future SUFT needs to balance these three dimensions simultaneously. It aims to find an optimal solution which is not the best solution for one dimension.

Although most of the cities have formulated the sustainable development agenda, thus far, the transportation systems in most of the cities and urban areas are unsustainable. The main reason is that ineffective and fragmented urban governance is hard to generate a systematic agenda of sustainable urban planning with a long-term view (UN-Habitat 2016). Meanwhile, the urban planning system is focused principally on passenger transport (Behrends et al. 2008). This has caused urban freight to remain marginalized in sustainable urban planning. This finding reveals that the future SUFT needs to comprehensively consider the urban development to formulate sustainable strategies, which contribute to connecting to the sustainable urban development strategies at the city level. Additionally, the notion of smart cities has changed the original sustainable urban planning agenda. Although the universal agreement of the definition is lacking, academia has agreed that it radically influences the building allocation and urban transport. The development of ICT and IoT is also an emerging challenge for the information security of urban freight customers and logistics providers. Therefore, future SUFT also needs to reduce the risks of information security as much as possible, thereby promoting sustainability in the social dimension.

3.9   Conclusion of This Chapter

This chapter presents a theoretical research framework of future sustainable urban freight transport, while to discuss the appropriate methodologies. At present, to the best of our knowledge, the long-term planning of SUFT is lacking. Accompanied with the urban development and application of distribution innovations, this gap is possible to restrict the further sustainability of UFT in the future cities. City development has exacerbated the challenges of city logistics, particularly on the large/megacities around the world. The trends of city development as the exogenous trends of urban freight have motivated the logistics providers to find endogenous solutions to cope with these challenges. From a short-term view, usage of urban distribution innovations is an efficient solution to promote the sustainable urban freight system. Nevertheless, considerable research has paid scant attention to the impacts of both urban development and distribution innovations on the conventional urban freight system. For responding to this gap, applying the foresight methods is an efficient solution for the research on the long-term planning of SUFT in these two aspects.

Given that, this chapter employs the SLR to detect the literature on foresight research published in 2003–2018. Subsequently, the impacts of exogenous and endogenous trends on future SUFT are systematically discussed. This step contributes to selecting the appropriate research methodologies to construct the theoretical framework. Meanwhile, the theory of transition perspective is integrated into the theoretical framework to improve its feasibility. A combination of existing and emerging elements is a critical component of the current urban freight system, which makes the transition to the future system. This combination is involved in the infrastructures, transport modes, policies, etc. Due to urban freight transport is a complex system, multiple dimensions need to consider in the research of city logistics comprehensively. Based on the theoretical framework, the dimensions of stakeholders, policy, risk evaluation, and management have also discussed.

The limitations of this chapter include the followed aspects: First, urban development is also influenced by the decision of the local government. The authorities are to adjust the model of urban development based on the investment environment, economic positioning, and geopolitics. This framework did not further discuss this point. Additionally, this framework did not further discuss the impacts of external technologies on sustainable urban logistics, such as the 3D-Printer. Hence, future studies will involve these limitations to strengthen and test the framework. this chapter can assist practitioners and researchers to better orient their efforts on promoting sustainable city logistics in the future.

Future Trends of SUFT

4

4.1 Logical Arrangement of the Chapter

This chapter presents the conceptual model of sustainable inner-urban intermodal transportation (SIUIT), which can be used as the future operational model of urban freight transportation. This chapter followed both the research framework of this work (in Chapter 2) and the theoretical framework of foresight research (in Chapter 3). In Chapter 2, the systematic literature review determined 11 urban distribution innovations in sustainable urban logistics. Nevertheless, relevant research lacks a systematic analysis in aspects with applied status and usage restrictions on distribution innovations (Gap 2 as mentioned in Chapter 2). It is noteworthy that fulfilling this gap is critical to developing the operational model of future SUFT. To this end, this chapter focuses on the analysis of the implemented status and the applied restrictions on these innovations, thereby proposing the conceptual model of SIUIT. Figure 4.1 depicts the logical structure of this chapter.

This chapter was published as an article[1] in the *Sustainablility*. The content exposed in this chapter aims to resolve four sub-questions of this work as below:

- What is the status of the applications and research of these innovations in urban freight transport?
- What are the restrictions and suitability of these innovations in urban freight transport?
- What is the future transport model in urban freight system?

---

[1] He, Z and Haasis, H.D (2019). Integration of Urban Freight Innovations: Sustainable Inner-Urban Intermodal Transportation in the Retail/Postal Industry. *Sustainability 11*(6), 1749.

Z. He, *Future Sustainable Urban Freight Network Design in the Large Cities and Megacities*, Sustainable Management, Wertschöpfung und Effizienz, https://doi.org/10.1007/978-3-658-34203-6_4

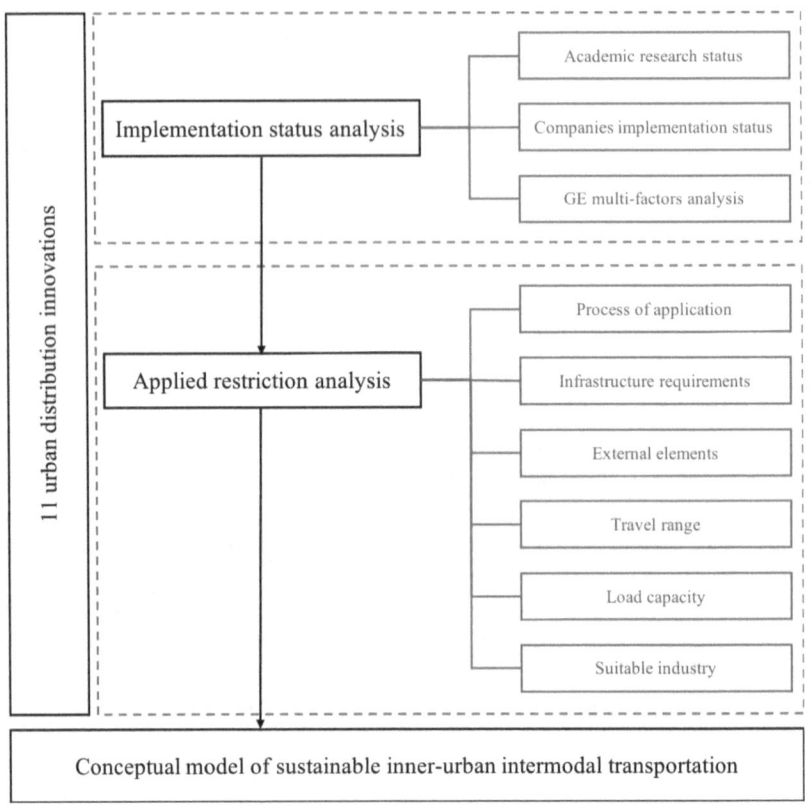

Figure 4.1 Structure of Chapter 4

As published paper, this chapter is organized as below: Section 4.2 introduces the research background and motivations of this chapter. Section 4.3 is the research question and methodology in the published paper. Section 4.4 presents a systematic literature review to identify the concept of urban distribution innovations. Section 4.5 employs the method of GE multi-factors analysis to discuss the applied status of these distribution innovations from both dimensions of academic research and company implementation. In Section 4.6, the applied restrictions of these 11 innovations are discussed from the six dimensions (as mentioned in Figure 4.1). According to the previous discussion, the conceptual model of sustainable inner-urban intermodal transportation is constructed to address Gap 1 as mentioned in Chapter 2.

This model is based on the application of standardized small-containers in urban logistics. In the end, the conclusion of this chapter is in Section 4.7.

Urban population growth has permanently increased the commodity demands and freight flow within urban areas. The retail/postal industry is intent on finding appropriate internal approaches and a new business model to respond to the adverse impacts generated by urban freight activities. Usage of emerging transport modes is an efficient solution for these industries. Nevertheless, considerable research has paid less attention to the implementation status of distribution innovations, as well as to their suitability and application restrictions. Concurrently, a comprehensive consideration of various distribution innovations that operate together as a system is lacking. To this end, this chapter adopted a literature review method and GE multifactorial analysis. Specifically, this chapter reviewed the related articles published in 2013–2018 to define the concept of distribution innovations. In addition, the approach of GE multifactorial analysis is adopted to analyze the application status of distribution innovations from the perspective of academic research and company implementation. Following the suitability assessment and application of restriction analysis, the concept of sustainable inner-urban intermodal transport (SIUIT) is formulated for the retail/postal industry. This chapter contributes to the sustainable urban freight literature by exploring possible future research directions of SIUIT.

4.2   Introduction

Urban demographic expansion has led to persistent issues and emerging urban challenges, for instance urban sprawl and an aging urban population (UN-Habitat 2016). These issues and challenges are an exogenous trend that has radically influenced the urban freight system. The commodity demand growth and consumer behavior changes have continually increased the frequency of freight activities within urban areas, particularly in the retail and postal industries, which has been accompanied by significant e-commerce growth since the year 2000, increasing on average 10–20% per year for online retail (Rodrigue et al. 2016). This increased activity implies that the high frequency of parcel delivery will exacerbate emission and urban congestion, as it is the primary model of transporting goods to consumers for e-commerce. For the retail industry, urban population expansion has increased the commodity demands and freight flows within urban areas. It is estimated that urban freight accounts for 10–15% of vehicle equivalent miles on a city street (ALICE/ERTRAC Urban mobility WG 2015). In addition, freight and the city maintain a set of core relations, as the city is an entity where production, distribution, and consumption movements are used and compete for scarce land (Rodrigue et al. 2016). To this end, the retail/postal enterprises have increasingly become concerned with balancing the relation between economic benefits and the urban environment.

Despite the fact that urban freight movements have continually contributed to the economic growth of cities, this has caused more environmental externalities within urban areas. These externalities primary consist of air pollution, congestion, noise, etc. (Anderson et al. 2005; Wittlöv 2012). While cities are responsible for more than 70% of global carbon dioxide emissions (UN-Habitat 2016), almost 5.5% of the total annual greenhouse gas emissions are generated by the logistics and transport sectors, around 57% of which are caused by road freight transport (Doherty and Hoyle 2009). In addition, congestion is also a major issue created by urban freight. Urban freight transport (UFT) is responsible for 10–15% of vehicles equivalent miles traveled on urban streets (ALICE/ERTRAC Urban mobility WG 2015). Of these vehicles, only 42.6% of the miles traveled were full load, and approximately 25% were entirely or half empty loaded (Bureau of Transportation and Statistics, Research and Innovation Technology 2009). Nevertheless, simultaneously solving these issues is difficult in the current circumstance. Hence, from the views of local authorities and urban inhabits, these externalities have fundamentally required the retail and postal industries to choose more suitable transport modes and operational strategies for the various segments of urban freight transport. Additionally, for companies that are involved in the retail/postal industry, the commodity demand growth and consumer behavior changes have resulted in companies attempting to find appropriate internal approaches and new business models to accommodate these challenges created by exogenous trends. To this end, several enterprises involved in retail/postal have used emerging transport modes while developing an innovative urban freight concept to cope with these environmental externalities in cities. For instance, *Yamato Transport Co., Ltd.* (Tokyo, Japan) has utilized the tram to transport parcels in the city of Sapporo since 2012 (Kikuta et al. 2012), and the result has presented that this system has reduced CO_2 emissions and almost halved the number of trucks used for delivering parcels within urban areas (Taniguchi et al. 2016). In 2007, the initiative *Vracht Door De Gracht* (freight through the canal) in Amsterdam was launched by *Mokum Mariteam*, where the inland waterway was used to transport retail goods to consumers; it is equipped with a low-noise electrical engine that generates a reduction of energy usage, as well as PM10 and CO_2 emissions (Maes et al. 2015). The results have demonstrated that these distribution innovations have enabled the effective mitigation of congestion and emission issues created by the conventional urban freight model. It is noted that, accompanied by both digital transformation and the development of information communications technologies (ICT), a majority of technology companies have developed new distribution innovations for the urban freight system. For example, *Starship Co., Ltd.* (Liverpool, U.K.) has developed the delivery robot for last-mile delivery, which is capable of carrying goods no more than 100 pounds (Starship nd). Mercedes-Benz Co., Ltd. (Stuttgart, Germany) has launched *Vision Vans* to deliver goods on the urban freight network, which will be equipped with two delivery drones (Mercedes-Benz 2016). Therefore, applying distribution innovations is an efficient solution for the retail/postal companies in the future city while enabling the provision of individual logistics services, thereby increasing the enterprises' competitiveness.

However, much less research has paid attention to the application status of distribution innovations and their suitability assessment. In addition, comprehensive consideration of operation strategies and risk evaluations, particularly on various distribution innovations that operate together as a system, is lacking. Concurrently, the distribution innovations research of academia and the development projects of companies have appeared as a highly asymmetric trend. To this end, this chapter adopts the literature review approach and the method of GE multifactorial analysis to respond to these issues. First, Section 4.4 reviews articles published in 2013–2018 from the Scopus database. The distribution innovations are consist of 11 emerging transport modes from the view of the retail/postal logistics system. In Section 4.5, GE multifactorial analysis is used to analyze the status of these distribution innovations from the two perspectives of academia and companies. Section 4.6 demonstrates the suitability assessment of these innovations and proposes the concept of sustainable inner-urban intermodal transport (SIUIT).

4.3   Research Question and Methodology

A considerable body of research has paid little attention to the application and research status of distribution innovations, as well as to the comprehensive consideration of their restrictions and suitability. This chapter intends to analyze their application and research status and to assess their restrictions and suitability in urban freight transport. As previously mentioned, the concept of distribution innovations does not have an accurate definition, so the first research question (RQ.1) addressed in this chapter is as follows:

RQ.1: In recent years, what are the emerging transport modes for distribution innovations in urban freight transport?

The related companies aim to utilize the emerging transport modes to balance the relations between economic benefits and environmental externalities by freight activities. For academic research, scholars are more concerned with the planning scheme design, impacts/risks evaluation, and policy discussions. Nevertheless, the research and application status of distribution innovations in urban freight transport reveals an asymmetry. This asymmetry is capable of restricting the application and promotion of these innovations in the urban freight system. Consequently, the principal second research question (RQ.2) is the following:

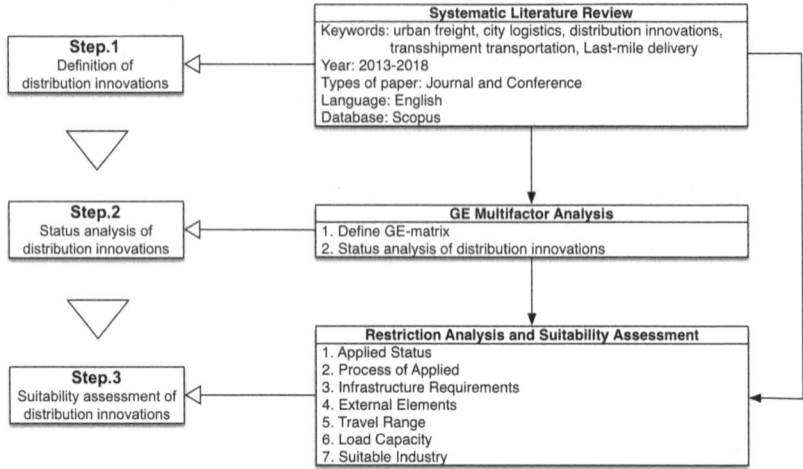

Figure 4.2 Research methodology

RQ.2: What is the status of the applications and research of these innovations in urban freight transport?

As mentioned previously, a lack of a comprehensive consideration of restrictions and suitability regarding the emerging transport modes exists. Given that these transport modes need to be integrated with the conventional/new modes, assessing the restrictions and suitability of them is necessary. To this end, the last research question (RQ.3) is as follows:

RQ.3: What are the restrictions and suitability of these innovations in urban freight transport?

To respond to the above research questions, this chapter opted for the approach of systematic literature reviews (SLR) and the method of GE multifactorial analysis. The research methodology is presented in Figure 4.2). First, this chapter systematically reviewed the related articles published in 2013–2018 from the Scopus database. According to the literature review, we defined the concept of distribution innovations in urban freight transport, thereby answering RQ.1. Furthermore, GE multifactorial analysis was used to formulate the GE matrix from the views of academic research and company applications. Then, the GE matrix is used to analyze the status of these distribution innovations. Finally, this chapter assessed the restrictions and suitability of these innovations through the previous SLR, as well as the related reports from companies. Concurrently, the concept of sustainable inner-urban intermodal transport is constructed to integrate these distribution innovations into one system.

4.4 Literature Review of Distribution Innovations

In recent decades, numerous emerging technologies have been widely implemented in the urban freight system. Urban distribution innovations refer to the transportation enterprises that apply the emerging urban transport mobility to the transship/delivery of goods within urban areas and are intended to reduce the negative impacts created by freight movements and provide the diversification of logistics services. For instance, electric vehicles and cargo bikes are such innovations. However, the lack of a comprehensive analysis regarding the various distribution innovations and their application range remains. To this end, this chapter adopted the literature review approach to understand the distribution innovations and analyze the research and implementation status of these emerging technologies. Table 4.1 demonstrates the indicators of the paper selection.

According to the indicators of the paper selection, the titles and abstracts of the selected papers were reviewed for each paper. After a discussion and analysis, papers that were unrelated to the research topic were removed from the bibliography corpus. Moreover, almost 70 papers were not strictly concerned with emerging transport modes in transshipment transportation or last-mile delivery.

Table 4.1 Paper selection

Items	Description
Main keywords	Urban Freight Transport, City Logistics, Transshipment transportation, Last-mile delivery
Inclusion criteria	Transportation, Economic, Management
Language	English
Document types	Journal Articles and Conference Papers
Source	Scopus
Time interval	2013–2018

Table 4.2 Topics in the paper corpus of distribution innovations

Topic	Description	Transshipment Transportation	Last-Mile Delivery
Electric vehicles	Applied the E-vehicles to transport the goods in urban areas	Rizet et al. (2016); Lebeau et al. (2015b); Giordano et al. (2018); Teoh et al. (2018); Koháni et al. (2017)	Cagliano et al. (2017); Franceschetti et al. (2017); Taefi et al. (2017); Wątróbski et al. (2017); Cossu (2016); Taefi (2016); Yang et al. (2016); Ahani et al. (2016); Lebeau et al. (2016); Schau et al. (2016b); Quak et al. (2016); Rizet et al. (2016); Taefi et al. (2016); Schau et al. (2016a); Liakos et al. (2016); Lebeau et al. (2015b,c); Schau et al. (2015); Lebeau et al. (2015a); Taefi et al. (2015); Roumboutsos et al. (2014); Lebeau et al. (2013); Melo et al. (2014); Macharis et al. (2013); Van Duin et al. (2013); Giordano et al. (2018); Teoh et al. (2018); Pelletier et al. (2018); Morganti and Browne (2018); Mirhedayatian and Yan (2018); Muñoz-Villamizar et al. (2019); Lebeau et al. (2018); Koháni et al. (2017)
Modular E-vehicles	The special type of vehicles is used to deliver the goods to consumers by carrying one or multiple cabin modules		Rezgui et al. (2015); Andaloro et al. (2015); Aggoune-Mtalaa et al. (2015)

(Continued)

Table 4.2 (Continued)

Topic	Description	Transshipment Transportation	Last-Mile Delivery
Public transit system	Integrated the passenger and freight activities (i.e., tram, subway, bus)	Kelly and Marinov (2017); De Langhe (2017); Gonzalez-Feliu (2016b); Strale (2014); Wang and Deng (2013); Regué and Bristow (2013); Liu et al. (2018); Behiri et al. (2018); Ozturk and Patrick (2018); Gonzalez-Feliu (2016a); Zhao et al. (2018); Serafini et al. (2018); Dong et al. (2018); Pimentel and Alvelos (2018)	Ewedairo et al. (2018)
Urban waterway logistics	Utilized a ship to transfer goods to the transit points by the inland waterway of the city	Labanauskas (2016); Janjevic and Ndiaye (2014); Seidlová et al. (2020)	Maes et al. (2015); Seidlová et al. (2020)
Taxi logistics	Applied the taxi to transport goods; the purpose is reduce traffic congestion		Chen and Pan (2016); Eidhammer et al. (2016); Li et al. (2014); Zhang and Wang (2018); Gao et al. (2018)
Cargo bike	Use of a cargo-bike for freight distribution in city centers		Rudolph and Gruber (2017); Melo and Baptista (2017); Anderluh et al. (2017); Koning and Conway (2016); Schier et al. (2016); Choubassi et al. (2016); Gruber and Kihm (2016); Gruber et al. (2015); Schliwa et al. (2015); Gruber et al. (2014); Lenz and Riehle (2013); Sárdi and Bóna (2018); Arnold et al. (2018); Lopez (2018)

(Continued)

Table 4.2 (Continued)

Topic	Description	Transshipment Transportation	Last-Mile Delivery
Robotic vehicles	Use of autonomous (robotic) vehicles for freight distribution in city areas		Vleugel and Bal (2018); Haas and Friedrich (2017); Mitrea and Kyamakya (2017); Yu and Lam (2017); Molfino et al. (2014); Dinale et al. (2013); Muscolo et al. (2018); Scherr et al. (2018b); Beirigo et al. (2018)
Delivery drones	Use of drones for freight delivery in city areas		Kunze (2016); Mckinnon (2016); Mbiadou Saleu et al. (2018); Boysen et al. (2018)
Parcel lockers	The implementation of parcel lockers aims to reduce the traffic congestion in residential areas and enhance the efficiency of delivery		Lemke et al. (2016); Iwan et al. (2016); Deutsch and Golany (2018)
Mobile depot	A mobile depot is a trailer fitted with a loading dock, warehousing facilities, and an office		Arvidsson and Pazirandeh (2017); Verlinde et al. (2014); Marujo et al. (2018)

These papers have instead focused on particular issues, for instance health, social perspectives, and urban planning. Furthermore, some papers that utilized methods with different logistics or management, such as chemical or environmental approaches, were excluded. Meanwhile, this work removed the articles that were not related to the previous definition of urban distribution innovations. For example, some papers focused on the goods consolidation between various companies out of the urban consolidation center (e.g., Cepolina (2016); Lewandowski (2014); Moutaoukil et al. (2015)); many articles studied the application of internet communication technology to design new delivery strategies (e.g., Bates et al. (2017); Dablanc et al. (2017); Cardenas et al. (2017); Allen et al. (2018); Pan et al. (2017); Köster et al. (2015); Wang (2015)). Finally, 93 papers were analyzed and classified in the bibliography corpus that were published in 2013–2018. The main topics of these papers contained two types: transshipment transportation and last-mile delivery. The results of the topics identification are reported in Table 4.2.

Figure 4.3 demonstrates the distribution by year of the papers in the corpus. The number of papers regarding distribution innovations reveals a spurt in growth trends, particularly in the year 2016. Concurrently, the peak of conference papers also occurred in this year, almost 14 papers. In contrast, the peak of the journal articles related to distribution innovations occurred in 2018 since some journals have called for papers regarding their Special Issues in the year 2018, for instance Transportation Science.

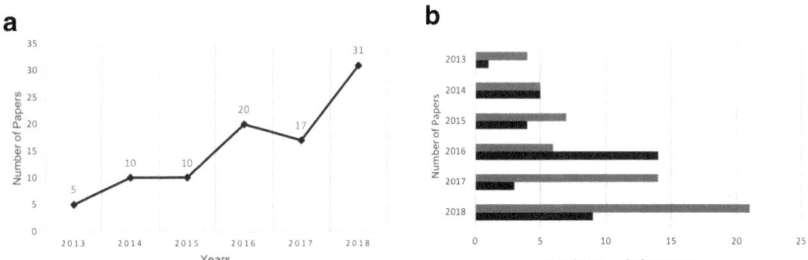

Figure 4.3 Description of bibliography corpus (**a**) is the number of papers by year, and (**b**) is the number of papers by classification

As mentioned previously, the bibliography corpus involves 93 papers in terms of the distribution innovations in the urban freight system. Commonly, the investigation of distribution innovations has focused on the process of transshipment transportation or last-mile delivery. According to a systematical literature review, some research has considered both of these processes. For instance, the papers regarding electric vehicles have simultaneously discussed the application and promotion in both processes (Giordano et al. 2018; Rizet et al. 2016; Lebeau et al. 2015b). Therefore, the number of papers on transshipment transportation and last-mile delivery was 22 and 77, respectively. Although the Scopus database lacks the literature of the delivery robot, this chapter also considering this emerging transport mode. Table 4.3 shows that 11 topics have discussed distribution innovations.

The results illustrates that the topics regarding electric vehicles and cargo bikes had received more attention in 2013–2018 since these innovations are able to mitigate congestion and environmental externalities created by freight activities within urban areas. This notwithstanding, these two topics have been given more attention regarding last-mile delivery (47 papers), and only five articles were related to transshipment transportation. It is noted that some papers on last-mile delivery have mentioned transshipment transportation or urban freight network structure design, but these are not the main research question in these papers, for instance Arvidsson and Pazirandeh (2017).

Therefore, according to the systematic literature review, this chapter defines the scope of distribution innovations (as presented in Table 4.3). There are eleven emerging transport modes/concepts that are included in it. However, little research has focused on the implementation status of these distribution innovations and their application restrictions in urban areas. To this end, this chapter adopts the GE multifactorial analysis approach to discuss these questions from the perspective of academia and companies.

Table 4.3 Research range and methodology

Items	Description
Research objectives	Electric vehicles, modular E-vehicles, cargo bikes, delivery drones, public transit system, robotic vehicles, taxi logistics, urban waterway logistics, parcel lockers, mobile depots, delivery robot
Research method	GE multifactorial analysis
Research perspectives	Academic research, company application

4.5   Implementation Status Analysis of Distribution Innovations

4.5.1   Definition of Implementation Status

GE multifactorial analysis was first developed by McKinsey for General Electric in the 1970s. It is a method used in brand marketing and product management to assist a company in deciding what product(s) to add to its product portfolio and which opportunities in the market that they should continue to invest in (Wikipedia nda). In general, there are two dimensions used to evaluate the existing portfolios of strategic business units. Each dimension is classified into three levels to create the two-dimensional matrix. The GE matrix is able to assist a strategic business unit to evaluate its overall strength, as each product, service, and brand is mapped in this two-dimensional matrix. The advantage of this method is an intuitive analysis of relevant elements, as well as the strength evaluation. Consequently, this chapter adopted GE multifactorial analysis method to analyze the implementation status of distribution innovations.

First, this chapter defines the two dimensions of the academia research phase and company implementation phase. Following a review of the related articles, we classified each dimension into three phases (as presented in Table 4.4).

Table 4.4 Research and implementation phase of two perspectives

	Low Phase	Medium Phase	High Phase
Academia research phase	Conceptual Model phase	Analysis and planning phase	Promotion and evaluation phase
Companies research phase	Theoretical research phase	Testing and development phase	Operation and improvement phase

According to the systematic literature review, the distribution innovations research in academia is capable of being classified into three phases: (1) conceptual model phase, (2) analysis and planning phase, and (3) promotion and evaluation phase. The definitions are as follows:

- The conceptual model phase refers to scholars proposing and designing the conceptual model/framework to respond to social economic questions. This is the initial stage for studying the innovative technology. Examples include the use of the delivery drone in last-mile delivery (Kunze 2016; Mckinnon 2016) and the application of autonomous vehicles in urban freight transport (Molfino et al. 2014; Dinale et al. 2013; Yu and Lam 2017; Mitrea and Kyamakya 2017).

- The analysis and planning phase is based on the specific parameters of the technology, thereby analyzing the future risks, costs, and the possible impacts of the technology application while planning both the operational scheme and the ex ante evaluation. An example is the integrated system of passenger and freight transport (Li et al. 2014; Chen and Pan 2016).
- The promotion and evaluation phase refers to scholarly discussions regarding alternative strategies that aim to promote the use of innovative technologies in urban freight transport and the evaluation of costs, as well as impacts to improve the policy or strategy. Commonly, this approach is based on private enterprises, and local authorities have already used these technologies. An example is the research regarding electric vehicles (Giordano et al. 2018; Ahani et al. 2016; Taefi et al. 2017; Wątróbski et al. 2017) and cargo bikes (Rudolph and Gruber 2017; Choubassi et al. 2016).

From a transition perspective, history has shown that established technologies are often slowly replaced with emerging technologies (Arvidsson and Pazirandeh 2017; Geels 2005). Hence, the application of emerging technologies should consist of these three phases.

According to the review of the research reports (e.g., Kersten et al. (2017)), the case studies in the articles (e.g., Verlinde and Macharis (2016)), and the official websites of enterprises (e.g., Workhorse Group (2016); Mercedes-Benz (2016)), this chapter defines the application phases from the perspective of the company. This approach also enabled a classification into three phases: (1) theoretical research phase, (2) testing and development phase, and (3) operation and improvement phase. The specific definitions are as follows:

- The theoretical research phase is the initial phase for the companies, which proposes the technology's theoretical model and conceptual model. The purpose is to identify the application range and features of technologies. For example, in 2018, Germany's Volkswagen proposed a project that integrates autonomous vehicles into the mobile depots.
- The testing and development phase is based on the result of the theoretical research phase and aims to develop the technology physical model. Concurrently, the performance is tested, and the possible risks are evaluated. An example is the use of drones to deliver goods within urban areas (e.g., Amazon Prime Air (nd)).

- The operation and improvement phase describes how the companies have used the established technologies to provide the logistics service while improving these technologies and thereby reducing the costs and risks. An example is the utilization of cargo bikes in last-mile delivery (e.g., Melo and Baptista (2017)).

Therefore, the company application phase of technology consists of three phases. In addition, these three phases correspond to the academic research phases on the technology application. Based on these, the GE matrix of the implementation status analysis is established (as demonstrated in Figure 4.4).

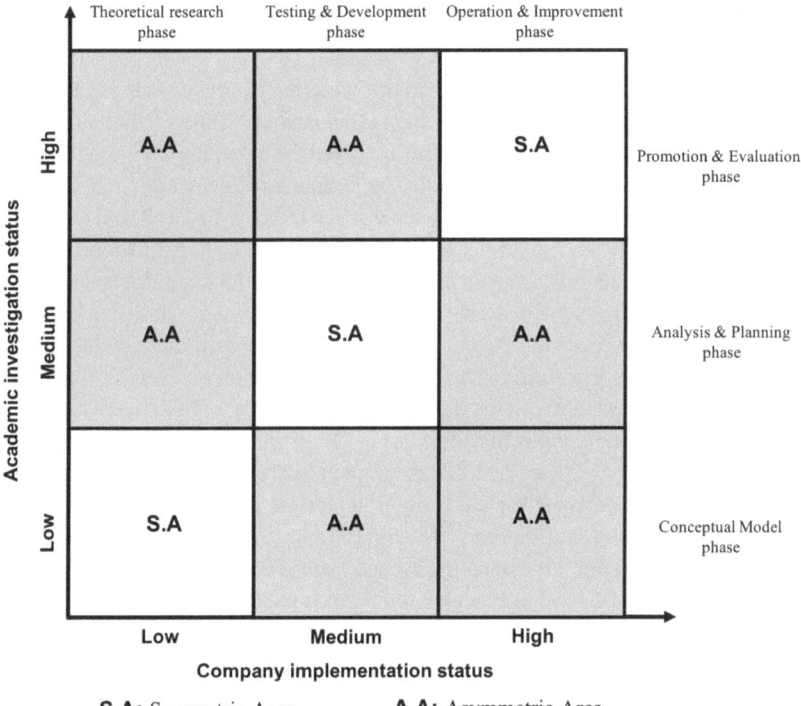

Figure 4.4 The GE matrix of the implementation status analysis. (Source: Author's own elaboration)

4.5.2   Analysis of Implementation Status

As mentioned by the German logistics company BVL International in its publication *Trends and Strategies in Logistics and Supply Chain Management-Digital Transformation Opportunities* in 2017, they adopted the questionnaire approach to understanding the status of applying technologies in the logistics industry. In this report, the questionnaire was used in conducting interviews with 38 experts in manufacturing, logistic services, trade, and consultancy. In addition, "the result was taken further quantitatively in an online survey with 1351 participants, of which 363 completed data sets assured a statistically reliable and detailed analysis" (Kersten et al. 2017).

Kersten et al. (2017) described the relevance and implementation status of technologies and defines the innovative technology concepts in logistics. The autonomous vehicles, drones, robots, and driverless transport systems are at a very low level regarding the aspect of implementation status. It is noted that this report has presented that 73% of companies have approved the emerging technologies, giving rise to the development of substantial opportunities (Kersten et al. 2017). The notwithstanding, more than 50% of the enterprises indicated a "wait-and-see" attitude until tried and tested solutions are available for practical application (Kersten et al. 2017). Consequently, logistic enterprises currently lack an efficient integration solution to the implementation of innovative technologies, while considerable research has paid little attention to the relevance among the different technologies.

According to the literature review, applying the autonomous vehicles in urban freight transport is currently in the theoretical research stage. There were nine articles related to autonomous vehicles (AVs) in urban freight transport. Mitrea and Kyamakya (2017) have discussed the assessment and prediction of the impact of various autonomous driving use cases on urban freight transport. Vleugel and Bal (2018) have indicated that the AVs are able to reduce the use of space (50%) in cities and emissions by this transport. Yu and Lam (2017) have proposed the AV logistic system (AVLS) and used a quadratic-constrained mixed integer linear program to formulate the joint routing and charging problem. The result indicated that AVLS can effectively utilize excessive renewable energy and satisfy all logistics demands. Haas and Friedrich (2017) have developed a microsimulation tool for AVs used in city logistics from the perspective of the travel time. Molfino et al. (2014) and Dinale et al. (2013) have designed a conceptual architecture of a robotic vehicle that integrates a robotic handling device that is positioned in the vehicle. These papers imply that the research regarding autonomous vehicles is in the conceptual model stage. In regards to companies, Mercedes-Benz is developing Vision Vans as autonomous vehicles to deliver goods in the urban freight network

(Mercedes-Benz 2016). The British company Ocado has trialed driverless vans to transport commodities in London, which will be in operation in all of Britain by 2019 (Kleinman 2017). This progress illustrates that the relevant companies are in the testing and development stage.

Delivery drones are commonly used in the last-mile delivery in urban freight transport. According to the literature review, the studies related to delivery drones are also in the conceptual model stage. For instance, Kunze (2016) has proposed the concept of "Post 4.0", which integrates ground drones and small unmanned aircraft systems (sUAS) in the future urban freight system. In addition, some scholars are involved with cooperation among delivery drones and other innovative technologies. For example, Mckinnon (2016) have discussed and analyzed the possible impacts of 3D-printing and drones on last-mile delivery. Additionally, the relevant enterprises are actively developing and improving the performance of delivery drones used in the last-mile delivery that are equipped with a delivery drone in various vehicles. Amazon is developing a UAV delivery system called Amazon Prime Air, which is a cargo airline and conceptual drone-based delivery system, and goods can be delivered to customers just in 30 min (Amazon Prime Air nd). The *Workhorse Group* has developed the *HorseFly UAV Delivery* system, which is fully integrated with electric/hybrid delivery trucks, while UPS has tested residential delivery with a drone launched from Atop Package Car (Workhorse Group 2016). Mercedes-Benz is developing *Vision Vans* that will be equipped with two delivery drones (Mercedes-Benz 2016). It is noteworthy that several logistic companies have utilized drones to deliver special goods to consumers. For instance, in 2013, DHL Parcel launched a research project on the use of a particular drone, dubbed the *Parcelcopter*, for transporting goods under real conditions to remote or geographically-challenging areas (Deutsche Post DHL Group 2018a). However, thus far, the use of delivery drones in urban freight transport is still in the development and testing phase for relevant companies.

The delivery robot is an emerging freight technology that enables reducing traffic congestion and saves labor costs. In the Scopus database, there is a lack of research regarding the use of the delivery robot in urban freight. Nevertheless, this innovative technology has received more attention in logistic corporations. For instance, the Starship firm has developed delivery robots to carry cargoes within the urban environment, and the capacity of cargo-carrying is no more than 100 pounds. (Starship nd). The Chinese retail companies JingDong, CaiNiao, etc., are also developing delivery robot networks and testing their performance. Hence, for the relevant companies, the delivery robot remains in the development and testing phase.

The advantages of electric vehicles (EVs) have been widely recognized by academia in recent years. Concurrently, many local authorities have also positively formulated a policy that aims to promote the application of EVs in urban freight. The reason is that much research on EVs is related to replacement strategies (Giordano et al. 2018; Ahani et al. 2016; Taefi et al. 2016; Lebeau et al. 2013) and cost evaluation (Taefi et al. 2017; Wątróbski et al. 2017; Taefi 2016; Lebeau et al. 2015c), as well as the choice of vehicle routing. Hence, the use of EVs in urban freight is in the operation and improvement phase.

The implementation status of cargo bikes is comparable to that of EVs. As mentioned in Section 4.3, there are 14 articles regarding the use of cargo bikes in the last-mile delivery. These studies have focused on operational strategies and impact analyses, as well as cost evaluation. In real-world settings, many logistics companies have applied cargo bikes to urban freight transport, such as DHL Germany. Moreover, some manufacturers have developed an innovative cargo bike to enhance the load capacity and delivery range within urban areas. For instance, the Velove Armadillo cargo bike produced by the Swedish company Velove (Velove Cororpation nd). Consequently, the implementation status of cargo bikes is in the operation and improvement phase.

Modular vehicles (MVs) are a particular type of vehicle that is used to deliver goods to consumers by carrying one or multiple cabin modules. In the papers corpus, there were three articles regarding this topic. Indeed, the modular vehicle is a special EV (Andaloro et al. 2015; Rezgui et al. 2015; Aggoune-Mtalaa et al. 2015). Notwithstanding, these articles are in the conceptual model phase. From the view of case studies in these papers, the logistic service companies and manufacturers are in the theoretical research phase.

The integrated system of passengers and freight transport consists of trams, metros, buses, and taxis. The relevant articles that have presented investigations of this topic are in the analysis and planning phase. For instance, Kelly and Marinov (2017) proposed a conceptual system of urban freight transport that integrated the light rail system. Chen and Pan (2016), as well as Li et al. (2014) discussed the feasibility of people and parcels sharing taxis. Indeed, the relevant enterprises and manufacturers have developed and tested the integrated system of passengers and freight transport. For example, the Yamato Transport Company has been utilizing a tram system for distributing goods to Arashiyama in Kyoto, Japan, since May 2011 (Japan for Sustainability 2011). However, thus far, many companies have not yet adopted this system to transport goods within urban areas due to financial reasons, possible risks, etc. Hence, from the perspective of the company, the integrated system of passengers and freight transport is in the testing and development phase.

Urban waterway logistics (Inland waterway) refer to using ships to transfer goods to the transit points by the inland waterway of a city. According to the literature review, the studies of the inland waterway in urban freight transport are in the analysis and planning phase. Due to the implementation condition that the city needs to have an inland waterway, the broad application of this system in the logistics service company is restricted. Hence, for the company, inland waterway transport is in the testing and development phase.

The parcel locker is commonly used in the parcel or B2C industry. According to the literature review, much research is analyzing and evaluating the application of parcel lockers (Lemke et al. 2016; Iwan et al. 2016). Indeed, a multitude of logistics service companies have used the parcel locker in urban freight transport, such as Amazon Co. and DHL Co.

A mobile depot is a trailer fitted with a loading dock, warehousing facilities, and an office. In the Scopus database, only four articles were related to this topic. The literature review indicates that these research studies consist of a conceptual model design (Verlinde and Macharis 2016), cost analysis, and evaluation (Arvidsson and Pazirandeh 2017; Verlinde et al. 2014; Ducret 2014). In these papers, TNT Express in Brussels has used this system in urban freight transport (Verlinde and Macharis 2016; Verlinde et al. 2014). Hence, thus far, the mobile depot is in the testing and development phase from the perspective of companies.

Based on the previous analysis, Figure 4.5 demonstrates the implementation status of distribution innovations based on the GE two-dimensional matrix. Currently, modular E-vehicles are still at the low-low phase. Electric vehicles and parcel lockers have been at the high-high level of application, and academia and companies have paid more attention to them as replacement policies and promotion strategies within urban areas. In contrast, delivery drones, delivery robots, mobile depots, and robotic vehicles have so far still maintained a medium-low level of application. The costs and external elements (e.g., weather, vandalism) have radically restricted their wide application in enterprises. Moreover, the taxi delivery is at the low-medium level, where immature technology and local transport policies are the primary barriers for applying these in urban freight transport. It is noted that public transit systems and inland waterway transportation are at the level of medium-medium. This observation implies that the integrated freight and passenger model in urban freight transport has increasingly become the future operational measure in city logistics. This notwithstanding, the enterprises still need to promote the implementation phase of these emerging technologies to the next level actively, while academic research has to consider comprehensively the relevant elements to evaluate risks and make the operational measures and policies for local authorities and private companies. In addition, applying the cargo bike to the delivery of goods has received more attention in recent years. A majority of tech companies have developed innovative cargo bikes equipped with a large container and mechanical transmission devices to enhance the delivery range, for instance the cargo bike of Velove Armadillo developed by Velove Corporation (Velove Cororpation nd), which was utilized by DHL in German cities in 2018. However, academic research is still in the analysis and planning phase. The future research direction of the innovative cargo bike is in the promotion and evaluation phase. In summary, the various distribution innovations are in different implementation phases. These innovative units have formed the new urban intermodal transportation concept, which is a necessary consideration in the future agenda of urban freight planning.

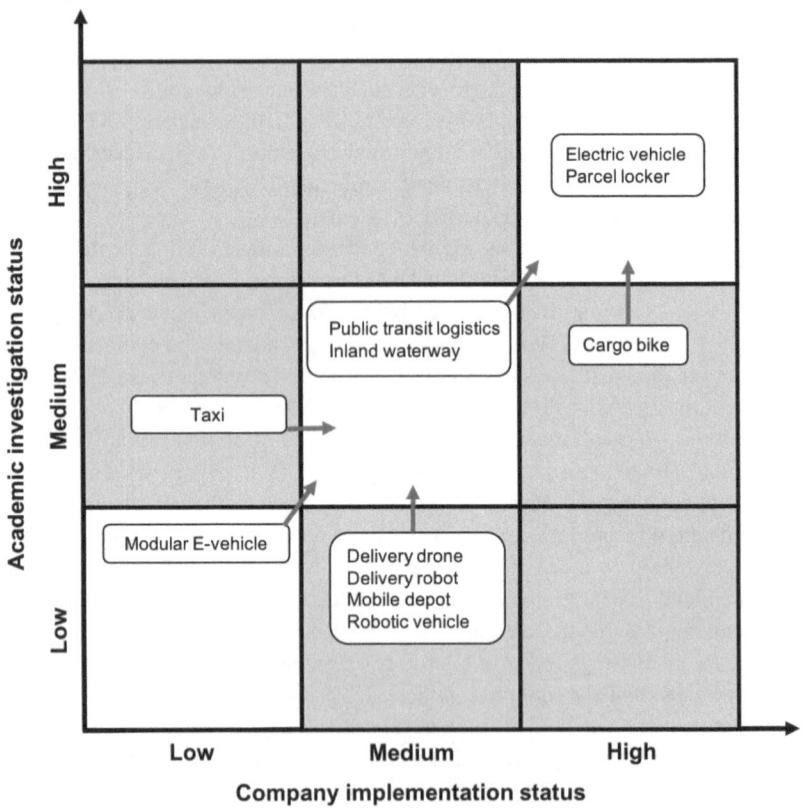

Figure 4.5 The technology implementation status in urban freight transport. (Source: Author's own elaboration)

Nevertheless, there is a lack of a comprehensive consideration regarding the integration of all emerging technologies. A considerable body of research has paid scant attention to feasibility analyses and risk evaluations of urban intermodal transport with these emerging technologies. Hence, future research is needed to consider the interrelation and interplay among the various innovative technologies on urban freight transport. Additionally, it is necessary to consider the network structure of urban freight transport. From a view of urban freight network design, the application of emerging technologies and freight network structure are the primary influence factors that need to be analyzed. Understanding the implementation status regarding these technologies contributes to future network design on urban freight transport.

4.6 Application Restriction and Scope of Distribution Innovations

4.6.1 Applied Restriction of Distribution Innovations

As mentioned previously, much research lacks a comprehensive consideration of the combined applications of the emerging transport modes as a system. The research of various distribution innovations is highly fragmented. The primary barrier that exist for the application restrictions of these innovations concerns the operational processes within urban areas. For instance, such processes include weather, urban freight policy, urban topography, and technical limitations. Hence, this chapter has assessed the restriction of these 11 emerging transport modes from seven aspects:

- Status: This is based on the previous GE-matrix analysis. According to the analysis of the implementation status of the distribution innovations, some of them are in the low-low phase. This status poses challenges in finding the technical data of these transport modes because they are in the development phase for the related companies, for instance modular E-vehicles.

- Process of application: As mentioned previously, the processes of city logistics consist of transshipment transportation and last-mile delivery. The capacity and size of distribution innovations have restricted their application process in urban freight transport. For instance, the delivery drone is generally only utilized in the last-mile delivery.

- Infrastructure requirements: The infrastructure requirements of various innovations are different. For example, the use of electric vehicles should consider the location of the charge station and the application of delivery drones should not only consider this critical point, but also consider the control platform and loading dock.

- External elements: In addition to the technical limitation itself, external elements have influenced the application of these distribution innovations on urban freight transport. Weather is a critical impact factor for the application of distribution innovations. Storms, wind, and snow are unfavorable to the use of these innovations (delivery drone, delivery robot, etc.). In addition, the external elements are associated with urban freight policies, related laws, urban topography, and so on.

- Travel range: This is a crucial indicator for assessing the suitability of transport modes. Concurrently, this indicator contributes to the selection of transport modes for the companies, particularly to address distinct delivery demands and complex urban topography.

- Load capacity: This is a pivotal criterion to measure a suitable industry for transport modes. The distribution innovations with a small capacity generally have been used in parcel delivery, such as the delivery drone/robot. However, the load capacity of some distribution innovations appears to be flexible and uncertain. For instance, public transit logistics are based on the spare capacity of the tram/bus/subway Behiri et al. (2016); Masson et al. (2017). The load capacity of taxi logistics depends on the taxi types, which in general is approximately 0.5–2 m^3 (Auto-Date nd; Mercedes-Benz nd).

- Suitable industry: As the research perspectives of this chapter are related to the retail and postal industries, this study have analyzed the suitable industries of these emerging transport modes from these two aspects. Generally, the load capacity and travel range are critical factors for measuring their suitable industries. It is noted that the transshipment transportation process of the parcel industry also requires vehicles with a large load capacity. Consequently, flexibility and sustainability are also the key points for analyzing suitable industries.

Table 4.5 demonstrates the suitability assessment of distribution innovations. The technical data regarding the travel range and load capacity of modular e-vehicles and robotic vehicles are difficult to find. The problem is that both of these innovations are still in the exploitation phase for technology companies. In addition, taxi logistics are still in the testing and planning phases, and the load capacity data are based on the taxi types from the official report of Mercedes-Benz.

Table 4.5 Suitability assessment of distribution innovations

	Status	Process of Application	Infrastructure Requirements	External Elements	Travel Range	Load Capacity	Suitable Industry
Electric vehicles	High–high phase	Transshipment transportation/ last-mile delivery	Charge station	Urban topography	100–500 km (Lebeau et al. 2016, 2015c)	3–20 m^3 (Lebeau et al. 2016, 2015c)	Retail/Post
Modular E-vehicles	Low–low phase	Transshipment transportation/ last-mile delivery	Charge station	Urban topography	N.A.	N.A.	Retail/post
Public transit logistics	Medium–medium phase	Transshipment transportation	Integrated station of transit and freight	Off-peak periods of passenger	Based on the range of the public transport network	Standardized box is approximately 1.5–2 m^3 (Kelly and Marinov 2017), and the number of boxes is based on the spare capacity of public transit modes (approximately 15 boxes) (Behiri et al. 2016; Masson et al. 2017)	Retail/post
Urban waterway logistics	Medium–medium phase	Transshipment transportation	Multiple canal loading docks or ship equipped with a hydraulic crane that delivers the goods to the quays	City's extensive canal network, weather	Based on urban canal network	30–85 m^3 (Maes et al. 2015)	Retail/post
Taxi logistics	Low–medium phase	Last-mile delivery	No special requirements	Urban transport policy, taxi policy	600–1000 km (Auto-Date nd)	Based on the taxi types, generally is approximately 0.5–2 m^3 (Auto-Date nd; citealtbenz1)	Post

(Continued)

Table 4.5 (Continued)

	Status	Process of Application	Infrastructure Requirements	External Elements	Travel Range	Load Capacity	Suitable Industry
Cargo bike	High-medium phase	Last-mile delivery	Charge station	Weather, urban topography	13–100 km (Rudolph and Gruber 2017)	Approximately 1–2 m³ (Velove Cororpation nd)	Post
Robotic vehicle	Medium-low phase	Transshipment transportation/ last-mile delivery	Charge station, controller platform, urban road network	Urban freight policy, law allows	N.A.	N.A.	Retail/post
Delivery drone	Medium-low phase	Last-mile delivery	Charge station, controller platform, loading depots/trucks	Weather, human damages, law allows	A range of about 20–30 km (Agatz et al. 2018; Boysen et al. 2018: Deutsche Post DHL Group 2018b)	Approximately 2–4 kg (Agatz et al. 2018; Boysen et al. 2018: Deutsche Post DHL Group 2018b)	Post
Delivery robot	Medium-low phase	Last-mile delivery	Charge station, controller platform, loading depots/trucks	Weather, topography, law allows, human damages	Within a 3-km radius (Starship nd)	No more than 50 pounds (Starship nd)	Post
Parcel locker	High-high phase	Last-mile delivery	No special requirements	Weather	N.A.	Approximately 1.36–25.84 m³ (KEBA nd)	Post
Mobile depot	Medium-low phase	Last-mile delivery	NO special requirements	Urban freight policy, parking limitation	Depends on the type of tractor and urban acreage	Fits 4 large and 7 smaller cages (STRAIGHTSOL 2012)	Retail/post

In summary, these 11 distribution innovations have been/will be used in city logistics. The result of the suitability assessment has indicated that the application of these innovations is a viable and efficient solution for urban freight transport in the future. Their advantages are that they mitigate the conflict between the city and freight aspects regarding land, while alleviating the negative impacts for urban environments. In addition, the use of delivery drones and delivery robots will provide increasingly more individualization of logistics services, thereby increasing enterprises' competition ability and economic scale. However, research attention is lacking on the operation of these innovations together as a system. Regardless, in the literature review of distribution innovations, this work determined that some innovations have operated together. For instance, the mobile depot has operated with cargo bikes and small E-vehicles (Arvidsson and Pazirandeh 2017; Verlinde et al. 2014). Some companies have utilized a combination of vans to transport small containers to the locations where cargo bikes are then responsible for the last-mile delivery. For example, DHL company has implemented this approach.

4.6.2   Sustainable Inner-Urban Intermodal Transportation

As mentioned previously, some companies have operated one or two distribution innovations together as a system. Following the literature review of these distribution innovations, this chapter determines that some city logistics providers and technology enterprises have launched new concepts of integrated operation among these technologies, while they have begun to test them in the real world. For instance, Swedish company Velove has proposed the concept of the containerized urban last-mile delivery solution. This refers to parcels being placed in containers at the sorting terminal, using an electric vehicle equipped with a special trailer to transport containers to handover points, so that cargo bikes are able to pick the containers up to do the last-mile delivery (Velove Cororpation nd). In 2017, DHL Express piloted the City Hub concept in Frankfurt, Germany, and Utrecht, Netherlands (Deutsche Post DHL Group 2017). The concept of City Hub is similar to the idea from Velove, the vehicles combined with a customized trailer carrying up to four containers, then use of DHL Cubicycles (a cargo-bike able to carry a container) to complete last-mile delivery (Deutsche Post DHL Group 2017). In addition, the concept of mobile depot is also a typical integration case. In May of 2013, TNT Express introduced the mobile depot in Brussels (TNT Express 2013), which is used to load the goods that will be then driven to a central parking location in the city and be carried out by several electric tricycles as the last-mile delivery (Verlinde et al. 2014). Concurrently, some vehicle manufacturers have also launched new future transport modes to city logistics. For example, in Hannover Messe 2018, Volkswagen (Berlin, Germany) has put forward the concept of Future Urban Freight Mobility as well as a 1:10 model, which is a mobile depot with autonomous driving, equipped with the several delivery robots for carrying goods within urban areas. In summary, the logistics providers and technology enterprises have begun to integrate the various distribution innovations to construct the new distribution concept of urban freight transport, which has an extensive consensus for coping with the environmental externalities. However, the lack of a systematic analysis of the current status on integration of distribution innovations can be observed.

To this end, this chapter systematically analyzes the current status of integration on these 11 emerging transport modes through the literature review. As depicted in Table 4.6, the result has demonstrated that many researches have begun to integrate among the several transport modes. Due to some types of innovative transport modes still being in the theoretical research or testing phase, as well as their applied restriction as mentioned before, their integration status is unable to be further analyzed, such as delivery robots and taxis. According to the relevance analysis in Table 4.6, the electric vehicle and the cargo bike have been extensively used in the operations with the other emerging transport modes. It is noted that these operating modes have applied the standardized box/container (the capacity is approximately 1–2 m^3) (DHL nd; Behiri et al. 2016; Masson et al. 2017; Velove Cororpation nd). From the application results of these companies, this delivery model has radically reduced emissions and congestion while increasing the enterprises' competitive ability (DHL nd; Deutsche Post DHL Group 2018b; Maes et al. 2015; TNT Express 2013; Kikuta et al. 2012). Meanwhile, for the some future integration concepts, they mentioned the feasibility and suitability of the standardized box/container as well. For example, James Kelly and Marinov (Kelly and Marinov 2017) suggested urban freight distribution using a light rail system based on standardized box/container; Yamato has used a similar concept of a standardized container to transport goods in the urban tram system (Kikuta et al. 2012). Hence, using a standardized container/box is a key element for the integration of these distribution innovations. Indeed, this integrated operational scheme is obviously a special type of intermodal transportation within urban areas. This notwithstanding, the analysis result also indicates that less research has comprehensively considered the inner-urban intermodal transport from the viewpoint of the retail/post industry.

Table 4.6 also indicates that the integration of urban freight innovations is an efficient solution to promote a sustainable and livable city. Much research and some enterprises have proposed one or two transport modes operated together as a system. For instance, mobile depots have been discussed with the use of cargo bikes to deliver goods (Arvidsson and Pazirandeh 2017; Verlinde et al. 2014; Ducret 2014), and the

Table 4.6 Relevance analysis of various technologies

	Electric Vehicles	Modular E-vehicles	Cargo Bikes	Delivery Drones	Public Transit System	Robotic Vehicles	Taxi	Inland Water-way	Parcel Lockers	Mobile Depots	Delivery Robot
Electric vehicles	/		✓	✓	✓			✓	✓	✓	
Modular E-vehicles		/									
Cargo bike	✓		/		✓			✓	✓	✓	
Delivery drones	✓			/		✓			✓		
Public transit system	✓		✓		/					✓	
Robotic vehicles	✓			✓		/					
Taxi							/				
Inland waterway	✓		✓					/			
Parcel lockers	✓		✓	✓					/		
Mobile depots	✓		✓		✓					/	
Delivery robot											/

use of delivery drones was discussed in the application of parcel lockers (Deutsche Post DHL Group 2018a). Hence, urban intermodal transport is the future research and application direction, aimed at applying the various emerging technologies in the urban freight system. However, a considerable body of research has paid little attention to the integrated application of these emerging transport modes, in particular to their combined operation as a system. Concurrently, comprehensively considering the application restrictions of these transport modes in the urban areas is necessary. Therefore, this chapter has proposed sustainable inner-urban intermodal transport for future freight within urban areas.

Intermodal transportation refers to using multiple modes of transportation in an intermodal container or vehicle, from origin to destination, without handling of goods themselves or changing the type of their unitization (UNCTAD. Secreteriat 2001; Munim and Haralambides 2018; Wikipedia ndb). Urban intermodal transportation (UIT) involves the integrated use of a high carrying capacity mode (rail or barge) to transport the containers between the port and intermodal terminals, after which trucks are used to transport these goods to the consumer location/warehouses (Meyrick and Associates 2006; Teye et al. 2016). Indeed, an important definition of the intermodality is the ability to consider many transport modes (e.g., rail, trucks) that operate together as a system (Cuncev 2004). According to the literature review and analysis of the implementation status, there are eleven emerging transport modes that will be applied in the future urban freight transport. Hence, the concept of sustainable inner-urban intermodal transport (SIUIT) is developed for the future urban freight transport (as depicted in Figure 4.6). The concept of SIUIT is defined as the combined use of various emerging transport modes (e.g., tram, bus, cargo bike) to transport goods by small modular containers from a city's logistics center to consumers. As mentioned previously, inner-urban intermodal transport has received more attention in recent years, in particular with the postal and retail industries. Using various innovative transport modes in different logistics processes, it is able to provide an individual logistics service while reducing the negative impacts and costs, thereby improving the competitiveness of the enterprise, as well as achieving a livable and sustainable city.

The integration of the various distribution innovations is a challenge for urban freight transport. The existing issues include the special infrastructure construction (e.g., urban freight tram station (Kelly and Marinov 2017)), structure changes of the urban freight network (e.g., the urban freight network of triple helix model (Verlinde and Macharis 2016)), software platform establishment (e.g., usage of delivery robot and drone), as well as the formulation of urban freight policy and laws, etc. In addition, urban development is also radically impacted by freight transport due to the city and freight having maintained a set of core relations (Rodrigue et al. 2016). However, considerable research has paid less attention to links between city development and the integration of urban freight distribution based on the previous analysis. To this end, further research of SIUIT needs to consider comprehensively the future trends of urban development. For example, urban population growth causes increasing freight flow; urbanization and suburbanization lead to the growth of delivery range; as well as a sustainable and livable city desired by urban residents. Besides these, according to relevance analysis of distribution innovations in Table 4.6, this work have found that integrating all 11 distribution innovations into one system is unnecessary. Not only the purpose of these integration modes is to radically relieve the environmental externalities created by city logistics, selected parts of innovations to construct a suitable scheme of SIUIT are necessary. Hence, the selection and integration between the distinct innovations produce the different operational scheme of SIUIT. Which type of SIUIT is suitable for different a city environment needs to be further investigated. This chapter aims to develop the concept of SIUIT, as well as the direction of further research.

As a consequence, SIUIT is the future trend of urban logistics, whose operational measures and existing risks should be integrated into the planning phase of the urban freight system. The advantages of this concept are its use of standardized small boxes/containers to transport goods in the various segments of urban freight transport while applying these emerging transport modes to alleviate environmental externalities.In future research, the suitability of SIUIT needs to be based on a cost-benefit analysis. In addition, the application limitations and existing risks need

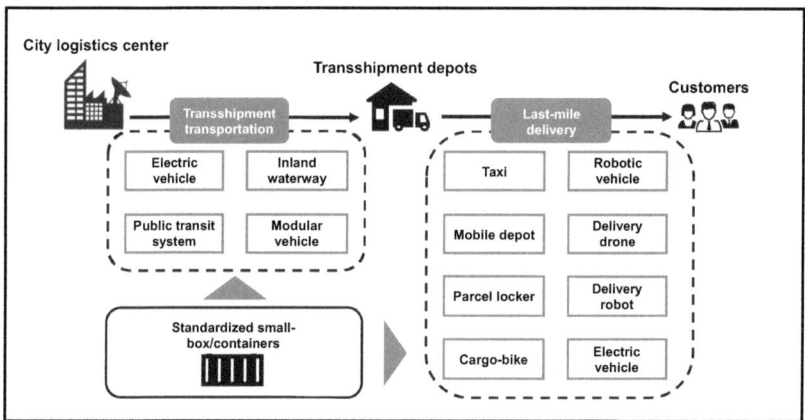

Figure 4.6 The concept of sustainable inner-urban intermodal transportation. (Source: Author's own elaboration)

further analysis and assessment. Currently, it is noted that the combined operation of these emerging modes as a system has demonstrated effectiveness, particularly in the aspects of congestion and emissions. However, these results were solely obtained for the integrated operation between one or two emerging transport modes. Therefore, future research needs to consider comprehensively the combined operation of all emerging technologies, namely sustainable inner-urban intermodal transport.

4.7   Conclusions of This Chapter

This chapter reviews the articles regarding the emerging transport modes that were published in 2013–2018. Following the literature reviews, the concept of distribution innovations is defined, which consist of eleven emerging transport modes. The results indicates that the research of various distribution innovations is highly fragmented. A considerable body of research has paid scant attention to the application status of these innovations. To this end, the approach of GE multifactorial analysis is employed to analyze the implementation status from the perspectives of academia and companies. There were six types of emerging transport modes in the asymmetric application phase. According to the GE matrix, this chapter shows the future direction of these six types of modes from the academia and company perspectives separately. Concurrently, the literature review indicated that the research on suitability assessments of distribution innovations is extremely scarce. Hence, this chapter reviews the related enterprises' official reports and case studies in articles, thereby assessing the suitability and limitations of these emerging transport modes. Finally, this work develops the concept of SIUIT and a further research direction for future urban freight transport.

This chapter aims to develop the concept of SIUIT based on the status analysis of the distribution innovations, as well as their suitability assessment, this chapter did not further analyze the applied restriction of SIUIT in future urban development and their potential issues, as well as the selection and combination scheme of distribution innovations in SIUIT. For this reason, further research can be as follows: (1) comprehensively considering the future urban development to design a feasible scheme of SIUIT from the viewpoint of management and economic; (2) further analysis and design of the network structure of urban freight to which SIUIT is applicable and suiting the future urban development; (3) from the perspective of the decision-makers and stakeholders, this study will attempt to further analyze the selection and combination scheme of these distribution innovations.

Future Network Design of SUFT

5

5.1 Logical Arrangement of the Chapter

This chapter illustrates the network model of 2.x-tier modular & sustainable urban freight transport, which by a systematic consideration of the tendency analysis on large and megacities and conceptual model of SIUIT. As mentioned in Chapter 1, this work aims to design an innovative urban freight network to respond to future challenges in large and megacities. To this end, the tendencies of urban spatial development on large and megacities, as the exogenous trends of SUFT, need to discuss further. Additionally, the integrations of distribution innovations, as the endogenous trends of SUFT, also need to determine the feasible solutions for the urban logistics providers. In conclusion, the systematic analysis of both trends is essential to design the future urban freight network. Figure 5.1 depicts the logical structure of this chapter.

The content exposed in this chapter aims to resolve three sub-questions of this work as below:

- What are the future trends of large/megacities and their impacts on future urban freight system?
- What are the future trends of UFT and their impacts on urban freight network structure?
- How to combine and select distribution innovations to design appropriate freight strategies?
- How to design the network structure of urban freight system to promote its sustainability and flexibility further?

© The Author(s), under exclusive license to Springer Fachmedien Wiesbaden GmbH, part of Springer Nature 2021
Z. He, *Future Sustainable Urban Freight Network Design in the Large Cities and Megacities*, Sustainable Management, Wertschöpfung und Effizienz,
https://doi.org/10.1007/978-3-658-34203-6_5

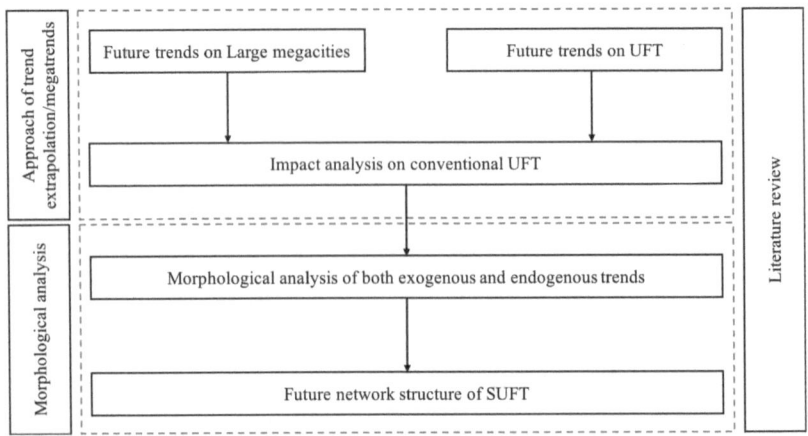

Figure 5.1 Structure of Chapter 5

Following Figure 5.1, this chapter organized as below: Section 5.2 introduces the research background and motivations of this chapter. Section 5.3 is a literature review of critical keywords of this chapter that are associated with the conventional urban freight network and urban distribution innovations. Section 5.4 described the research questions of this chapter as well as the research methodology. Section 5.5 analyzed the future trends of large/megacities by the approach of trend extrapolation/megatrends, while discussed their impacts on the urban freight network further. Section 5.6 used the same approach to analyze the future trends of urban distribution innovations, then discussed their impacts on the urban freight network. In section 5.7, the approach of morphological analysis is used to discuss both integrations of distribution innovations, thereby designing the 2.x-tier modular sustainable urban freight network.

This chapter aims to develop a flexible and sustainable urban freight network for the future large and megacities, which have systematically considered the trends of urban development and the integrations of distribution innovations. Although urban development has challenged city logistics, considerable research has paid scant attention to the links between city and freight with long-term planning. Additionally, the logistics providers devote to employ distribution innovations to decrease the negative environmental externalities caused by urban freight movements. Nevertheless, the impacts of integration of distribution innovations on urban freight networks have rarely considered. Given that, this chapter contributes to addressing the above gaps. First, this chapter proposes the two concepts related to integrating distribution innovations: operational integration and technological integration. After that, this chapter used the approach of morphological analysis to locate the possible solutions of these two integrations. Combined with the trends exploration of large/megacity development, the conceptual model of 2.x-tier modular & sustainable urban freight network has been developed. The objective of this model is to promote the flexibility and sustainability of future urban freight system. In the end, the limitations of this chapter and future research directions have been discussed.

5.2   Introduction

City and urban freight maintain a set of core relations, as the city is an entity where production, distribution, and consumption movements are used and compete for scarce land (Rodrigue et al. 2016). After the year 2000, urban population growth ceaselessly drives urban sprawl and urbanization process. These tendencies have challenged the performance of urban freight transport, particularly on the large and megacities around the world. In fact, the urban population growth is the primary element that caused persistent issues and emerging urban challenges (UN-Habitat 2016) such as, increased residency in slums and informal settlements, and urban area growth. Nevertheless, ineffective and fragmented urban governance poses significant challenges for the post-2015 development era across these vast urban regions (UN-Habitat 2016). Moreover, considerable research has paid scant attention to the links between urban freight planning and urban development (Cui et al. 2015). This observation reveals that the conventional network structure of the urban freight system that has possibly become inflexible along with the urban sprawl.

For improving environmental sustainability, the city logistics providers are intent on employing innovative transport modes to decrease the negative environmental externalities caused by urban freight activities. These externalities primarily consist of air pollution, congestion, and noise (Anderson et al. 2005; Wittlöv 2012). According to the literature review, thus far, the urban distribution innovations include electric vehicle, modular E-vehicle, public transit system, urban waterway logistics, taxi logistics, cargo bike, robotic vehicle, delivery drone, parcel locker, and mobile depot (He 2020). However, less research focuses on the various distribution innovations that operate together as a system (He and Haasis 2019). Meanwhile, the impacts of integrating distribution innovations on conventional urban freight networks have been rarely considered He (2020). It is noteworthy that several logistics providers and technology enterprises attempt to adopt standardized small-containers/boxes to promote collaborations of the partial distribution innovation. An example is that *Yamato Transport Co., Ltd.* (Tokyo, Japan) has used a similar concept to transport goods in the urban tram system Kikuta et al. (2012). Additionally, some technology enterprises have launched the concept of technology integration that is between these distribution innovations. An example is a concept of "*Future urban freight mobility*" that was proposed by the Volkswagen (Germany) in 2018, this vehicle has integrated the function of the mobile depot, robotic vehicle, and delivery robots together. To sum up, there are indeed two types of integration between these distribution innovations. Nevertheless, thus far, considerable research has paid scant attention to the two types of integrations in the urban freight system and their impacts.

According to the literature review, some research has discussed operational integration on distribution innovation. For example, He and Haasis (2019) shared the concept of sustainable inner-urban intermodal transportation (SIUIT) that refers to the combined use of various emerging transport modes to transport goods by small modular containers from an urban logistics center to customers. Although the fact is that SIUIT is a possible solution for the future urban freight system, it is lack of a systematical analysis of the combined & selected strategies on various distribution innovations. From a view of long term planning, the future trends of city development also need to be systematically considered into the urban freight network planning. To this end, this chapter employed the approach of morphological analysis to study the possible solutions of two integrations of distribution innovations based on the concept of SIUIT. Moreover, the impacts of future trends of large- and megacities development on urban freight systems are discussed, which are integrated to design the innovative structure of the urban freight network.

5.3   Research Questions & Methodology

As mentioned previously, urban freight planning lacks a systematic consideration of the future challenges that caused by urban spatial development on large and megacities. Moreover, considerable research has paid scant attention to the two types of integration of distribution innovations and their impacts on conventional urban freight networks. Despite the logistics providers individually employing one or more distribution innovations to promote sustainability, these applications possibly influence the flexibility of conventional urban freight networks within a long-term perspective. This chapter contributes to fulfilling these gaps, while the research questions of this chapter are as following:

RQ.1 What are the future trends of large/megacities and their impacts on future urban freight system?

RQ.2 What are the future trends of UFT and their impacts on urban freight network structure?

RQ.3 How to select and integrate distribution innovations to construct the appropriate freight strategies?

RQ.4 How to design the network structure of the urban freight system to promote its sustainability and flexibility further?

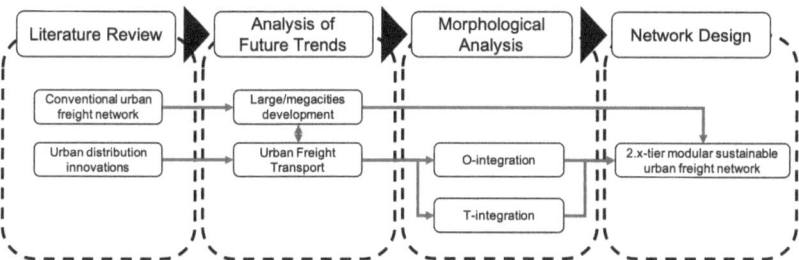

Figure 5.2 The framework of research methodology

For responding to the above questions, this chapter constructed the research methodology presented as Figure 5.2. First, the relevant research of conventional urban freight networks and urban distribution innovations is discussed. After that, this chapter separately analyzes the future tendencies and impacts on conventional urban freight network in aspects of large/megacities' development and urban freight transport. Subsequently, this chapter employs the method of morphological analysis to determine the feasible solutions for two types of integration in the future urban freight transport. Based on the identified solutions, this chapter develops the conceptual model of the 2.x-tier modular & sustainable urban freight network and discussed the future research directions.

5.4   Review of Critical Words

5.4.1   Conventional Urban Freight Network

Urban freight transport (UFT) is defined as a process and a system to collect, transport, and distribute goods within the urban environment. According to the literature review, some research has defined the terms *City Logistics* (CL) as the process for optimizing urban freight activities by stakeholders, aim to decrease the primary negative of freight activities and balance the links with urban economic scale (Taniguchi et al. 1999; Taniguchi 2015; Savelsbergh and Van Woensel 2016). Notwithstanding, a majority of scholars interchangeably used the terms CL and UFT in the papers, their definitions are the same (Lagorio et al. 2016; Neghabadi et al. 2016). Additionally, the synonym of UFT is also frequently used in this research field (e.g., urban logistics, city freight). In this work, the definition of UFT and CL is a process or a system of describing freight activities within urban areas.

As summarized by Benjelloun and Crainic (2009), and Gragnani et al. (2004), the conventional network/system structure of UFT generally consists of two types: Singer-tier and Two-tier. The former refers to delivery paths that are performed directly from the city logistics center (CLC). The two-tier urban freight system constructed by the two components: CLC and shipping terminal/depot (Figure 5.3). The CLCs constituted the first tier of UFT and located on the urban suburbs (Benjelloun and Crainic 2009). The second tier is formed by shipping terminals/depots, where the freight flow is coming from the CLCs. This process is defined as line-haul transportation or transshipment transportation (Ehmke 2012). Eventually, the goods of other external points may be transferred to and consolidated into vehicles adapted for utilization in dense city zones (Benjelloun and Crainic 2009). In this process, city logistics service providers pick up the commodities and deliver them to customers in terms of last-mile delivery (Ehmke 2012). In last-mile delivery, the shipping terminal/depot commonly uses the vehicles with a relatively small capacity to travel along any street in the city areas (Benjelloun and Crainic 2009; Ehmke 2012).

The single-tier system is generally used in small or medium-sized cities, and the two-tier system is more suitable for large or megacities (Dablanc 2007; Benjelloun and Crainic 2009). Commonly, the selection of the urban freight system is based on the urban population density and the needed coverage of delivery. For large and megacities, the single-tier system is incapable of satisfying the delivery demand. The reason is that the single-tier system exacerbates the negative environmental externalities in large and megacities, particularly on the aspects of congestion and contamination. Additionally, operational cost growth and a wide range of delivery also prevent this structure from being used in large or megacities. Therefore, this chapter concentrates on the two-tier system in large and megacities.

Although the conventional freight network structure owns high stability, it possibly causes inflexibility and unsustainability with urban logistics expansion. The reason is that the logistics providers commonly employ short-term solutions based on the conventional network structure, such as infrastructure expansion and freight vehicle fleet increase to enhance the delivery range and freight efficiency. In recent decades, urban spatial development and technological innovations also radically influence freight demands and logistics service mode within urban areas. For instance, urban sprawl increases the delivery range, the rapid growth of the urban

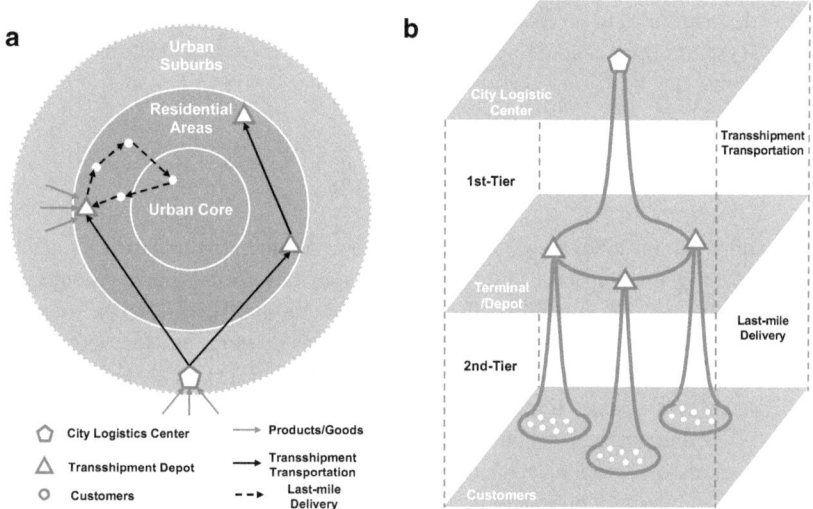

Figure 5.3 Two-tier system of UFT on large and megacities. (Based on Benjelloun and Crainic (2009), Gragnani et al. (2004))

population increases the commodity demands and freight frequency, and consumer behavior changed by the "business to customers" (B2C) requires efficient and secure delivery. These exogenous challenges have aggravated the conflict between stability and flexibility regarding the urban freight network structure. It is noteworthy that urban population growth is the primary element in causing these challenges. In 1990, almost 43% (2.3 billion) of the world's population lived in urban areas. However, by 2015, these numbers had increased to 54% (4 billion) (UN-Habitat 2016). Furthermore, in the period of 1900-2000, urban population growth has increased the built-up area by 28% in cities around the world, and the population grew at a rate of 17% on average (Albrechts et al. 2003). By 2030, the urban population will double, and the land area will triple (Ali and Keil 2006). The data exposes that urban spatial development challenges the performance of urban logistics network from the view of long-term planning. Nevertheless, the links between urban freight planning and city development are rarely considered. This observation implies that short-term solutions are possible to restrict the sustainability and flexibility of urban freight transport from a long-term perspective. Therefore, designing an innovative network contributes to promoting the sustainability and flexibility of future urban freight system, taking accounting into the urban spatial development and distribution innovations.

5.4.2   Urban Distribution Innovations

Urban distribution innovations refer to the usage of emerging transport modes to reduce the negative impacts caused by urban freight movements, thereby promoting the environmental sustainability of city logistics (He and Haasis 2019). According to the literature review, a considerable body of research has focused on the 11 distribution innovations as follows: electric vehicles (EVs), modular E(electric) vehicles (MEVs), public transit logistics, urban waterway logistics, taxi logistics, cargo bikes, autonomous (robotic) vehicles (AVs), delivery drones, delivery robots, parcel lockers, and mobile depots (He and Haasis 2019). As mentioned previously, the two-tier urban freight system is consists of two processes: transshipment transportation and last-mile delivery. To understand the applicable process of these innovations, this chapter detects the research papers published in 2014–2018. The article source is the Scopus database. Table 5.1 demonstrates the indicators of the paper selection. Following the literature retrieval and filtering, the titles and abstracts were reviewed for each selected paper. After the discussion further, research articles unrelated to the research topic were removed from the bibliography corpus. Almost 60 papers were not stringently concerned with applying the emerging transport modes in the two processes of UFT, and instead focused on some special issues (e.g., health, social perspectives, and urban planning). Consequently, these articles were removed. Additionally, this research excluded some papers that applied methods that are different from logistics or management, such as chemical or environmental approaches. Meanwhile, some papers' topics not match the definition of distribution innovations and were removed, such as the units consolidation and ICT solutions. After the literature filtering, 83 papers are related to the 10 urban distribution innovations. It is noteworthy that the literature on delivery robots was not found in the Scopus database.

Indeed, delivery robots have increasingly become a popular topic in the urban freight system. An example is that *Starship Co., Ltd.* (Liverpool, U.K.) has developed the delivery robot for last-mile delivery, which is capable of carrying goods no more than 100 pounds (Starship nd). Moreover, several Chinese retail companies develop delivery robot networks and testing freight ability, such as *JingDong, CaiNiao*. Therefore, the application of delivery robots is also a critical component of the future urban freight system. Given this, the delivery robot is also necessary to analyze and

Table 5.1 Paper selection

Items	Description
Main keywords	Urban Freight Transport, City Logistics, Transshipment transportation, Last-mile delivery
Inclusion criteria	Transportation, Economic, Management
Language	English
Document types	Journal Articles and Conference Papers
Source	Scopus
Time interval	2014–2018

discuss further. Although the relevant literature is lacking, this research determines that delivery robots are suitable for last-mile delivery by analyzing the technical data and enterprise report (He and Haasis 2019).

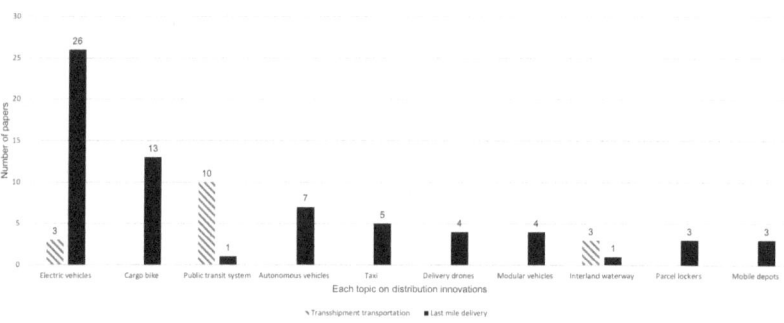

Figure 5.4 Number of papers of each topic on distribution innovations

Figure 5.4 illustrates the number of papers of each topic on distribution innovations. Considerable research has concentrated on EVs, cargo-bikes, and public transit logistics. The related articles expose that these three innovations can drastically reduce both emission and congestion caused by freight movements. Additionally, the case studies and performance assessment on these papers reveal that these three innovations are extensively used in urban logistics systems in the next few years. It is noted that the public transit logistics system is based on the public transit station that integrates passenger and freight, which radically changes the conventional

Table 5.2 Distribution of the eleven topics in distribution innovations

Topic	Transshipment transportation	Last-mile delivery
Electric vehicles	×	×
Modular E-vehicles		×
Public transit logistics	×	×
Urban waterway logistics	×	×
Taxi logistics		×
Cargo bike		×
Robotic vehicles		×
Delivery drones		×
Delivery robots		×
Parcel lockers		×
Mobile depot		×

freight network structure. This finding establishes that the applications of distribution innovations indeed challenge the network structure of the conventional urban freight system.

Following further analysis of the 83 papers, the applicative process of the 11 distribution innovations has been identified. As depicted by Table 5.2, only three distribution innovations are appropriate for applying in the transshipment transportation process: EVs, public transit logistics, and urban waterway logistics. In contrast, all of these innovations can be utilized in last-mile delivery.

5.5   Future Trends on Large/Megacities and Impacts Analysis

To respond to RQ.1, the method mix of trend exploration and literature review is adopted to discuss the future trends of large and megacities. These two methods are extensively used in foresight research, and the applied frequency of their method mix is very high (Popper 2008). The trend exploration approach is commonly adopted to forecast future tendencies based on the assumption that the future is a continuation of the past (Popper 2008). The method of literature review provides argumentative support for the continuation of the past. Consequently, this section employed the method mix of these two methodologies to analyze the future urban spatial development trends on large and megacities. Additionally, the authoritative reports/ data from the *United Nations* have been discussed to ensure the reliability of tendency forecasting.

5.5.1 Future Trends on Large/Megacities

The *United Nations*' reports have mentioned that urban population growth is a critical element for generating urban issues. For example, *World City Report 2016* that was published by the *United Nations Human Settlements Programme* (UN-Habitat), and the report of *World Urbanization Prospects* that is regularly issued by *Population Division of the United Nations Department of Economic and Social Affairs* (UN DESA) since the year 1988. Therefore, it is essential to understand the growth trends of the urban population and its impacts on large and megacities.

UN-Habitat (2016) has mentioned that the urban demographic expansion has engendered some persistent issues and emerging urban challenges, which include urban growth, change in family patterns, increased residency in slums and informal settlements, challenges in providing urban service, climate change, exclusion, and rising inequality, insecurity, as well as the upsurge in international migration. In which, Urban growth, climate change, and the challenges in providing urban services have radically challenged urban freight transport. Although the city and freight have maintained a set of core relations (Rodrigue et al. 2016), considerable research has paid scant attention to the links between urban development and city logistics planning (Cui et al. 2015). Given that, understanding the future tendencies of large and megacities contributes to urban freight planning and the formulation of operational strategies. It is noted that the average annual rate of changes in the urban population has appeared a downward trend, but the world urban population has still appeared the spurting growth since the year 1995. Due to the city creates more employment opportunities, better conditions on health care and education, improved quality of life, and the perfect infrastructure, that has continuously motivated the people to migrate to the city. Additionally, some multilateral and bilateral organizations recommend policies to encourage migration to enable the poor to move from lagging to leading areas(Albrechts 2001). These circumstances have promoted the urban population worldwide to maintain an increasing tendency.

Figure 5.5 demonstrates the world's urban population and the average annual rate of changes in 1995–2018, and the prediction until the year 2030. By 2015, 54% (4 billion) of the world's population lived in urban areas (UN-Habitat 2016). By 2030, the world's urban population will reach more than 5 billion; by 2050, 68% of the world's population is predicted to be living in the city (UN DESA 2018). This

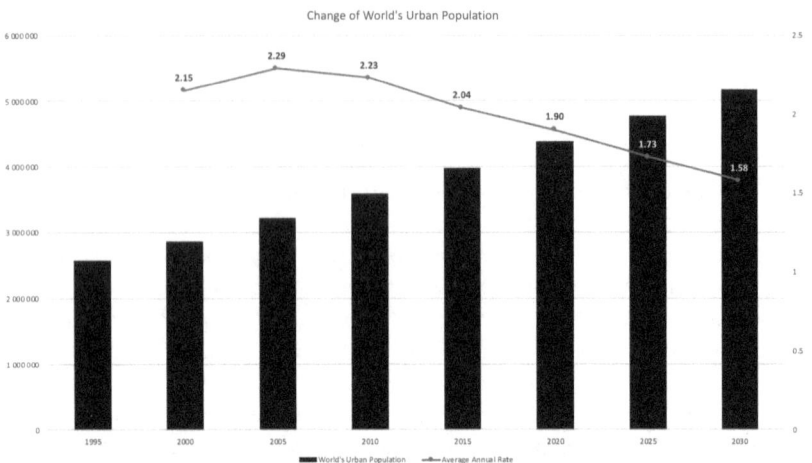

Figure 5.5 The change of world's urban population. (Adapted from UN DESA (2018))

growth leads to the sharply surged on numbers of Large and megacity worldwide. In 1995, there were 22 large cities and 14 megacities; by 2015, both categories of cities had doubled, as there were 44 large cities and 29 megacities (UN-Habitat 2016). By 2030, the world is projected to have 43 megacities with more than 10 million inhabitants (UN DESA 2018). According to the linear prediction, there are approximately 67 large cities by 2030 (as depicted by Figure 5.6).

Additionally, urban population growth leads the land area occupied by cities to increase an even higher rate (UN-Habitat 2016), particularly in the residential and commercial areas within city areas. The reason is that housing accounts for more than 70% of land use in most cities and determines urban form and densities; by 2025, one billion new homes are necessitated worldwide (UN-Habitat 2016). This finding suggests that urban freight demands and frequency will remain increased tendency at a higher rate, which exacerbates challenges on the performance of existed urban logistic systems. Furthermore, urban economies are evolving rapidly towards a higher level of material intensiveness (Rodrigue et al. 2016). These trends have caused the volume of commodity demands on urban residents to radically increased. It is noteworthy that urban population growth and urban land sprawl are crucial features for urbanization. Over the last two decades, more dispersed urbanization patterns in the form of suburbanization, peri-urbanization, or urban sprawl have constituted a significant trend (UN-Habitat 2016). The economic factors and quality of life have enormously motivated the inhabitants to move outside the congested urban core. Because both land and housing in the suburbs are cheaper

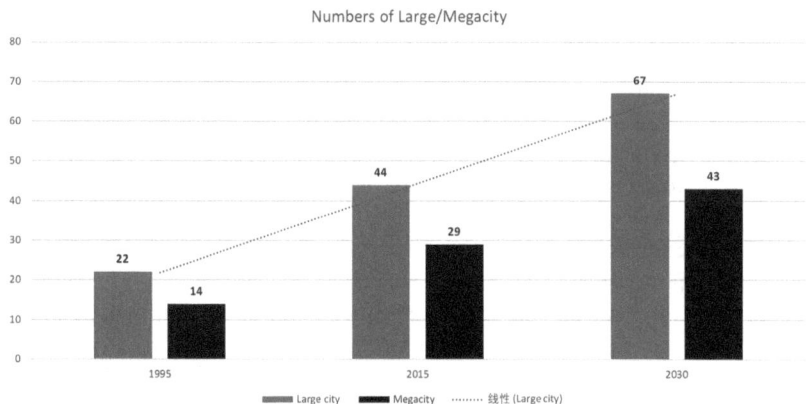

Figure 5.6 The change of number of large and megacities. (Adapted from UN DESA (2018), UN-Habitat (2016))

than city core areas, with low-density living, often resulting in a better quality of life and improved access to amenities (UN-Habitat 2016). The ensuing urban development pattern consists of the displacement of population, industries, and services from the city center to the periphery, and the creation of new centers with their own economic and social dynamics (UN-Habitat 2016). This transformation implies that establishing the brand new commercial areas in the urban suburbs is an irreversible trend. From a view of the urban logistics providers, the above trends have required the logistics companies need to construct the new infrastructure and provide better logistics services. These requirements imply that conflict of land use among the urban sprawl and urban logistics will further exacerbation. Therefore, it is essential to comprehensively consider the future city development trends in urban freight network design.

Moreover, aging population growth has increasingly become one of the primary trends in the large/megacities, especially in the European (24% of the population is aged 60 or over (UN-Habitat 2016)). Globally, the population aged 60 or over is the fastest growing at 3.26% per year (UN DESA 2015a). By 2050, 25% of the population in all regions except Africa will be aged 60 or over (UN DESA 2015a). In opposite, youth population (aged 15 to 24) accounting for a further 17% (UN DESA 2015b). The high proportion of these two types possible caused the commodity demand polarization. For example, the aged population has mainly concerned with the product related to health care, daily necessities, and the youth population has more interest in electrical products and clothing. Owing to the aged people with mobility difficulties, they desire the logistics carriers to deliver goods at any time and provide a convenient pick-up method. In contrast, the young group has more concern with delivery security and transport duration. This disparity passively increases the urban delivery frequency, which causes to exacerbate traffic congestion and emission within urban areas. Additionally, body reasons for the aged population imperiously require individualized delivery services in the last mile delivery. This requirement undoubtedly increases total costs for the logistics service provider and reduces their cost-benefit. Consequently, the future urban freight network planning needs to comprehensively consider the population age structure and the possible issues caused by commodity demand polarization in the large and megacities.

In the recent two decades, global climate change is a popular topic in academic disciplines. Indeed, cities worldwide have played a negative role in this issue since cities are responsible for more than 70% of global carbon dioxide emissions (UN-Habitat 2016). In which of this, the logistics and transport sectors contribute almost 5.5% of the total annual greenhouse gas emissions generated, 57% of which result from road freight transport (Doherty and Hoyle 2009). Road freight transport is the primary distribution approach within urban logistics. In urban road networks, urban freight vehicles account for 10 to 15% of vehicle equivalent miles (ALICE/ERTRAC Urban mobility WG 2015). However, only 42.6% of the miles traveled were the full load; approximately 25% were entirely or half-empty load (Bureau of Transportation and Statistics, Research and Innovation Technology 2009). The low full-load of freight vehicles is a barrier to the sustainability of the urban freight system. Followed by urban sprawl and commodity demand increased, the traffic flows have exponential growth, whether it is from freight or passenger transportation. This increase implies that traffic congestions and emission will cause the exacerbation trend in the future large/megacities, especially lack the integrated governance strategy and the rational design scheme of the urban freight network.

5.5.2   Impacts Analysis on Urban Freight Network

As mentioned previously, the quantity and scale of the large and megacity present the spurting growth by 2030. Meanwhile, the urban population growth and suburban-ization trend lead to the construction of more residential and commercial areas (as depicted by Figure 5.7). To respond to this tendency, urban logistics providers commonly adopt some short-term solutions to increase the transport range and delivery frequency, such as infrastructure extension and increase vehicle fleets. Although these measures are efficient short-term solutions, Although these measures can satisfy the short-term freight demands, These measures partly exacerbate negative environmental externalities from a long-term view, such as land-use conflict. Besides that, the population's age structure and commodity demand polarization have required individualized delivery services, which further increased the congestion and emission. As discussed before, the logistics providers have used the two-tier freight network in the large and megacity. To respond to the challenges of freight demand growth, logistics providers possibly adopt infrastructure extension or increase vehicle fleets. From a long-term perspective, these strategies possibly cause that the two-tier freight network increasingly becomes inflexible and unsustainable. Nevertheless, considerable research is less attentive to links between city development and urban freight transport (Cui et al. 2015; Rodrigue et al. 2016; Taniguchi 2015). Concurrently, the long-term planning of sustainable urban logistics remains lacking He (2020). These findings highlight that these transforms based on the conventional freight network structure are hard to accommodate the challenges of future large and megacities. Consequently, it is essential to design an innovative network structure of urban freight transport for the future large and megacities.

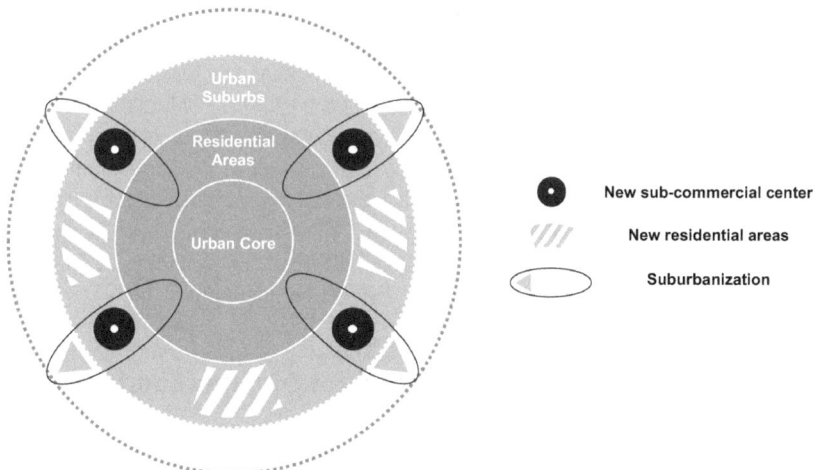

Figure 5.7 Future trends of urban spatial development on large and megacity. (Source: Author's own elaboration)

Although the fact is that considerable research has paid more attention to the impacts of urban population growth on urban logistics, a systematical consideration of urban freight planning and future urban development remains lacking. As mentioned previously, the urban logistics providers commonly employ some short-term strategies to cope with the freight challenges caused by urban population growth. It is noteworthy that these strategies are formulated based on the conventional two-tier urban freight network, which aims to address some specific issues of the short-term. For example, using EVs or other low-emission vehicles is an efficient solution to balance the cost-benefit and environmental externalities from a view of short-term planning. However, considerable research paid scant attention to the cooperation of EVs with other distribution innovations, and its impacts on the urban freight network (e.g., EVs equips delivery drone to deliver goods.) The above discussion implies that the short-sighted expansion of the conventional urban freight network is radically restricting the further promotion of its sustainability, partially due to complex freight demands and changeable tendencies of future urban spatial development.This finding also highlights that the conventional urban freight network possibly becomes inflexible, even unsustainable, from a long-term perspective. To improve the flexibility of the two-tier urban freight system, the long-term planning of SUFT needs to systematically consider the trends of spatial development on large and megacities.

Besides the above short-term solutions, urban logistics providers and relevant technology enterprises have also launched several innovative operational schemes and emerging transport modes to cope with urban spatial development challenges. For example, the scheme of urban consolidation center(UCC), the horizontal collaboration between the same level of stakeholders, integration of passenger and freight within urban areas through public transit system, as well as the application of the delivery robots. These strategies imply that the relevant companies are intent on finding the appropriate endogenous approaches to accommodate these exogenous trends. To this end, understanding the endogenous trends of urban freight transport is also a crucial component of long-term urban freight planning.

5.6   Future Trends on Urban Freight Transport and Impacts Analysis

Owing to the city and freight have maintained a set of core relations, UFT plays a crucial role in urban development (Rodrigue et al. 2016). However, the transport processes of urban freight have generated negative environmental externalities within city areas. The main negative impacts include congestion, crashes involving trucks, visual intrusion, barrier effects, noise, energy consumption, and emissions (Anderson et al. 2005; Wittlöv 2012). To this end, the logistics providers aim to balance the urban economic growth and negative environmental externalities through environmentally friendly strategies. Given the emission and congestions are primarily created by transport vehicles, the usage of emerging transport modes is an efficient solution for decreasing these externalities. Indeed, the emissions of road freight transport account for 57% of total emissions on city logistics (Doherty and Hoyle 2009), which has exacerbated the air quality, and the climate changed. To respond to this exacerbation, governing bodies and multilateral organizations have called for immediate action through the promotion/formulation of new policies or agendas. For example, the *European Commission* calls for halving the use of "conventionally-fuelled" cars in urban transport by 2030, "phasing them out in cities by 2050" and necessarily achieving "CO_2-free city logistics in major urban centers by 2030" (European Commission 2011). The formulation of these agendas highlights that the usage of urban distribution innovations is an efficient solution for promoting the sustainability of future urban freight. To this end, this section employed the method of literature review to understand the future trends of urban freight transport, while further analyzed their impacts.

5.6.1 Distribution Innovations on the Large/Megacity

According to the systematical literature review, the future trends of urban freight transport are constructed by eleven distribution innovations that are presented in Section 5.4. For addressing RQ.2, the implications of these innovations on future urban freight networks need to be further analyzed. For addressing RQ.2, the implications of these innovations on future urban freight networks need to be further analyzed. To this end, the full-text of the selected article has been reviewed and discussed This analysis aims to understand the restrictions of these innovations and their implications on the conventional urban freight network structure. The objective is to design an innovative urban freight network to cope with future challenges by urban spatial development.

Electric vehicles (EVs): As mentioned previously, some government agendas have encouraged city logistics providers to employ the EVs, while motivated local authorities to formulate the relevant promoted or replacement policies. Correspondingly, considerable research has concerned with evaluating the cost (Taefi et al. 2017; Wątróbski et al. 2017; Taefi 2016; Lebeau et al. 2015c), replacement strategies (Giordano et al. 2018; Ahani et al. 2016; Taefi et al. 2016), and the choice of delivery routing based to the charged station. This finding highlights that the usage of EVs on urban freight transport has been an inevitable tendency. However, electric vehicles remain some restrictions, such as high purchase costs and limited driving range (Apel et al. 2015; Lebeau et al. 2015a; Taefi et al. 2015; Liakos et al. 2016; Lebeau et al. 2016). It is noteworthy that these papers extensively discussed the usage of EVs on the conventional urban freight network. For instance, the research of Giordano et al. (2018); Rizet et al. (2016); Lebeau et al. (2015b) focused on the application of EVs on the transshipment transportation process of the two-tier urban freight network. In contrast, a majority of research has paid more attention to the last mile delivery (e.g., Cagliano et al. (2017); Franceschetti et al. (2017); Taefi et al. (2017); Wątróbski et al. (2017); Giordano et al. (2018); Cossu (2016); Taefi (2016); Yang et al. (2016); Ahani et al. (2016); Lebeau et al. (2016); Schau et al. (2016b); Quak et al. (2016); Rizet et al. (2016); Taefi et al. (2016); Schau et al. (2016a); Liakos et al. (2016); Lebeau et al. (2015b); Schau et al. (2015); Lebeau et al. (2015a); Taefi et al. (2015); Roumboutsos et al. (2014); Melo et al. (2014); Lebeau et al. (2015c)). Indeed, the EVs are better than conventional fuel vehicles in the aspect of energy consumption, which is zero emissions in the freight process. The implications of EVs on urban freight network include the location and distribution of the charge station and the formulation of charging schedules. Although EVs' application requires to increase charging infrastructures and equipment, this adding does not gravely change the urban freight network structure. Nevertheless, thus far, the literature of EVs has also less mention the promotion of flexibility on conventional urban freight networks.

Modular electric vehicles (MEVs) is a particular type of EVs, which is delivering the goods to consumers through carrying one or multiple freight cabin modules (Rezgui et al. 2015; Andaloro et al. 2015; Aggoune-Mtalaa et al. 2015). Thus far, Modular E-vehicles remain in the theoretical & development phase from a view of technology enterprises (He and Haasis 2019). This observation implies that the actual technical data of MEVs is still lacking. Furthermore, the relevant literature has concentrated on the applicability assessment of the conceptual model of MEVs and the fleet routing problem. According to the literature review, the impacts of MEVs on urban freight network is similar to the EVs. It is noteworthy that the reviewed results also demonstrated that the usage of MEVs is capable of decreasing the emission and enhancing distribution efficiency. Although actual technical data is lacking, it is forecastable that the application of MEVs immensely improves both the sustainability and flexibility of the conventional urban freight system.

Public transit logistics refer to utilizing urban public passenger system to distribute goods within urban areas (e.g., tram, subway, and bus). In the 23 papers of public transit logistics, almost 90% of articles are related to the application of tram/metro/subway in the urban freight system. Given this, the urban tram/metro/subway system is the primary analysis object in this research. As mentioned before, urban freight transport has exacerbated traffic congestions. To alleviate this issue, in recent years, the usage of urban tram/metro in city transshipment transportation has increasingly become a popular topic in the field of sustainable urban logistics. Indeed, a considerable body of research has concentrated on using urban tram/metro/subway system to transport goods in the city interior (e.g.,Dinwoodie (2006); Browne et al. (2014); önke Behrends (2012); Behrends (2012); Motraghi and Marinov (2012); Robinson and Mortimer (2004); Behiri et al. (2016); Arvidsson (2010); Kikuta et al. (2012); De Langhe (2017); Gonzalez-Feliu (2016b); Dampier and Marinov (2015); Strale (2014); Masson et al. (2017); Liu et al. (2018); Gonzalez-Feliu (2016a); Dong et al. (2018)). These articles aim to reduce traffic congestions and air pollution through public transit logistics. The reason is that, in metropolitan areas, freight transport is almost exclusively done by conventional fuel trucks/vans, which have exacerbated the congestion and emission (Lindholm and Behrends 2012). Additionally, the relevant literature demonstrates that academics and practitioners reach a common consensus on the feasibility of using the tram to transport goods within metropolitan areas. Indeed, a majority of large and megacities worldwide own a significant network of subway and/or commuter (suburban) trains, which can be used to transport goods (Behiri et al. 2016). This circumstance has motivated some logistics providers to test and apply the urban tram logistics system within partial large and megacities. An example is that *Yamato Transport Co.* (Japan) has been adopting a tram system for delivering goods to Arashiyama in Kyoto since May of 2011 (Kikuta et al. 2012). Moreover, since January of 2001, *Volkswagen and Transportation Services of Dresden* has used cargo tram to transport spare parts between its distribution center and factory in Dresden city center (Arvidsson 2010). These research articles and relevant case studies expose that the public transit logistics system is an efficient solution for responding to traffic congestions and air pollutions. Moreover, considerable research has systematically discussed the tram system cooperates with the E-vehicles or cargo-bikes to deliver goods within urban areas (e.g., Kikuta et al. (2012); Kelly and Marinov (2017); Arvidsson (2010)). The results of relevant articles indicate that these cooperations can improve the environmental sustainability of the urban freight system. Responsively, the construction of the transshipment infrastructure/platform and innovative urban cargo containers have also received more extensive attention (e.g., Fatnassi et al. (2015), Kelly and Marinov (2017)). These findings highlight that integrating the urban passenger and freight system is a central tendency for future urban freight transport. Nevertheless, public transit logistics usage has radically changed conventional urban freight network structure due to the requirement of a particular infrastructure that can integrate passenger and freight activities. This influence even changed the hierarchical structure of the conventional urban freight network. An example is a three-tier logistics system (road-tram-road) on Amsterdam[1]. As dis-

---

[1] Benjelloun and Crainic (2009) cited from http://www.citycargo.nl/

cussed before, increasing the tier of logistics infrastructure based on conventional urban freight network is a short-term solution. This increase can only temporarily cover freight demand growth and delivery frequency increase caused by urban spatial development. From a view of future management on urban freight transport, this solution possibly restricts the flexibility of the urban freight transformation.

Urban waterway logistics refers to employ the floating ship (FS) to transfer goods to the transit points by the inland waterway of the city. Owing to this system needs to operate in the urban inter-land waterway, which restricts the extensive application of this system in the city logistics system (He and Haasis 2019). Indeed, the vast majority of large and megacities own one or two applicable inland waterways that can transport goods within urban areas (e.g., Berlin, Amsterdam, and New York). Given this, this system is a feasible measure for the large and megacities that owned the inland waterway. According to the literature review, urban logistics providers commonly adopt the floating ship to transport goods to the city center, and the commodity types primarily consist of retail, food, parcel, and mail (Maes et al. 2015). For example, *DHL Express Netherlands* has established the DHL express floating service center in Amsterdam since 1997 (DHL nd; Maes et al. 2015); In 2007, *Mokum Mariteam* (Amsterdam) was launched the initiative "Vracht Door De Gracht" (Freight through the canal) (Mokum Mariteam 2012), the cargo capacity is 85 m^3 and can take up to 56 t of cargo (Maes et al. 2015). In these cases, the freight ships commonly have operated with the cargo-bikes and E-vehicles responsible for conducting the last-mile delivery within urban areas (DHL nd; Mokum Mariteam 2012; Maes et al. 2015). These cases also indicate that the urban freight ship is customarily applied in the transshipment transportation process of the two-tier urban freight system. Indeed, large cargo capacity and reduce road traffic congestion have radically motivated logistics providers to adopt this urban freight strategy actively. However, urban geography restriction is a principal barrier to the extensive application of this system. After the systematical discussion, the impacts of urban waterway logistics on urban freight network structure is similar to the urban public transit system. From a future management perspective, this system remains lack a comprehensive consideration of flexibility on future urban freight.

Taxi logistics is an integrated transport strategy that combines freight and passenger into the taxi network (Li et al. 2014). The relevant literature indicates that this system can alleviate environmental externalities caused by freight activities, particularly for urban traffic congestions (Chen and Pan 2016; Eidhammer et al. 2016; Li et al. 2014; Zhang and Wang 2018; Gao et al. 2018). However, the extensive application of this system remains some barriers. For instance, transport policy differences between the distinct cities, taxi schedules need to integrate passenger and freight flow, the problem of the ride-sharing route, and the benefit allocation of collaboration between the taxi companies and logistics providers. Nevertheless, this integrated system is a feasible solution for large and megacities that owned many taxis. It is noteworthy that some articles proposed the construction of particular facilities (e.g., customer self-pickup facilities) in the taxi logistics network, but it challenges the two-tier system's network structure. An example is that Agatz et al. (2018) introduced the taxiCrowdShipping system, which is composed of customer self-pickup facilities that are 24 h shops in the city. However, taxi logistics less influence the conventional network structure of urban freight transport due to this system being generally used in the last-mile delivery.

Cargo-bikes (CBs) refers to adopt the particular bikes to freight distribution within urban areas. According to the literature review, most cities have utilized cargo-bike to conduct the last-mile delivery to customers, particularly in the European (Menge and Horn 2014). The advantages of the cargo-bikes are reducing emission and congestion in last-mile delivery. Even though cargo-bikes can be a particularly cost-effective and time-efficient solution to fulfill specific transport needs (Rudolph and Gruber 2017), the load capacity and travel range remain to constrain an extensive application of cargo-bikes. To this end, lots of technology companies devote to continuously improving the freight ability of cargo-bike and reducing manufacturing costs. An example is the cargo-bike of *Velove Armadillo* has produced by Sweden Velove company (Velove Cororpation nd). These enterprises are intended to achieve zero-emission in the last mile delivery while enhancing the load capacity and travel range of cargo-bikes. ISome research mentioned that introducing urban micro-consolidation centers (UCCs) is a prerequisite for exploiting the maximum potential of cargo-bikes (e.g., Conway et al. (2012),   Rudolph and Gruber (2017)). Leonardi et al. (2012) indicated that using cargo-bikes and electric vehicles under the system of urban consolidation center can be a drop in CO_2 emissions of 55%, during a potential 14% fall in vehicle miles. This finding exposes that operational integration between the cargo-bikes and other distribution innovations strengthens environmental sustainability. After discussing relevant articles, this research identified that considerable logistics providers utilize a similar system in real-world settings. An example is the UPS in Hamburg uses two different types of cargo-bikes for last-mile delivery under the UCCs (Behörde für Wirtschaft und Innovation 2015). Although the research on cargo-bikes paid less attention to the impacts on freight network structure (De Decker 2012; Lenz and Riehle 2013; Rudolph and Gruber 2017), applying alone cargo-bikes is less influence on the conventional urban freight network. It is noted that this operational integration is possible to change the network structure of the conventional urban logistics. Nevertheless, some companies have launched a similar innovative concept based on the conventional urban freight network, namely vertical cooperation between EVs and cargo-bikes in last-mile delivery. An example is DHL Express piloted the *City Hub* concept (2017) that is the vehicles combined with a customized trailer carrying up to four containers, then the use of DHL Cubicycles (a cargo-bike able to carry a container) to complete last-mile delivery (Deutsche Post DHL Group 2017). Followed the bibliometrics analysis of relevant literature, this research locates that considerable research has systematically considered the feasibility of vertical cooperation between the cargo-bikes and distinct distribution innovations. For instance, vertical cooperation with the mobile depot(e.g., Arvidsson and Pazirandeh (2017), Marujo et al. (2018), Verlinde et al. (2014)), and urban tram logistics (e.g., Kikuta et al. (2012)). However, it lacks a systematic consideration regarding the impacts of this vertical cooperation on the urban freight network structure. This research also did not find evidence of literature reviews with this aspect.

Autonomous vehicles (AVs) refers to applying driverless vehicles in the urban freight system. From the perspective of the technology company, autonomous vehicles remain in the testing and development phase (He and Haasis 2019). According to the literature review, much relevant research on AVs remains the discussion and analysis phase of the conceptual model. This finding implies that relevant research has not yet considered the impacts of AVs on urban freight network. Owing to AVs' essence is also a type of vehicle, the impacts on conventional urban freight network are similar to EVs.

Delivery drones (DDs) is a particular type of unmanned aerial vehicle (UAV) that is capable of transport goods in its flight range. Thus far, the flight range of delivery drones is generally in a range of 20–30km (Agatz et al. 2018; Boysen et al. 2018; Deutsche Post DHL Group 2018b). Due to the delivery drone usage that can significantly decrease the traffic congestions in last-mile delivery and provide individuated logistics services, urban logistics providers have commonly used it in the last-mile delivery. For example, *Amazon Co.* has proposed the project of *Amazon Prime Air* that is a cargo airline and conceptual drone-based delivery system, the package able to be delivered to the customers just in 30 minutes (Amazon Prime Air nd). In 2013, *DHL Parcel* launched a research project on the usage of a particular drone, dubbed the "DHL Parcelcopter", for transporting goods under real conditions to remote or geographically challenging areas (Deutsche Post DHL Group 2018a). In April of 2016, *Australia Post* started testing the UAV on the parcel delivery internally, which is supported by the *Civil Aviation Safety Authority* (Francis 2016). These cases expose that UAV usage in last-mile delivery is an irreversible trend for future urban freight system. The relevant literature demonstrated that the flexibility of the delivery drone and the cost-efficient motivate the logistics providers to promote this system actively. However, thus far, the technical restrictions and operational costs are principal barriers to applying the delivery drones on urban freight transport.

The partial reason is that the multi-propeller drones are currently practiced in most experiments, which only can carry goods of almost 2 kg over a range of around 20 km (Agatz et al. 2018). Given this, some research has concentrated on applying the truck as a mobile landing and takeoff platforms for the delivery drones (e.g., (Boysen et al. 2018; Mbiadou Saleu et al. 2018)). Correspondingly, some vehicle manufacturers propose an innovative vehicle-drone concept that can employ the delivery drone in the last-mile delivery as well. For example, *Workhorse Group* have developed the *HorseFly UAV Delivery* system that is fully integrating with the electric/hybrid delivery trucks, and UPS has tested residential delivery with Drone launched from Atop Package Car (Workhorse Group 2016). *Mercedes-Benz Co.* launches the project of the Vision Vans that would be equipped with two delivery drones (Mercedes-Benz 2016). Besides these, some research has paid attention to the operational integration of delivery drones with other technology innovations. For instance, Kunze (2016) has proposed the concept of "Post 4.0" that is integrated the ground drones and small Unmanned Aircraft Systems (sUAS) in the future urban freight system. Mckinnon (2016) has analyzed the possible impacts of 3D-printing and drones on last-mile delivery. These cases imply that vertical cooperation with other distribution innovations can improve the feasibility of applying delivery drones in last-mile delivery. It is noted that the current application of delivery drone remains based on the conventional network structure of urban freight, while usage of vertical cooperation devotes to avoid itself technical limitations. Furthermore, UAVs' application requires the technical support of relevant facilities that primarily includes the control platform, charging station, and pick-up equipment. Although the expansion of these facilities has less influence on the conventional freight network, vertical cooperation with other distribution innovations possibly change the network structure. Nevertheless, considerable research has paid scant attention to the impacts of this vertical cooperation on the flexibility of the freight network structure.

Delivery robots (DRs) refers to using the small robots to deliver commodities from a local depot to the final destinations. As mentioned previously, the Scopus database lacks the articles related to delivery robot partially due to the delivery robot remain in the testing and development phase from the technology companies' perspective (He and Haasis 2019). It is undeniable that the delivery robot has increasingly become a popular topic in sustainable urban logistics. Meanwhile, lots of relevant enterprises devote to develop delivery robots with higher performance. An example is *Starship Co., Ltd.* (Liverpool, U.K.) has developed the delivery robot for last-mile delivery, which is capable of carrying goods no more than 100 pounds (Starship nd). Given the delivery robot and the delivery drone own similar operation modes in urban freight transport, the impact of the delivery robot on the urban freight network is similar to the delivery drone.

Parcel lockers (PLs) is an unattended delivery machine composed by a group of cargo lockers and located at the chosen places within urban areas (Deutsch and Golany 2018; Iwan et al. 2016). The superiority of this system is both receive and send parcels 24 h a day, seven days a week (Iwan et al. 2016). Given the essential functions and applied restrictions of the parcel lockers, this system is generally used in the electronic commerce (B2C) distribution and parcel industry. From a view of freight network coverage, employing the parcel lockers can extend the cover range of the urban logistics service network. Indeed, this system only adds a consumer service terminal in the last mile delivery, which is fewer impacts on the conventional urban freight network. It is noteworthy that some technology companies launched the concepts that are the integration of parcel locker and other emerging transport modes. An example is that *ZF Friedrichshafen AG* (Germany) has launched the project of Autonomous Depot, which is a robotic vehicle equipped with the parcel lockers (as depicted by Figure 3.9). Nevertheless, from the future management perspective, considerable research paid scant attention to the feasibility of technology integration and the impacts on the urban freight system.

Mobile depots (MDs) is an emerging concept for urban freight transport in the large/megacities, which refers to a trailer fitted with a loading dock, warehousing facilities, and an office (Verlinde et al. 2014). Applying mobile depots is an efficient solution for sustainable urban logistics because it can effectively reduce congestion and emissions within urban areas (Arvidsson and Pazirandeh 2017; Marujo et al. 2018). Moreover, the flexibility of the mobile depot can radically relieve the conflict of land use between city and freight. The parking location of the mobile depot can be adjusted flexibly with the freight demands changed, while it is vastly expanding the service range of the original urban freight network. Concurrently, the general application of the mobile depot can decrease the construction and operation costs of the terminal/depot on the second tier, and improve the urban logistics performance to respond to the delivery range growth and freight frequency increase. These findings highlight that mobile depot is an efficient solution for future sustainable urban freight system. In recent years, some urban logistics providers already used this concept in urban freight transport. An example is that since May of 2013, *TNT Express* introduces the mobile depot in Brussels, equipped with four large and seven smaller cargo cages (TNT Express 2013; Kok 2013). Furthermore, in 2017, *DHL Express* piloted the "City Hub" concept in Frankfurt, Germany, and Utrecht, Netherlands (Deutsche Post DHL Group 2017). Indeed, the "City Hub" concept is similar to the mobile depot, which is the vans combined with a customized trailer carrying up to four containers, then using DHL Cubicycles (a cargo-bike able to carry a container) to complete last-mile delivery (Deutsche Post DHL Group 2017). These cases expose that urban logistics providers reach a common consensus regarding the flexibility and sustainability of the mobile depot. It is noteworthy that mobile depot changes the partial network structure of conventional urban logistics. Although mobile depot enables to increase the delivery range and to decrease the environmental externalities, it weakens the existing terminal/depot functions. Meanwhile, the application of mobile depots leads the conventional freight network structure to become more complicated than the fixed two-tier structure. From a perspective of applied conditions, mobile depot can be utilized as the second-tier infrastructure in the conventional urban freight system. However, mobile depots can be used at different tiers, even as the expansion tier of urban logistics from a view of freight network structure. After discussing the relevant literature, this research determines that the relevant research has paid scant attention to the appropriate network structure patterns for applying the mobile depot (e.g., Arvidsson and Pazirandeh (2017)). It is noteworthy that some vehicle manufacturers have launched the innovative concepts/projects of future urban freight vehicles that integrating the mobile depot and other distribution innovations to develop brand-new freight vehicles. An example is that *Volkswagen* (Berlin, Germany) has put forward the concept of Future Urban Freight Mobility, which is a mobile depot with autonomous driving, equipped with several delivery robots for carrying goods within urban areas (as depicted by Figure 5.8). The transition process of applying the innovative freight vehicle probably challenge the network structure of convention urban logistics. Given this, the future urban freight network design also needs to systematically consider the possible implementations of future urban freight vehicles. This consideration aims to improve the flexibility of conventional urban logistics transformation under the extensive usage of distribution innovations.

5.6.2 Impacts Analysis on Urban Freight Network

As mentioned before, urban distribution innovations involved 11 emerging transport modes. Urban logistics providers and technology enterprises devote to finding the appropriate transport modes to relieve the negative environmental externalities, thereby improving the sustainability of the urban freight system. Nevertheless, a considerable body of research has paid scant attention to the impacts of different distribution innovations on the urban freight network structure. In the previous section, the discussed findings demonstrate that adopting one or two distribution innovations appears less or even no influence on the conventional network structure of the urban freight system. However, in practice, city logistics providers commonly employ multiple distribution innovations to complete the entire process of urban distribution. This observation implies that the superpositions of multiple influences

Figure 5.8 Future Urban Freight Mobility proposed by Volkswagen. (Photo by Author, Hannover Messe 2018, Germany)

probably exacerbate the flexibility of the urban logistics transformation and restrict the promotion of sustainability. Although the operational integration (O-integration) that various distribution innovations operate together as a system has received extensive attention from urban logistics providers, the possible combinations of different distribution innovations lack a systematic consideration. In contrast, relevant technology companies are more attentive to the technological integration that combines multiple transport modes to design brand new freight vehicles. It is foreseeable that these two integrations are the primary endogenous trends of future urban freight transport and challenge the flexibility of urban logistics transformation, particularly on the transition between the new and old technologies. Given this, a comprehensive consideration of both integrations is necessary, thereby designing an appropriate network structure for the future sustainable urban freight system.

According to the above discussion, this research determines that O-integration is an efficient solution and an irreversible trend on the future urban freight system. O-integration refers to selecting various distribution innovations to construct emerging freight measures, thereby achieving sustainable urban logistics. An example is that the mobile depot can operate with cargo-bikes and deliver the goods from the city logistic center to the destination without using the terminals/depots (Arvidsson and Pazirandeh 2017; Verlinde et al. 2014). From a view of the logistics providers, using the standardized small-box/container can promote the extensive application of O-integration on future urban freight system. For example, the concept of *City Hubs* proposed by DHL Express (Deutsche Post DHL Group 2017) that uses the standardized small-box/container called City Container (the capacity is 1 m³) that are produced by the Swedish companies Velove (Velove Cororpation nd). Moreover, *Yamato Transport Co., Ltd.* (Tokyo, Japan) has employed the small-containers of two sizes (the capacity is approximately 0.2–0.3 m³) in the subway-integrated city logistics system (Kikuta et al. 2012). In the previous chapter, the conceptual model of sustainable inner-urban intermodal transportation (SIUIT) has been developed to promote the extensive implementation of O-integration. SIUIT refers to integrated usage of various emerging transport modes (e.g., tram, cargo bike) to transport goods by small modular containers from an urban logistics center to consumers (He and Haasis 2019). According to the discussion in the previous chapter, the concept of SIUIT can decrease the negative environmental externalities caused by conventional freight activities, enhance economic sustainability, and provide the individual logistics services to the consumers. It is noted that the SIUIT challenges the network structure of conventional urban freight system (He and Haasis 2019). Therefore, it is essential to further discuss the possible solutions of two integrations and design the appropriate urban freight network structure to improve the flexibility of urban freight transformation. Before urban freight network design, it needs to determine the feasible combinations of distribution innovations based on the SIUIT.

In contrast to the O-integration, technological integration (T-integration) is defined as that relevant technology enterprises selected several distribution innovations to design a brand new urban freight vehicle by integrating technologies. The previous discussion mentioned that most companies launch similar projects to the concept of T-integration. For instance, the project of *Future Urban Freight Mobility* that is proposed by Volkswagen (Germany); ZF Friedrichshafen AG introduces the project of *Autonomous Depot*. Although these projects remain the development and testing phase, it is essential to comprehensively consider the future freight vehicles to design the appropriate network structure. However, thus far, the systematic method of predicting future freight vehicles remain lacking since this research did not find the literature evidence in this aspect. Consequently, understanding the possible tendencies of T-integration is essential to urban freight network design from the long-term perspective. Moreover, this systematic prediction contributes to relevant technology enterprises to develop brand new urban freight vehicles.

In sum, identifying the feasible solutions of both integrations contribute to designing a flexible and sustainable urban freight system to accommodate the urban spatial development. After the systematic discussion, this research finds that the 11 distribution innovations are fundamental components of both O-integration and T-integration. It is noted that these integrations are intent on finding the appropriate freight strategies to further promote sustainable urban logistics in the future. The previous analysis mentions that both integrations aim to find the appropriate freight strategies to further promoting future sustainable urban logistics. Additionally, applying both integrations can increase the cost-benefit of logistics providers and enhance enterprise competitiveness by providing personalized logistics services. However, thus far, it remains lacking the systematic approaches to determine feasible solutions for both integrations. To this end, the morphological analysis method is adopted to discuss the feasible solutions of O-integration and T-integration based on the theoretical framework proposed by Chapter 3. After that, the transition perspective theory is integrated to design an appropriate network structure of future sustainable urban freight transport.

5.7   The 2.x-tier Modular Sustainable Urban Freight Network Design

The previous findings indicate that the exogenous trends of urban freight transport are caused by city development and exacerbate the challenges on the flexibility of conventional urban freight network. Given that, city logistics providers and relevant technology enterprises commonly adopt the endogenous approach to cope with the exogenous trends. Nevertheless, systematic consideration of the integration of distribution innovations remains lacking in urban freight planning (He 2020). From a long-term perspective, this gap restricts the urban freight system to promote sustainability further. Therefore, this research utilized the morphological analysis method to discuss the feasible solutions for both integrations.

5.7.1   Morphological Analysis of the Integration of Distribution Innovations

Morphological analysis (MA) was proposed by Fritz Zwicky in the 1940s, which is a method for systematically structuring and comprehensively studying the total set of relationships contained in multi-dimensional, non-quantifiable, problem complexes (Zwicky 1969; Ritchey 1998). Given that MA is a method of systematically predicting the possible future technologies and feasible solutions, this research selected this approach to analyze both O-integration and T-integration for future urban freight transport (He and Haasis 2020). Figure 5.9 presents the process steps of morphology analysis that includes five steps as follows: (Zwicky and Wilson 1967; Ritchey 1998):

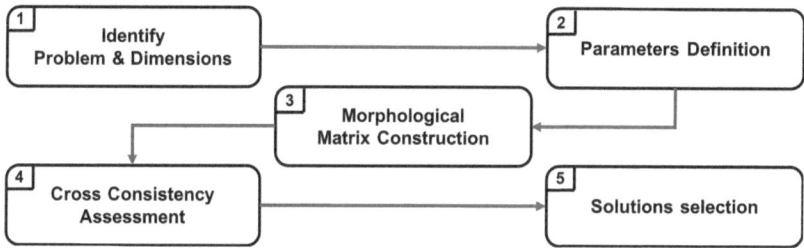

Figure 5.9 Process steps of morphological analysis. (Source: based on Zwicky and Wilson (1967))

- Identify problem and dimensions refer to the solved problem must be precisely formulated, then identify and properly define the dimensions of the problem
- Parameters definition refers to all of the parameters which might enter into the solution of the given problem that must be localized and characterized.
- Morphological matrix construction is defined as that utilizes all of the solutions/dimensions to the given problem to construct a morphological (multidimensional) matrix.
- Cross consistency assessment is that closely analyzed and evaluated all of the solutions which are contained in the morphological box, thereby achieving the purposes. According to the assessment of this step, the inconsistent combination is removed.
- Solutions selection refers to comparing and analyzing the distinct solutions/combinations that are used to find the available result.

For addressing RQ.3, this chapter followed the process steps of morphological analysis to determine the feasible solutions of both concepts of integration for the future urban freight system. First, the research problem was formulated as two components: determining the feasible combinations of O-integration and forecasting future possible distribution innovations regarding T-integration. According to the previous discussion, the critical dimensions of both types of integration were determined.

Furthermore, the distinct parameters are defined through the suitability and applied restriction of 11 distribution innovations discussed in Chapter 4.

Table 5.3 and 5.4 demonstrate the morphological matrices of both integrations separately. The matrix of O-integration includes nine dimensions as below: urban geography, urban weather, urban traffic, freight destination, the facility that needs to retrofit in the city logistics center (CLC), freight modes selection in the trans-shipment transportation process, using or not the existed second-tier infrastructure of existed urban freight system, transport modes selection in last-mile delivery, and the co-operation possibility with the other distribution innovations in last-mile delivery. After that, the relevant parameters of these dimensions were set based on the discussion of Chapter 5. This matrix is intent on determining feasible solutions of O-integration on sustainable inner-urban intermodal transportation. In contrast, the morphological matrix of T-integration is intended to predict the possible future transport modes based on the 11 distribution innovations. Given that, this matrix includes six dimensions as follows: operational models, driving models, modularization, basic module, installable module, as well as co-operation module.

After constructing the morphological matrices, the cross-consistency assessments are conducted separately. Cross-consistency assessment (CCA) refers to "reduce the total set of (formally) possible configurations in the problem space to a smaller set of internally consistent configurations representing a solution space" (Ritchey 1998). CCA is based upon the observation that there possibly be various pairs of conditions in the morphological field that are mutually incompatible (Ritchey 1998). All parameter values (conditions) in the morphological field are compared with one another, pair-wise, in the manner of a cross-impact matrix. This analysis process aims to detect each pair, whether they can coexist or need to be based on what extent. In common, there are three types of inconsistencies (or conflict) as follows (Ritchey 1998): purely logical contradictions, empirical inconsistencies, and normative constraints.

(1) Feasible Solutions of O-integration

As illustrated by Table 5.5, all parameter values in the morphological matrix of O-integration have been assessed. The relative inconsistencies are marked in the matrix by the symbol "×", and the related solutions are removed. For example, the freight float ship requires that the city owns the inland waterway, and both delivery robots and delivery drones are unable to be used in extreme weather (e.g., snowy, windy, and stormy). Besides these, public transit logistics requires the integrated transit station that integrates the freight and passenger, which is not an essential facility for the other innovations. Therefore, the integrated transit station has inconsistencies with the other distribution innovations apart from the public transit mobilities.

Table 5.3 Morphological matrix of O-integration

Urban Geography	Urban Weather	Urban Traffic	Freight Destination	Facility in CLC	Transshipment transportation	Depot /terminal	Last-mile delivery	Co-operation
Owned inland waterway	Sunny	Owned metro system	City core area	Loading docks	Electric vehicle	Use existed infrastructure	Electric vehicle	No Co-operation
No inland waterway	Rainy	No metro system	Residential areas	Charge stations	Freight float ship	No use existed infrastructure	Robotic vehicle	Delivery Drone
Steep terrain	Windy	Low-density road network	Sub-residential areas	Controller platform	Modular E-vehicle	Integrated transit station	Delivery Drone	Delivery Robot
Flat terrain	Snowy	High-density road network	Sub-commercial centre		Robotic vehicle		Parcel locker	Cargo-bikes
	Stormy				Bus		Delivery Robot	Parcel locker
					Tram		Cargo-bikes	
					Mobile depot		Taxi	
							Modular E-vehicle	

Table 5.4 Morphological matrix of T-integration

Operational Model	Driving Model	Modularization	Basic Module	Installable Module	Co-operation Module
Flight model	Autonomous Driving	Modularization design	Electric vehicle	Delivery Drone	Delivery Drone
Land model	Human Driving	Non-Modularization design	Float ship	Delivery robot	Delivery robot
Waterway model			Modular vehicle	Cargo-bikes	Cargo-bikes
			Robotic vehicle	Parcel locker	No Co-operation module
			Bus		
			Mobile depot		
			Taxi		
			Tram		

These five pairs are also removed from the final solutions. In the end, almost 495 feasible solutions are determined based on SIUIT, which can use the standardized small container/box in the urban freight process. The objective is to understand the commons of the different solutions, thereby determining the processes of future urban freight system

Figure 5.10 presents the feasible solutions of O-integration For resolving RQ.4, the feasible solutions are classified based on the applied process characterizes of distinct modules. Section 5.3 mentions that the conventional two-tier system is composed of the two components: transshipment transportation process (TTP) and last-mile delivery process (LDP). The transshipment transportation process refers to using freight vehicles transport goods from the CLC to the second-tier infrastructures. In contrast, the last-mile delivery process is defined as distributing goods to the customers or final destination. It is noteworthy that partial distribution innovations can directly transport goods from the CLC to customers without relying on the existing second-tier facilities. This observation implies that the last-mile delivery of future urban logistics is distinct from the conventional urban freight system. Based on the feasible solutions of O-integration, the last-mile delivery can be classified into three types:

Table 5.5 The cross-consistency assessment matrix of O-Integration

Option	Owned Inland waterway	No Inland waterway	Steep terrain	Flat terrain	Sunny	Rainy	Windy	Snowy	Stormy	Owned metro system	No metro system	Low-density road network	High-density road network	City core area	Residential areas	Sub-residential areas	Sub-commercial centre	Loading docks	Charging stations	Controller platform	Electric vehicle	Freight float ship	Modular E-vehicle	Robotic vehicle	Bus	Tram	Module depot	Use existed infrastructure	No use existed infrastructure	Integrated transit station	Electric vehicle	Robotic vehicle	Delivery Drone	Parcel locker	Delivery Robot	Cargo-bikes	Taxi	Modular E-vehicle
Urban Weather — Sunny																																						
Rainy																																						
Windy																												×					×					
Snowy																												×	×				×	×				
Stormy																												×	×				×	×				
Urban Traffic — Owned metro system																																						
No metro system																																						
Low-density road network																																						
High-density road network																																						
Facility In CLC — Loading docks																																						
Charging stations																																						
Controller platform																																						
Freight Destination — City core area																				×																		
Residential areas																			×	×																		
Sub-residential areas																			×	×																		
Sub-commercial centre																		×	×	×																		
Transshipment Transportation — Electric vehicle																		×																				
Freight float ship		×																																				
Modular E-vehicle																																						
Robotic vehicle																																						
Bus																																						
Tram																																						
Mobile depot			×																																			
Depot/Terminal — Use existed infrastructure																					×	×	×	×			×											
No use existed infrastructure																																						
Integrated transit station											×																											
Last-mile Delivery — Electric vehicle																																						
Robotic vehicle																																						
Delivery Drone																																						
Parcel locker																																						
Delivery Robot																																						
Cargo-bikes																																						
Taxi																																						
Co-operation — No Co-operation																																						
Delivery Drone																																						
Delivery Robot																																						
Cargo-bikes			×																																			
Parcel locker																																						

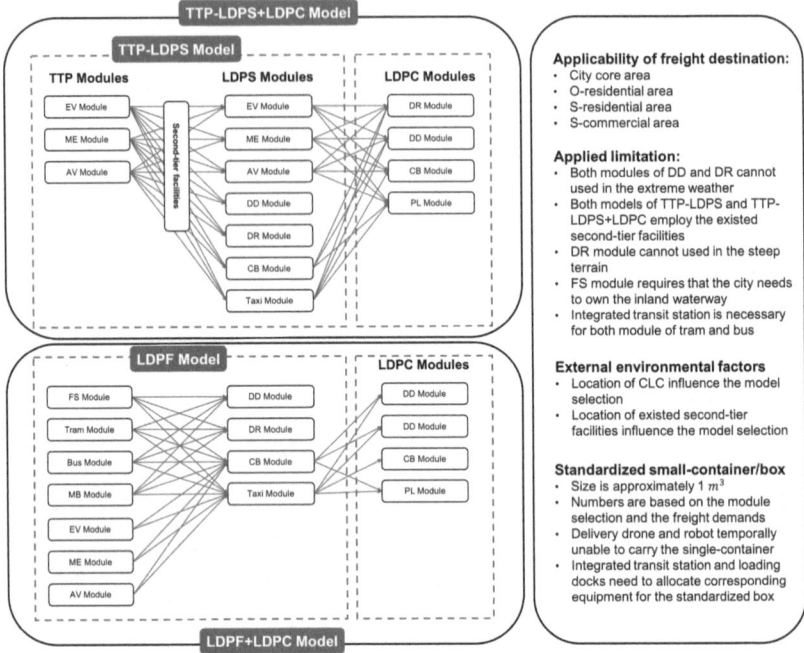

Figure 5.10 Feasible solutions of O-integration. (Source: Author's own elaboration)

- The last-mile delivery process based on first-tier (LDPF) refers to the last-mile delivery conducted from the first-tier infrastructure;
- The last-mile delivery process based on second-tier (LDPS) refers to the last-mile delivery conducted from the second-tier infrastructure;
- The last-mile delivery process with cooperation (LDPC) is defined as the transport modes co-operate with other distribution innovations to deliver goods to customers.

Based on the above definition, the feasible solutions of O-integrations can be classified into the four models as below: the TTP-LDPS model, the TTP-LDPS+LDPC model, the LDPF model, and the LDPF+LDPC model. The modules' definitions are presented as follows:

- TTP-LDPS model: urban logistics providers can employ the urban mobilities to tranship goods to the existing second-tier facilities (e.g., depot or terminal), then to deliver goods to the final destination. This model can deliver goods to the city core area, existing residential area, sub-residential area, and sub-commercial area. The suitability of delivery destination selection depends on the delivery range of the second-tier facilities.
- TTP-LDPS+LDPC model: adding the LDPC process based on the above model. The purpose is to increase the delivery range without building new second-tier facilities. Meanwhile, the other distribution innovations can co-operation with the freight vehicles of LDPS. An example is that EV is equipped with the trailer to transport the small standardized containers from the second-tier facility to the immediate areas of the final destination, then last-mile delivery is conducted by the delivery robots, delivery drones, and cargo-bikes. This model enables to reduce the traffic congestion and land-use conflicts while saving costs of logistics infrastructure expansion.
- LDPF model: compared with the previous two models, the difference of this operational model is that the logistics providers are unnecessary to use the existing second-tier facilities to transship goods. The urban freight carriers can use the vehicle to transport goods from the CLC to the specified location and then use the other modes to complete the last-mile delivery. An example is that Yamato Transport Co. (Japan) employs the tram logistics system, and cargo-bike is in charge of last-mile delivery (Kikuta et al. 2012).
- LDPF+LDPC model: it is integrating the LDPC model into the LDPF model. This model is similar to the TTP-LDPS+LDPC model. LDPC model can enhance the delivery range of the LDPF model.

For the urban logistics providers, the model selections are commonly based on the three dimensions: urban geography environment, urban road network, and customers locations. From a long-term view, the logistics providers also need to comprehensively consider all external challenges caused by urban spatial development to select appropriate solutions. This consideration contributes that the selected models and combinations are able to construct appropriate freight network to future sustainable urban freight system. Owing to the four models are based on the concept of SIUIT, both method of modular combination and the non-expansion of second-tier facilities can improve the flexibility of urban freight transformation. Concurrently, these basic modules of transport modes are composed of zero-emission mobilities, which can further promote the environmental sustainability of the urban freight system. However, applying the four models based on the conventional urban freight network is a short-term solution because the urban spatial development exacerbates the challenges of the sustainable urban freight system. Given that, design an innovative urban freight network structure is essential to long-term planning of sustainable urban logistics. Besides the urban spatial development, systematic consideration of future distribution innovations, namely T-integration, can improve the feasibility and flexibility of the designed urban logistics network.

(2) Feasible Solutions of T-integration

The previous discussion mention that some technology enterprises have launched the brand new concepts of future urban freight mobility. Meanwhile, the discussion indicates that a method of predicting future urban freight vehicles is lacking. According to the relevant case analysis, this research locates that the enterprises commonly integrate the partial advantages/functions of 11 distribution innovations to design a brand-new urban freight vehicle, namely technology integration. According to the systematic analysis of existing cases, this research identifies the six criteria to analyze and predict the feasible design schemes of future urban freight vehicles. These six criteria consist of the operational model, driving model, modularization, basic module, installable module, and co-operation module. Following the steps of morphological analysis, the cross-consistency assessment matrix of the T-integration is constructed.

As presented in Table 5.6, all parameter values of the T-integration have been assessed. The relative inconsistencies have marked in the matrix by the symbol "×", and the related solutions are removed. An example is that electric vehicles cannot be designed as the base transport mode in the inland waterway. It is noted that this research sets the hypothesis for the matrix: future urban freight vehicles can be used in the SIUIT, namely owning the ability to use standardized small-container/box. Therefore, the matrix does not consist of the parameter regarding this aspect.

Followed the cross-consistency assessment, almost 500 feasible solutions of T-integration are identified as depicted in Figure 5.11. It is noted that the previous hypothesis implies that they can employ the standardized small-container/box in future urban logistics. Feasible solutions can be classified into three types: flight model, land model, and waterway model. Flight model refers to the particular freight vehicle that owns the flight ability. An example is that *PAL-V International B.V.* (Netherlands) develops the PAL-V Liberty that is a vehicle that can both fly and land driving (PAL-V International B.V. 2018). The flight model is an efficient solution for both reducing traffic congestion and enhancing urban distribution efficiency. It is noted that the current technological and manufacturing materials are not sufficient for developing mature products of flight mode in the short term. In contrast, the land model is a common freight solution within urban areas. Hence, lots of enterprises have launched the concept of future urban freight mobility based on

Table 5.6 The cross-consistency assessment matrix of T-Integrtion

		Operational Model			Driving Model		Moduli-zation		Basic Module								Installable Module						
		Flight model	Land model	Waterway model	Autonomous driving	Human driving	Modulization design	Non-Modulization design	Electric vehicle	Freight float ship	Modular E-vehicle	Robotic vehicle	Bus	Mobile depot	Taxi	Tram	Electric vehicle	Freight float ship	Modular E-vehicle	Robotic vehicle	Bus	Mobile depot	Tram
Driving Model	Autonomous driving																						
	Human driving																						
Modulization	Modulization design																						
	Non-Modulization design			×																			
Basic Module	Electric vehicle	×	×																				
	Freight float ship			×				×															
	Modular E-vehicle			×				×															
	Robotic vehicle			×																			
	Bus			×																			
	Mobile depot																						
	Taxi			×																			
	Tram			×																			
Installable Module	Electric vehicle																						
	Freight float ship																						
	Modular E-vehicle																						
	Robotic vehicle																						
	Bus																						
	Mobile depot																						
	Taxi															×							
Co-operation Module	Delivery drone																						
	Delivery robot															×							×
	Cargo-bikes																						
	No Co-operation module																						

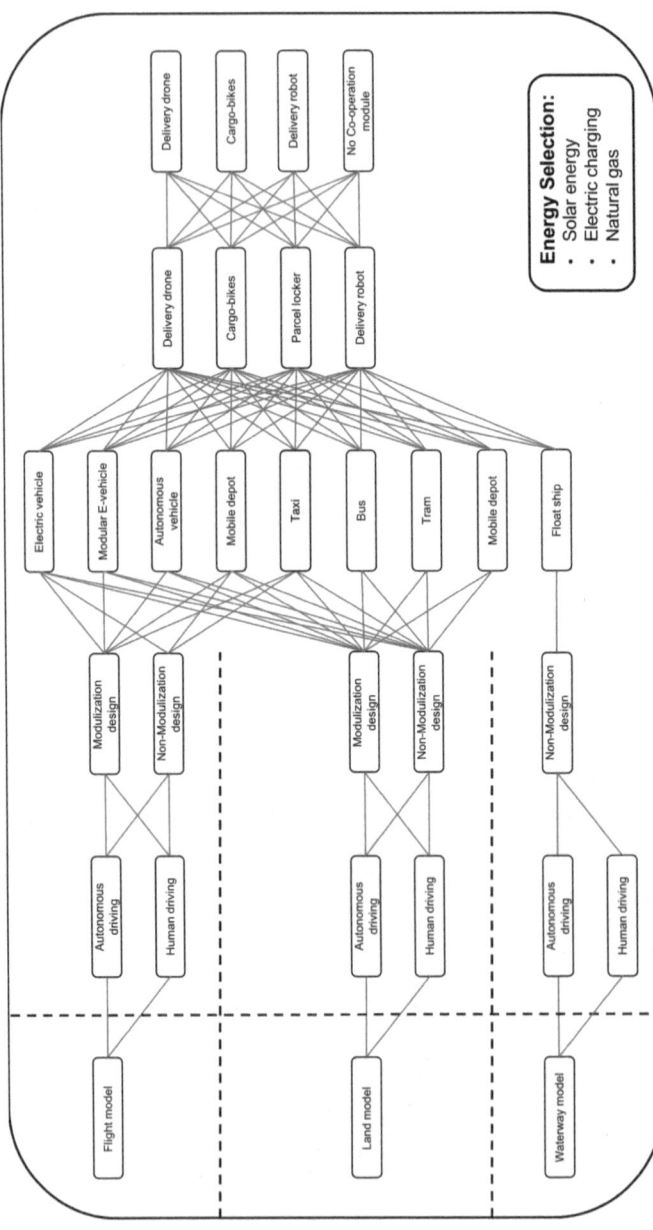

Figure 5.11 Possible solutions of T-integration. (Source: Author's own elaboration)

land model. These companies attempt to integrate two or multiple distribution inno-vations to design the brand new transport tool for future urban freight transportort. For example, *Autonomous Depot* (Figure 3.9) proposed by ZF Friedrichshafen AG, and *Future Urban Freight Mobility* (Figure 5.8) launched by Volkswagen. Indeed, developing new freight vehicles needs to consider technological support, manufac-turing materials, urban freight policy, and other limitations. The waterway model is commonly based on the floating ship and unable to integrate the modularization into the design scheme. To sum up, the feasible solutions are difficult to extensive appli-cation in the short term, particularly as mature products. Given that, this research selects one solution to discuss.

Figure 5.12 presents the conceptual model of future urban tram based on T-integration, which integrates the freight and passenger within urban areas. Concur-rently, this tram integrates the mobile depot's advantages, which can tranship goods within urban areas. The details of this conceptual model are introduced below: The tram can be equipped with different functions tram cabins that are used to passenger or freight. Freight cabins can carry cargo-bikes, delivery drones, delivery robots, and cargo-module of standardized small-containers. The MEVs can directly load cargo-module to save the passenger's waiting time when the tram needs to unload the freight. Simultaneously, drones and robots can deliver goods to the destination to reduce traffic congestions and improve delivery flexibility. Although the solution cannot be developed or implemented in the short term, relevant enterprises are able to design the appropriate freight vehicles based on the solution. Owing to vehicle manufacturing also involved the other disciplines, this research does not discuss further the applicability.

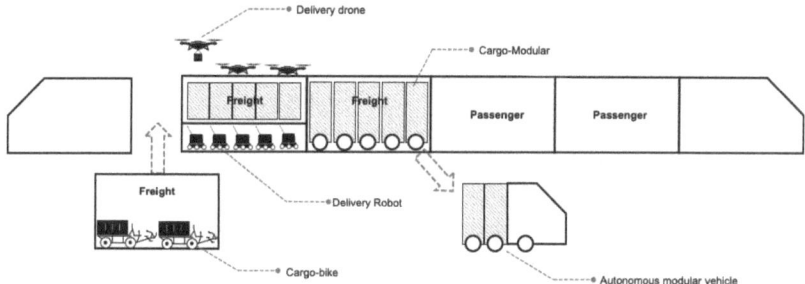

Figure 5.12 Future urban tram based on T-integration. (Source: Author's own elaboration)

Despite the fact is that these possible solutions remain some technological limitations, these feasible solutions provide a systematic thinking mode to relevant enterprises to design future urban freight modes. After developing innovative transport modes, the urban logistics carriers can use the morphological matrix of O-integration to determine the operation strategies of the new vehicles in the urban freight system. Indeed, the morphological matrix of T-integration is intended to propose a systematic method for the relevant companies to design the innovative urban freight modes. Meanwhile, understanding the possible future freight vehicles contributes to improving the flexibility and applicability of the designed network structure within a long-term view. From a view of foresight research, this matrix contributes to logistics providers design a flexible network of urban freight to accommodating the technological transformation. These findings also expose that morphological analysis of T-integration can be as a design methodology and thinking mode to relevant technology enterprises. According to the systematic discussion, this research determines that all T-integrations solutions can be used in the four future urban freight process models, namely TTP-LDPS, TTP-LDPS+LDPC, LDPF, and LDPF+LDPC model. It is noteworthy that partial T-integration solutions drive the entire urban logistics system to transform into the LDPF+LDPC and LDPF models. This finding implies that the future urban freight system is possible to transfer to the LDPF+LDPC and LDPF models entirely.

5.7.2   Network Structure of 2.x-tier Modular Sustainable Urban Freight

The previous discussion indicates that sustainable urban freight planning lacks a comprehensive consideration of urban spatial development. Given this, the sustainable urban logistics strategy needs to discuss the impacts of urban spatial development on the existing logistic system. According to the morphological analysis, this research determines that the modularization approach is an efficient solution for promoting the flexibility of sustainable urban freight transformation. Consequently, this research develops a conceptual model of 2.x-tier modular & sustainable urban freight network (2.x MSUFN) based on the findings of morphological analysis and the future tendencies of urban spatial development. This model aims to improve the flexibility of sustainable urban freight transformation within a long-term perspective.

As presented by Figure 5.13, the 2.x-tier modular & sustainable urban freight network (2.x MSUFN) is constructed by the four freight models. As discussed before, urban logistics providers commonly employ short-term solutions based on the conventional urban freight network to respond to the delivery range growth and freight demand increase. For example, expanding the logistics infrastructure and increasing the freight vehicle fleets. From a long-term perspective, the short-term solutions not only exacerbate the land-use conflicts between the city and logistics, but they also raise the costs of the logistics providers. The advantage of 2.x MSUFN is using existing second-tier facilities without logistics facility extension. In this model, logistics providers can use the existing facilities to construct TTP-LDPS and TTP-LDPS+LDPC models without facility expansion. Meanwhile, applying LDPF and LDPF+LDPC models are capable of enhancing the delivery range and reducing environmental externalities. Furthermore, the T-integration analysis demonstrates that the future urban freight system is possible to transfer to the LDPF+LDPC and LDPC models entirely. Although the feasible solutions of T-integration cannot be implemented as mature products in the short-term, the modularization approach indeed promotes the flexibility of urban logistics transformation. Additionally, the morphological analyses of O-integration and T-integration are able to construct a closed-loop system to enhance the flexibility and applicability of 2.x MSUFN.

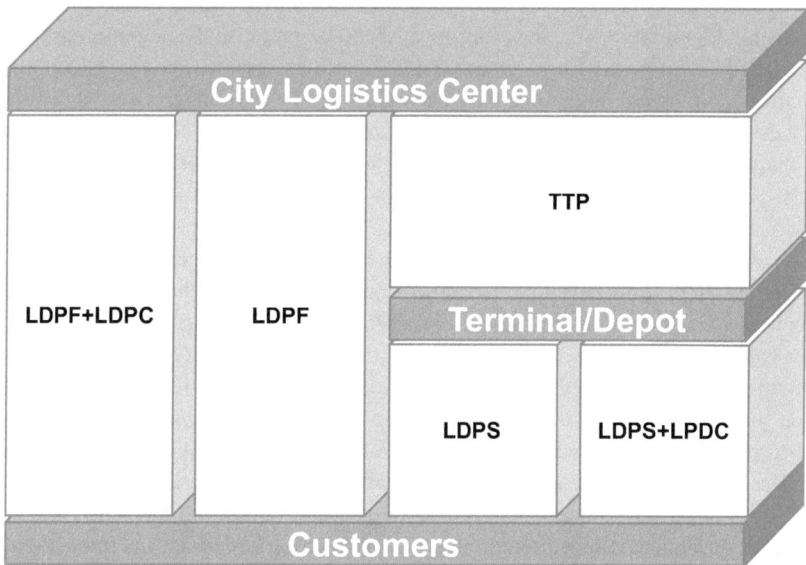

Figure 5.13 The 2.x-tier modular & sustainable urban freight network. (Source: Author's own elaboration)

Figure 5.14 presents the operational details of 2.x MSUFN based on the morphological analysis. As mentioned previously, 2.x MSUFN includes the four modules: TTP-LDPS module, TTP-LDPS +LDPC module, LDPF module, and LDPF +LDPC module. Urban logistics providers can select several feasible solutions of O-integrations to construct the appropriate urban freight strategies. Owing to the O-integration is based on the conceptual model of sustainable inner-urban intermodal transport, small standardized containers/boxes can be used extensively in the 2.x MSUFN system. It is noted that, thus far, the size of the container/box remains lack standardization or general protocol. Therefore, the suitable size of the container/box is dependent on urban logistics providers. Moreover, these four modules or partial modules can be simultaneously using in the single urban freight system. The morphological analysis of T-integration demonstrates that the future urban freight system on large and megacities possibly constructed by the LDPF and LPDF+LDPC modules without the other two modules. The reason is that the future freight vehicle can deliver commodities without the transshipment from the existing second-tier facilities. Therefore, the module selections and combinations are dependent on the logistics providers and urban circumstances.

Although the T-integration analysis contributes a systematical thinking model to technology enterprises, thus far, most of the schemes on T-integration are not launched yet in a real-world setting. Given that, this research only considers the innovative transport modes that have been launched by these enterprises. However, the 2.x MSUFN system has systematically considered the impacts of feasible solutions of T-integration on future urban freight systems. After developed emerging transport vehicles, logistics providers can add the vehicles in the morphological matrix of O-integration, thereby formulating the appropriate freight measures.

To sum up, the advantage of the 2.x MSUFN system is promoting the flexibility of the sustainable urban freight transformation to accommodate urban spatial development and distribution innovation's applications. Moreover, the feasible solutions for each module have been determined by morphological analysis. Owing to the circumstances that have the difference between various cities, the decision-makers can select suitable solutions to construct appropriate freight measures with a long-term perspective. However, this research remains some limitations. For instance, risk management of 2.x MSUFN, the impacts of technological innovations on 2.x MSUFN (e.g., 3D-printers), decision support system of 2.x MSUFN, costs assessment of different combined solutions, stakeholders transformation, and future urban freight policymaking. Consequently, future research directions can launch systematic discussions in these aspects.

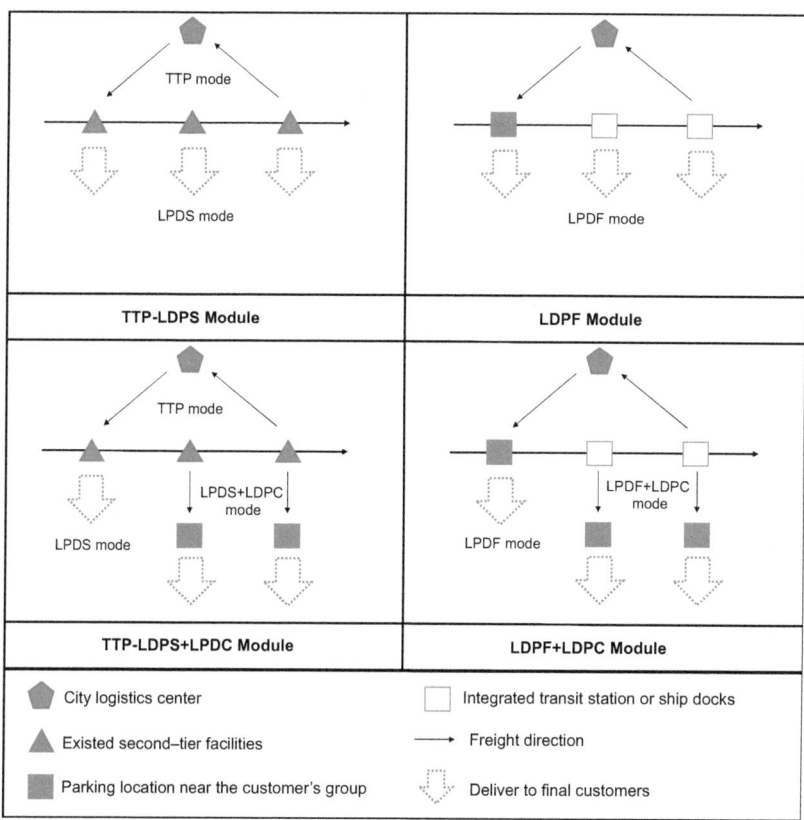

Figure 5.14 Operational model of 2.x-tier modular & sustainable urban freight system. (Source: Author's own elaboration)

5.8   Conclusion of This Chapter

This chapter proposes the two concepts of integration on distribution innovations: operational integration and technological integration. The morphological analysis method is used to determine the feasible solutions of O-integration and T-integration separately. Combined with the trends exploration of urban spatial development, the conceptual model of the 2.x-tier modular & sustainable urban freight network (2.x MSUFN) is developed. This model aims to improve the flexibility of sustainable urban logistics transformation from the long-term strategy. The relevant literature demonstrates that a considerable body of research has paid scant attention to the long-term planning of urban freight transport. Given that, this chapter contributes to resolving this gap. The advantage of 2.x MSUFN can promote the urban logistics to employ the long-term solutions to improve flexibility and sustainability of urban logistics in large and megacities.

Additionally, the morphological analysis determines many feasible solutions regarding O-integration, which can construct various freight measures to accommodate different cities. The logistics providers and decision-makers can select suitable schemes to combine the operational modules. In contrast, the morphological analysis of T-integration systematically predicts future possible freight vehicles, which provide a systematic thinking model to technology enterprises to develop innovative freight vehicles. Besides the research limitations as discussed before, some others also need to be further discussed and analyzed, such as the ICT platform of the 2.x MSUFN, decision support system of selecting O-integration measures, and standardization framework of future sustainable urban logistics.

Scenario Analysis on 2.x MSUFN

6

6.1   Logical Arrangement of the Chapter

Scenario analysis (SA) is a systematical method that is not only to describe a sample prediction about the future, but also a description of a set of possible eventualities relating what the world may look like over a certain time horizon (Tourki et al. 2013; Porter and Kramer 2002; Schwartz 2012; Van der Heijden 2011; Jarke et al. 1998; Cornish 2004; Scholz and Tietje 2002; Duinker and Greig 2007). Hickman et al. (2012) mentioned that "SA is conceivably essential here in helping us to begin to 'think the unthinkable,' while it is increasingly being used in the transport field". Given this work is foresight research on SUFT that involved the future urban freight transport, the approach of scenario analysis is a reliable solution for evaluating the 2.x modular & sustainable urban freight system. To this end, this research employed the scenario analysis approach to evaluate the suitability of the 2.x modular & sustainable urban freight network (2.x MSUFN) and further discussing the future research direction.

This chapter aims to evaluate the 2.x MSUFN and conceptual model of SIUIT from the three time-dimensions: now, 15 years later, and 30 years later. Figure 6.1 presents the logical structure of this chapter. Following this structure, this chapter is organized as below: Section 6.2 is regarding the scenario definition, includes a description of the example city, development hypothesis of distribution innovations based on the GE matrix of the implementation status analysis, and infrastructure locations of city logistics in the example city. Based on the previous setting, Section 6.3 demonstrates systematically discuss and compare the three scenarios. Scenario I is the conventional two-tier system in the three time-dimensions.

Z. He, *Future Sustainable Urban Freight Network Design in the Large Cities and Megacities*, Sustainable Management, Wertschöpfung und Effizienz, https://doi.org/10.1007/978-3-658-34203-6_6

Scenario II is the 2.x MSUFN system in the 15 years later. Scenario III is the 2.x MSUFN system in the 30 years later. Section 6.3 is scenario evaluation according to the comparison between the three scenarios.

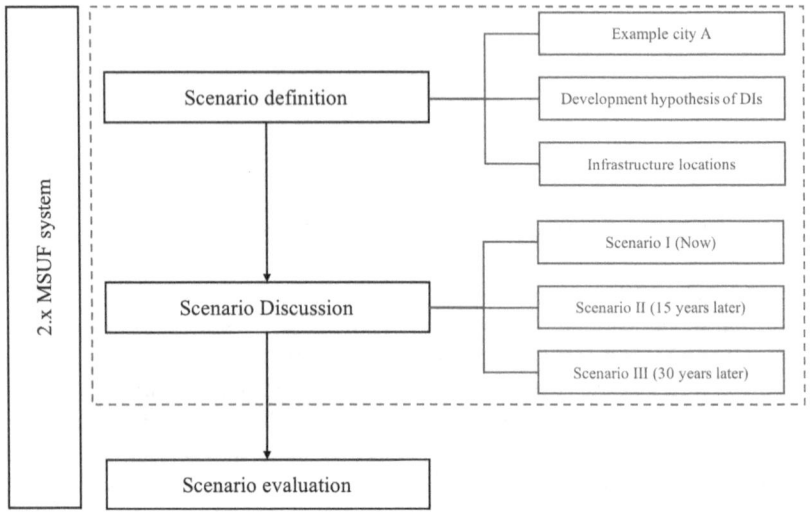

Figure 6.1 Structure of Chapter 6

6.2   Scenario Definition

Scenario definition refers to set several hypothesis conditions to construct an appropriate scenario that is provided for further analysis. Following the logical structure of this chapter, defining the scenarios and setting hypothesis conditions are critical components of the scenario analysis. As mentioned in the Introduction, this research aims to design an innovative urban freight system to respond to future challenges of large and megacities. Nevertheless, the urban governance and urbanization process have discrepancies between each actual city. The discrepancies are commonly created by multiple factors associated with urban policy differentiation, urban function positioning, And structure of the urban population. Given that, to ensure the evaluation is objective and valid, this chapter sets a virtual city as an example to conduct the scenario analysis.

Table 6.1 Scenario Definition

	Scenario I	Scenario II	Scenario III
Example city	City A		
Time-dimensions	Now, 15 years later	15 years later	30 years later
City change	Large city	Large city	Megacity
City logistics	Two-tier system	2.x MSUFN system	2.x MSUFN system
Industry selection	Post industry		
Freight destination	Residential area (RA) and commercial area (CA)		
Freight modes	Development hypothesis of 11 distribution innovations		

Table 6.1 demonstrates the scenario definition. Owing to this work focuses on the foresight research of future SUFT given long-term planning, the scenarios' setting follows the long-term time-dimensions (future 15–30 years). Based on the analysis of urban population growth in Chapter 5, the scenario definition set that example city A remains a large city in the next 15 years. After 30 years, city A increasingly transforms into a megacity along with the urban population growth. Scenarios are setting below: Scenario I involves the conventional two-tier system in the example city A (now) and the possible change of urban logistics network after the 15 years. Furthermore, Scenario II is involved in the city A of 15 years later that employe the 2.x MSUFN system. Scenario III is the megacity A of 30 years later, which continues the 2.x MSUFN system. For the logistics providers, the post industry is selected as the analysis target. Given that, the scenario analysis focus on the residential area (RA) and commercial area (CA).

Additionally, the freight modes are evolving along with technology innovations. Consequently, the application status of distribution innovations has made a systematic assumption based on Chapter 4. This assumption aims to ensure the authenticity and reliability of the set scenario in the time dimension. Meanwhile, further analyzing freight modes development contributes to evaluating the 2.x MSUFN system and the research limitations. For the example city, Section 6.2.1 describes the urban specific situations and analyzes the urban spatial change in the three time-dimensions. For freight destinations, this analysis selects the residential and Commerical areas in the example city. Owing to the urban sprawl radically increase the numbers and range of RA and CA, the transformations of both RA and CA in three time-dimensions need to be discussed based on the systematic assumption.

6.2.1   Example City A

The high authenticity of the example city contributes to assessing the feasibility
of the 2.x MSUFN system. Due to the real circumstances of large and megacities
are complicated (e.g., road network structure), the scenario setting needs to sim-
ulate the actual urban situation. The environment hypothesis of the example city
A is constructed as presented by Table 6.2. The description of city A is composed
of the following aspects: urban types, urban population, city acreage, geography
environment, and infrastructures.

Table 6.2 Circumstance description of example city A

Item	Description
Urban types	Inland large city
Urban population	Almost 9.23 million
Urban acreage	Almost 10,232 square kilometers
Geography environment	Inland river, lakes plain area
Urban infrastructures	Airport, freight train station, interstate highway, beltway
Public transit system	Urban tram, bus

Based on Table 6.2, the example city A is described as a large inland city located
in the plains and owns almost 9.23 million residents and covers an area of approximately 10.232 square kilometers. City A owns the inland rivers and small lakes.
Meanwhile, the floating ships can be used in the river A for passenger and freight. In
City A, the public transit system is consists of the urban tram system and bus system.
Moreover, the road network is composed of the interstate highway, the beltway, and
the inner-urban road. To add authenticity to the example city, this research references
maps and environmental details of Beijing and Berlin. After that, the EdrawMax
software is utilized to design the map of City A as depicted in Figure 6.2.

Based on the analysis of Chapter 5, the spatial sprawl of city A is systematically
assumed alone with the three time-dimensions. After referencing the actual maps of
Beijing and Berlin, the major RA and CA are selected as the evaluated objects. These
areas are set on the primary functional zones on the City A, which are referenced
the zone allocations of Beijing and Berlin to ensure its authenticity and reliability.

Following the previous definition and discussion, Figure 6.2 presents the map
of the example city A and the geographical distribution of primary RAs and CAs.
There are six interstate highways connected to this city, while two beltways have

Figure 6.2 The example city A (Now). (Source: Author's own elaboration)

been constructed based on the interstate highway network. Furthermore, river A crossed the entire city and linked the lake A and C. Lake B is located in the northwest of City A and linked with the small river B. Although the current City A is a large city, the population of almost 9.23 million is close to the urban population scale of the megacity. Although the current City A is a large city, the population of almost 9.23 million is close to the urban population scale of the megacity. Based on the trend exploration in Chapter 5, this analysis assumes City A will transform into a megacity after 20 years, and the urban population will more than 10 million. This transformation leads to urban spatial sprawl with urban population growth. Based on the above assumptions, this research sets the spatial alteration of City A in the future 15 years and 30 years. Figure 6.3 depicts the City A after 15 years.

Compared with Figure 6.2, after 15 years, the scale of City A (Figure 6.3) is larger than before. The urbanization process motivates urban sprawl and increases the number of architecture continually. Meanwhile, the coverage and denser of road

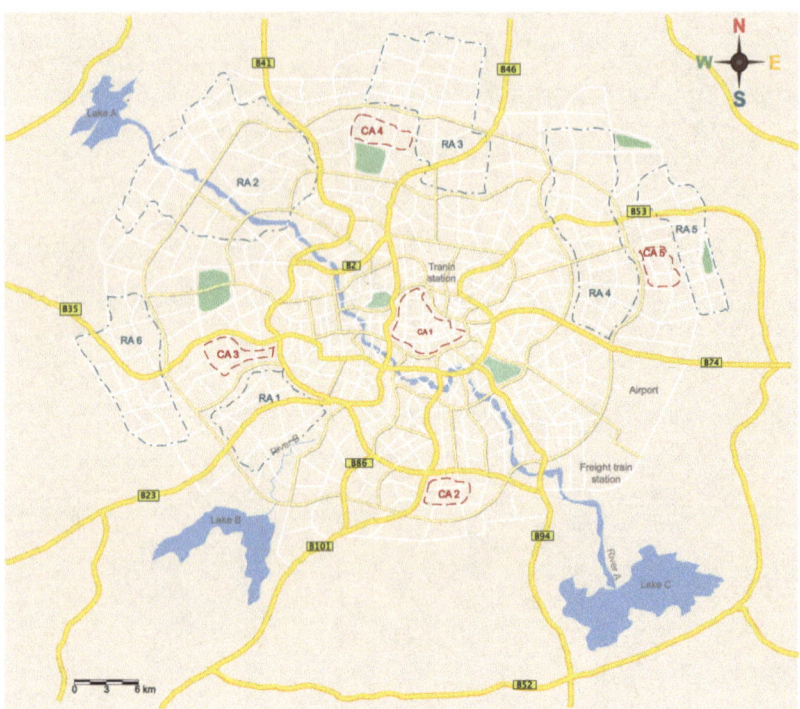

Figure 6.3 City A after 15 years. (Source: Author's own elaboration)

networks are rising. However, the urban demographic expansion causes the proportion growth of private vehicles on the streets, which challenges the performance of the urban traffic network. This finding implies that traffic congestions are possibly exacerbated in City A. To enhance the urban traffic performance, this analysis assumes that the local authority of city A launches the project of floating ships to transport passengers in the river A. This project aims to reduce the congestions and emission within urban areas. Considering City A remains a scale of a large city and cost budget, this analysis supposes that the local government still does not expand the beltway network on this time-dimension.

The trend exploration in Chapter 5 demonstrates that the urban population of city A possibly breaks 10 million after 30 years. This growth implies that city A increasingly transforms into the type of megacity after 30 years. Figure 6.4 presented the spatial scale of city A in this time-dimension.

Figure 6.4 City A after 30 years. (Source: Author's own elaboration)

After 30 years, the urban population growth makes the scale of city A to ultimately transform into a megacity. Compared between Figures 6.2 and 6.4, the urban area is almost double the scale of 30 years ago. The suburbanization tendency primarily prompts this transformation (UN-Habitat 2016). This finding exposes that urban traffic congestions and emission are possibly exacerbated than before with the urban areas increase. Given that, this analysis assumes that the local authority constructs a brand new beltway in this time-dimension to enhance the transport network's performance.

Accompanied by the urban population growth, the area of both RA and CA are spurt expansion. Compared with Figures 6.2, Figure 6.4 exhibits that the RAs in city A dramatically increase in aspects of the number and range, particularly on the RA 2, 3, and 6. Given to the CA1 is located in the core area of City A, this analysis assumes that its cover range is not changed in three time-dimensions. Moreover, Figure 6.3 shows that building CA 5 is based on the commercial demands of RA 4 and 5.

This hypothesis is following the trend exploration of urban spatial development in Chapter 5. Concurrently, the range growth of RA 4 and 5 promotes the expansion of CA 5 (Figure 6.4). Correspondingly, the expansions of CA 3 and 4 are also based on the commercial demands of near residential areas.

6.2.2   Development Hypothesis of Distribution Innovations

Following the scenario definition (Table 6.1), the distribution innovations need systematical assumptions based on the application status analysis (Figure 4.4 in Chapter 4). This analysis assumes that logistics providers extensively adopt distribution innovations of the high-high phase to transport goods within urban areas, and partial innovations of the high-medium phase are used simultaneously.

Figure 6.5 shows the current application status of eleven distribution innovations (as described in section 4.5). Given that, this research assumes that the post logistics provider has extensively employed electric vehicles and parcel lockers within areas of city A. Meanwhile, the company has used cargo bikes to conduct last-mile delivery in partial areas.

After 15 years, technology development promotes the extensive application of distribution innovations. This observation implies that partial innovations increasingly transform into the higher applied phase. Figure 6.6 demonstrates the applied status of distribution innovations after 15 years. The logistics provider extensively employs electric vehicles, parcel lockers, cargo-bikes, public transit logistics, and urban freight ships. Meanwhile, four distribution innovations of the high-medium phase are also used in partial urban areas: delivery drones, delivery robots, mobile depots, and robotic vehicles.

Corresponding to the urban spatial development with three time-dimensions, the last assumption of distribution innovations is related to 30 years later. Figure 6.7 indicates the applied hypothesis of distribution innovations after 30 years. Given that, the logistics provider widely adopts nine distribution innovations within urban areas: electric vehicle, parcel locker, cargo-bike, public transit logistics, urban freight ship, delivery drone, deliver robot, mobile depot, and robotic vehicle. In contrast, the modular E-vehicles are used to distribute goods within partial areas.

Although technology integration has been discussed by morphological analysis in section 5.7, the uncontrollability of future technologies restricts the reliability of scenario analysis. Additionally, Chapter 5 determines that the feasible solutions of T-integration can be used in the four modules of 2.x MSUFN. Given that the future distribution innovations are also based on the existing emerging transport modes,

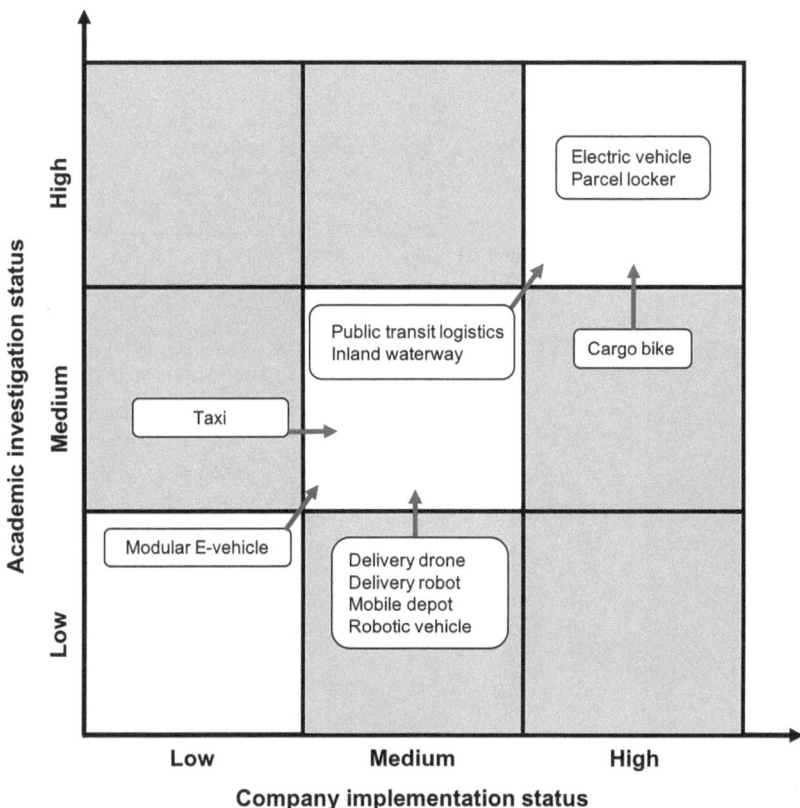

Figure 6.5 The application status of DIs (now). (Source: Author's own elaboration)

the scenarios analysis comprehensively considers the 11 innovations to ensure the authenticity of the scenario setting.

6.2.3   Logistics Infrastructure Locations

This section describes the infrastructure locations of the logistics provider A in City A. The logistics provider A currently employs the two-tier urban freight system since the city A is a large city. According to the discussion of section 5.3, the first tier infrastructure is the city logistics center (CLC) located in the urban suburbs (Benjelloun and Crainic 2009). The second tier facilities are formed by

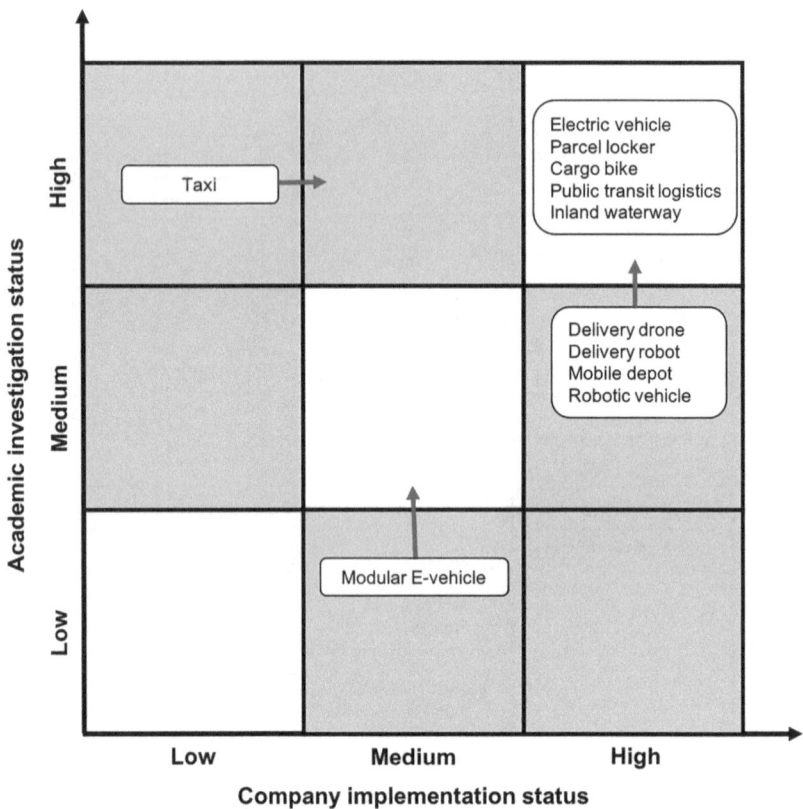

Figure 6.6 The application status of DIs (15 years later). (Source: Author's own elaboration)

shipping terminals/depots where the freight is coming from the CLCs. Moreover, these infrastructures are also consolidating the goods from other external points to transfer the commodities by vehicles for dense city zones (Benjelloun and Crainic 2009).

Based on the previous hypothesis and discussion, the locations of logistics infrastructures are set as depicted by Figure 6.8. The logistic provider constructs three major infrastructures: a CLC and two depots. The CLC is located on the outskirts of the urban zone near the freight train station, the airport, and the B94 interstate highway. The CLC location is based on a comprehensive consideration of transport capacity related to the goods from outside of the City A. The CLC location is based

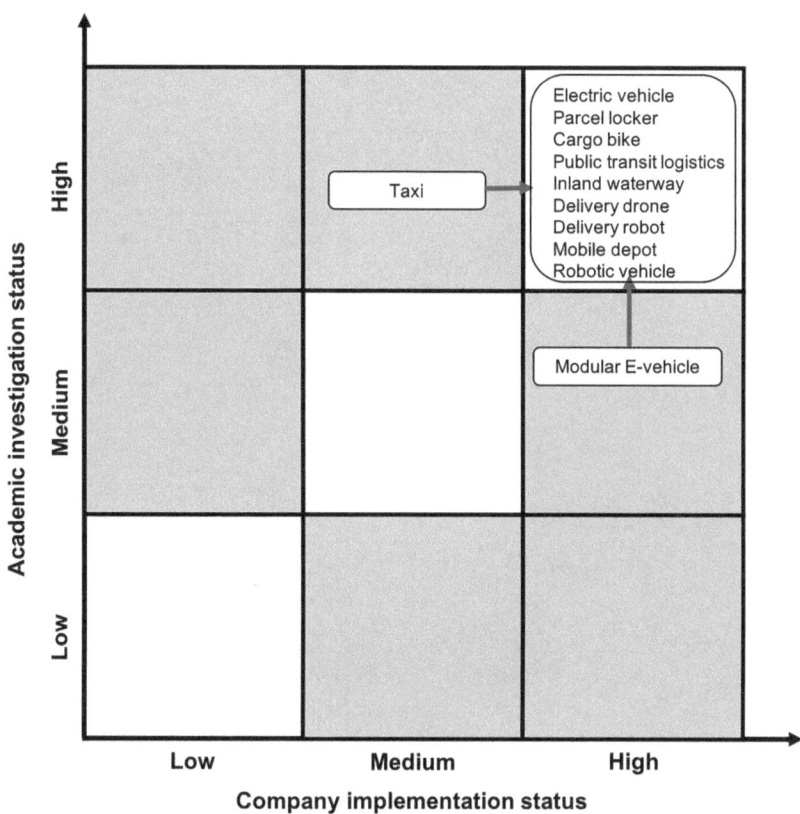

Figure 6.7 The application status of DIs (30 years later). (Source: Author's own elaboration)

on a comprehensive consideration of transport capacity related to the goods from outside of City A. The goods can be transferred by freight trains, flight, and road transportation. The second-tier infrastructures consist of depots 1 and 2 located on the northwest and southeast of the city separately. These two depots can consolidate the goods into the vehicles adapted for utilization in dense city zones and increase the delivery range of the logistics system.

Figure 6.8 Infrastructure locations of logistics provider A (Now). (Source: Author's own elaboration)

6.3   Scenarios Discussion

6.3.1   Scenario I

The Scenario I is defined as the logistics provider A uses the conventional two-tier urban freight system UFT to distribute goods to the customers within City A. In this time-dimension (now), the logistics provider A has employed the electric vehicles, parcel locker, and cargo-bikes to construct the urban freight network within City A. The selected transport modes is based on the analysis of the hypothesis of distribution innovations (Figure 6.5).

As depicted by Figure 6.9, the logistics provider uses the CLC to consolidate and transfers the goods to the two depots separately through the road transport network within urban areas. In common, the logistics provider A utilizes the trucks responsible for transshipment transportation. Despite the logistics provider A can transfer the goods by urban beltway network, this measure exacerbates the traffic congestions and emissions within City A. After the transshipment transportation, Depot 1 is responsible for distributing goods to the near residential and commercial areas: CA 1, CA 4, RA 2, RA 3, and RA 4. In contrast, Depot 2 is in charge of transport goods to CA 1, CA 3, RA 1, and RA 2. Given the location of CA 2 near the CLC, CLC distributes goods to this area directly.

Figure 6.9 Two-tier system of logistics provider A (now). (Source: Author's own elaboration)

As mentioned previously, three transport modes are adopted in this system. Hence, operation models are similar in different areas. Figure 6.10 exhibited that particulars freight activities of the conventional two-tier system in the residential and commercial areas. First, company A adopts the trucks to transfer goods from the CLC to the Depot 1 or 2. After the transshipment transportation, depots commonly use the small/standard size EVs responsible for the last-mile delivery in farther areas. An example is using EVs to transport goods from Depot 1 to customers who live in RA 2 and 4. For the surrounding areas of the depot, logistics provider A can utilize cargo-bikes to responsible for last-mile delivery. An example is using cargo-bikes is to deliver goods to the customers of RA 3.

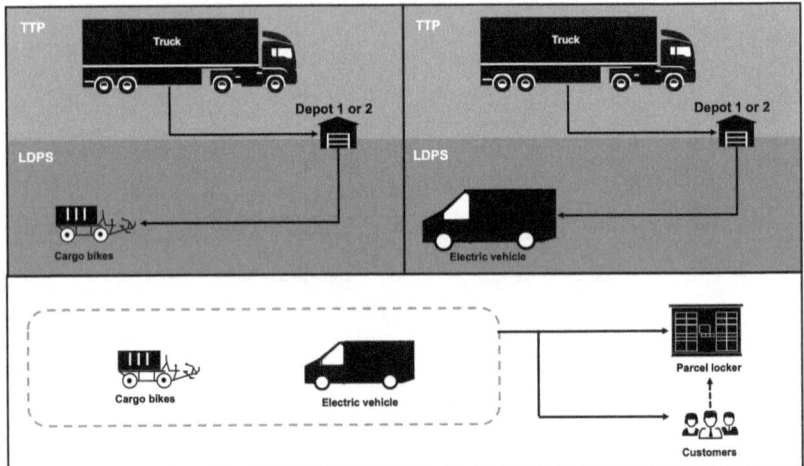

Figure 6.10 The operational model of two-tier system (now). (Source: Author's own elaboration)

Indeed, this conventional two-tier system of UFT is on some way to balance the economic growth and environmental externalities created by freight activities. However, urban spatial development has radically exacerbated the challenges of the conventional urban freight system. As mentioned previously, lots of logistics providers commonly adopt short-term solutions to accommodate these challenges.

Figure 6.11 demonstrates the transformation of the conventional two-tier system after 15 years, which is based on short-term solutions: infrastructure expansion and freight fleet increase. These solutions imply that the conventional urban freight system increasingly becomes a multi-tier system. Compared with Figure 6.9, the logistics provider A constructs Depot 3 that is responsible for delivering goods to CA 4, RA 2, and RA 3. Meanwhile, Sub-depot 1 is the third-tier facility in charge of distributing goods to RA 5 and CA 5. This expansion is caused by the range growth of residential areas and the generation of emerging commercial areas. Chapter 5 mentions that, thus far, urban logistics providers lack a comprehensive consideration of urban spatial development to make the long-term strategy of SUFT. To a certain extent, short-term solutions can improve urban logistics' performance in aspects of delivery frequency and transport coverage. However, from a long-term perspective, these approaches possibly restrict the further promotion of sustainable urban logistics. Therefore, applying short-term solutions under the two-tier system leads to an inflexible transformation of urban logistics.

Figure 6.11 Two-tier system of logistics provider A (15 years later). (Source: Author's own elaboration)

6.3.2   Scenario II

Scenario II is defined as that, 15-years later, logistics provider A constructs the 2.x MSUFN system within City A and using sustainable inner-urban intermodal transportation. Following the development hypothesis of distribution innovations (Figure 6.6), the operational measures of SIUIT can be primarily constructed by electric vehicles, parcel lockers, cargo-bikes, public transit logistics, and urban freight ships. Meanwhile, four distribution innovations (High-medium phase) are employed within partial urban areas: the delivery drones, delivery robots, mobile depots, and robotic vehicles.

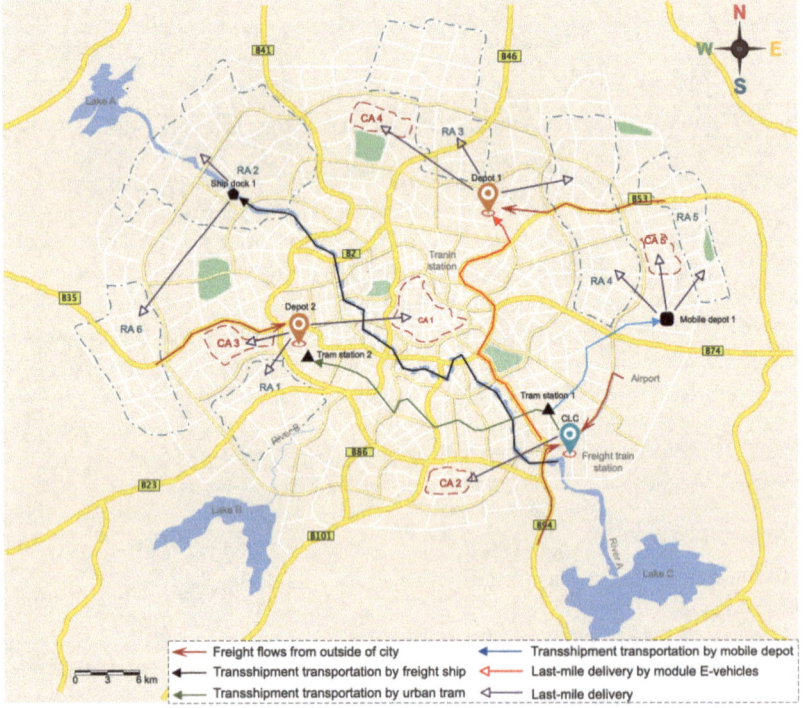

Figure 6.12 2.x MSUFN system of logistics provider A (15 years later). (Source: Author's own elaboration)

Figure 6.12 depicts the 2.x MSUFN system within City A after 15 years. The previous discussion mentioned that the expansion of RAs and CAs causes freight demand growth. This observation implies that the freight capacity of existing second-tier logistics facilities is impossible to provide efficient delivery services to respond to this growth. Given that, Scenario II adopts the 2.x MSUFN system based on the development hypothesis of distribution innovations. The operational measures are presented as follows:

- The urban freight ship is a component of the LDPF+LDPC module. Logistics provider A adopts the freight ships to transport standardized small-containers from CLC to the ship dock 1. After that, EVs and cargo-bikes can carry these small-containers to deliver goods to the customers in RA 2 and RA 6. Meanwhile, the EVs are able to be equipped with the delivery robots or drones to conduct cooperation in last-mile delivery. This cooperation can increase delivery range and freight efficiency.
- The urban freight tram is used to construct the TTP-LDPS module and the TTP-LDPS+LDPC module. Logistics provider A adopts the urban freight trams in the existing urban tram network. These trams are utilized to transfer the goods to Depot 2 and consolidating the goods into the standardized small-containers. After transshipment transportation, Depot 2 conducts last-mile delivery through EVs and cargo-bikes. The freight destinations of Depot 2 include CA 1, CA 3, and RA 1.
- The mobile depot is a critical component of the LDPS-LDPF+LDPC module. Owing to the new-built RA 5 and RA 4 growth, the original capacity of Depot 1 is unable to satisfy the freight demand increase. To reduce infrastructure expansion costs, the mobile depots can transfer the standardized small-containers from CLC to the parking near CA 5, RA 4, and RA 5. Concurrently, mobile depots can be equipped with cargo-bikes and delivery drones to conduct last-mile delivery.
- The conventional TTP-LDPS module is also used in the 2.x MSUFN system. The EVs fleet can transfer the standardized small-containers to the Depot 1. After that, Depot 2 is able to use the cargo-bikes and EVs to deliver goods within CA 4, RA 3, and RA 4.

According to the previous descriptions, Figure 6.13 demonstrates the operational models of the 2.x MSUFN system. In this scenario, logistics provider A employs long-term solutions to construct the urban freight network. For the logistics provider, the O-integration can enhance the delivery range and freight capacity without applying short-term solutions. Additionally, the O-integration is able to reduce facility expansion costs and land-use conflict.

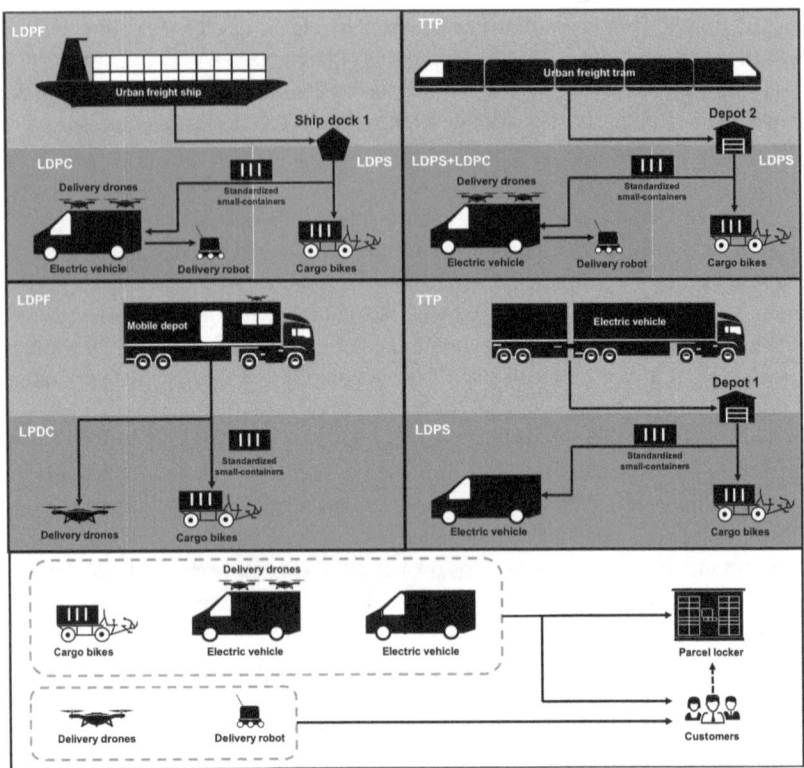

Figure 6.13 The operational model of 2.x MSUFN system (15 years later). (Source: Author's own elaboration)

6.3.3 Scenario III

Scenario III is defined as the logistics provider A expands 2.x MSUFN system to respond to the urban spatial development of City A (30 years later). On this time-dimension, City A increasingly transforms into a megacity. It is noteworthy that the expansion of 2.x MSUFN is based on the development of distribution innovations (Figure 6.7). Section 6.2.2 exhibits that nine distribution innovations are extensively implemented after 30 years: electric vehicles, parcel lockers, cargo-bikes, public transit logistics, urban freight ships, delivery drones, deliver robots, mobile depots, and robotic vehicles. Furthermore, the modular E-vehicles are applied to transport commodities within partial urban zones.

Figure 6.14 shows that, after 30 years, logistics provider A expands the 2.x MSUFN system based on the development hypothesis of distribution innovations. The scenario definition mentions that City A increasingly becomes a megacity alone with urban demographic growth. Urban sprawl and dense residential areas increase the number of high-rises architectures. This increase implies that logistics providers need to cost much delivery time on high-rises buildings. Moreover, freight demand growth requires high delivery frequency that causes traffic congestion. Therefore, after 30 years, the vehicle mode is not the primary component of transshipment transportation of the 2.x MSUFN system, such as using trucks and vans to transfer the goods. Based on the above discussion, the operational measures of the 2.x MSUFN system as follows:

Figure 6.14 2.x MSUFN system of logistics provider A (30 years later). (Source: Author's own elaboration)

- Besides to transfer goods to the ship dock 1, urban freight ships are also responsible for transport goods to the ship dock 2. After the transshipment transportation, the modular E-vehicles are in charge of distributing relevant commodities to the urban core area (CA 1). Considering the area sprawl of RA 2 after 30 years later, the existing capacity of ship dock 2 is only responsible for the freight demands of the RA 2 and CA 4.

- On this time-dimension (30 years later), the urban freight trams are used to transshipment transportation from CLC to the two depots. This scheme implies that no trucks/vans are driven within urban areas. It significantly reduced the traffic congestions and the issues of parking in the narrow street. Moreover, the delivery destinations of the two depots have changed due to the freight demands' growth of nearby residential and commercial areas. Based on the existed capacity of the two depots, Depot 1 is responsible for delivering goods to CA3 and RA 1, and Depot 2 is consolidating freight flows of RA 3 and RA 4. Additionally, the urban passenger tram can also be used in freight transportation, delivering goods to RA 6. This tram line needs to integrate the passenger and freight in tram station 3.

- Mobile depot 1 remains using to transfer standardized small-containers from CLC to the parking near CA 5 and RA 5. Considering the RA 4 expansion causes the freight demands growth, the capacity of depot 1 is unable to satisfy the entire freight demands of RA 4. To this end, mobile depot 1 assists Depot 1 to deliver partial goods to RA 4. With technology evolution, mobile depots increasingly perfect in aspects of capacity and flexibility. Based on the morphological analysis of T-integrations, mobile depots can be equipped with more than three delivery drones and adding a module of the delivery robots.

- The previous hypothesis mentions that technology evolutions can promote O-integration in the aspect of the LDPC module. The freight EVs can be replaced by robotic vehicles, which can be equipped with the delivery drones and robots. The delivery drones can be used to satisfy the freight demands of the high-rise architectures. Meanwhile, the extensive application of delivery robots is able to enhance the delivery frequency. Moreover, the parcel lockers can receive packages from the delivery drone and robots. This strategy can provide personalized logistics services to strengthen enterprise competitiveness.

- Although the modular E-vehicle is capable of reducing the congestion in the commercial areas, thus far, high costs are a barrier for extensive implementation within urban areas. Additionally, the modular E-vehicle can be equipped with a delivery drone to transport goods to the high-rise architectures located in the commercial areas.

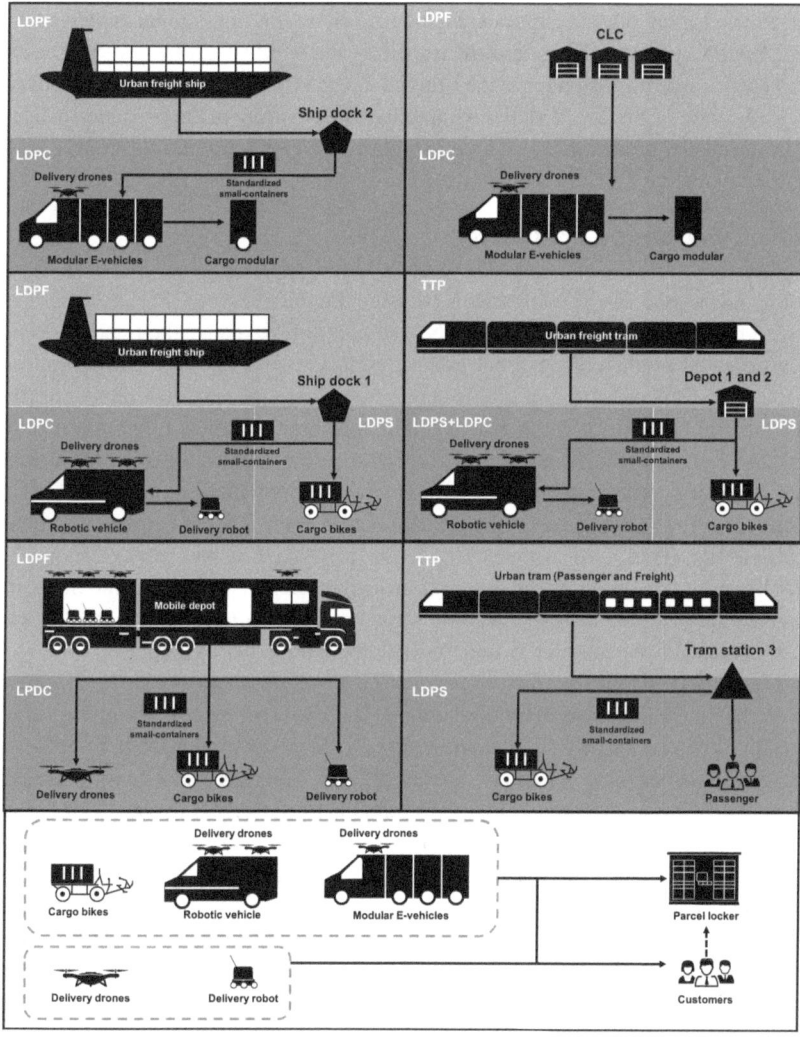

Figure 6.15 The operational model of 2.x MSUFN system (30 years later). (Source: Author's own elaboration)

Based on the previous descriptions, Figure 6.15 shows the operational models of the 2.x MSUFN system at this time-dimension. It is noteworthy that this system is based on a sustainable transition from the original 2.x MSUFN (Figure 6.13). Moreover, the expansion of the 2.x MSUFN comprehensively considers the possible changes of urban spatial development and the evolutions of distribution innovations.

6.4   Scenarios Evaluation

Following a systematic comparison between Figure 6.11 and Figure 6.12, this research identifies that the 2.x MSUFN system is able to reduce the freight vehicle flows created by the conventional urban freight vans/trucks. This finding implies that 2.x MSUFN can decrease traffic congestion within the existing urban transport network. In Scenario I, the logistics provider A employs short-term solutions to respond to urban spatial development (Figure 6.11), such as logistics infrastructure expansion and freight fleet increase. The previous discussion indicates that these solutions possibly causes the conventional two-tier system to transfer into the multiple-tier system. To further evaluate the 2.x MSUFN, this work deduces the possible transformation of the conventional urban freight system for the 30 years later. Figure 6.16 presents the network structure of the conventional urban freight system after 30 years, which is transformed into a three-tier system.

Figure 6.16 shows that this system can cover all urban areas, but it extremely exacerbates the land-use conflicts between the city and freight activities. Additionally, logistics facility expansion requires to increase freight fleets to enhance the delivery frequency. Although logistics providers can use EVs or cargo-bikes to decrease emissions, freight fleet growth remains to exacerbate traffic congestions. This observation exposes that short-term solutions are unable to continuously promote the sustainability of urban logistics from a long-term perspective. The findings of Chapter 3 illustrates that this situation caused by three aspects: (1) the long-term planning of SUFT is lacking; (2) the links between urban spatial development and urban freight planning have rarely considered; (3) the impacts of distribution innovations on the urban freight network structure have received scant attention. These gaps cause urban logistics providers to employ short-term solutions to balance the economy and environment. However, these solutions cannot promote sustainable urban logistics with a long-term perspective. Meanwhile, these measures restrict the flexibility of urban logistics transformation caused by the extensive application of distribution innovations.

Comparing Scenario II and Scenario III, this analysis locates that the 2.x MSUFN can systematically integrate different distribution innovations to promote them to

Figure 6.16 Three-tier system of logistics provider A (30 years later). (Source: Author's own elaboration)

operate as a system. Moreover, this system does not only enhances the urban delivery range and logistics performance, but it also reduces the operation costs growth and land-use conflicts caused by short-term solutions. It is noteworthy that the integration of passenger and freight is also launched in the 2.x MSUFN system (as depicted by figure 6.15). From a view of sustainable transition, this integration contributes the local authorities to reinforce urban governance, thereby achieving sustainable urbanization. For the sustainable transition, Chapter 3 mentions that it needs to be based on a systematic future prediction. From a view of the logistics providers, this prediction needs to consider urban spatial development, particularly for residential and commercial areas. Meanwhile, the tendencies of distribution innovations also need to integrate into this prediction. These discussions imply that the 2.x MSUFN system can be a feasible solution for long-term planning of sustainable urban logistics.

In the process of scenario analysis, this research located that some urban external factors can influence the construction of the 2.x MSUFN system. Indeed, there are numerous differences between the various cities. These differences influence the construction of the urban logistics network and the selections of urban freight strategies, such as geographic environment, economic scale (e.g., GDP, Per capita income), urban functional orientation, urban governance policy, architectural style (e.g., high-rise building, skyscraper). This observation implies that the 2.x MSUFN system and freight module selections also exist diverse in different cities. An example is Beijing, as the capital of China, is a megacity, and the urban population is more than 21.54 million. The high-speed economic growth of Beijing and it as the political core city that has motivated the migration of people to this city. Given that Beijing no owns the inland waterway, the urban freight ship cannot be used in this city. Additionally, the public transit system of Beijing is consists of the urban subway and bus. The integration of passenger and freight needs to be based on the public transit system. This requirement implies the urban underground logistics need to reconstruct the subway stations. However, this reconstruction is a considerable challenge for local authorities and logistics providers. Furthermore, thus far, Beijing has constructed the five beltways within urban areas. This situation implies that city logistics providers still use freight vehicles based on the road network in the short-term period. This example reveals that the existing urban transport network and infrastructure influence the module selection of the 2.x MSUFN system.

Besides these, urban geographic circumstances and architectural styles also challenge the construction of the 2.x MSUFN system. An example is Dubai as the capital of the Emirate of Dubai and is the largest and most populous city in the United Arab Emirates (UAE). In recent decades, the economic scale of Dubai has appeared the spurting growth. Although the fact that the current urban population of Dubai is almost 3.13 million, the spurting economic growth has motivated the demographic expansion in this city from a long-term view. It is foreseeable that Dubai gradually transformed into the category of a large city. It is noted that Dubai has constructed numerous skyscrapers within urban areas. This architectural style motivates that logistics provider can apply delivery drones to improve the urban freight efficiency. Nevertheless, the weather of Dubai restricts extensive applications of delivery drones and delivery robots. These examples reveal that the decision support system and module selection system is essential to construct 2.x MSUFN in different large and megacities. The reason is that the numerous external factors influence logistics providers to select the suitable solutions of O-integration, which retard the module formulation of the 2.x MSUFN system.

In conclusion, the scenario analysis determines three advantages of the 2.x MSUFN system: (1) The 2.x MSUFN system provides a feasible solution for long-term planning of sustainable urban freight transport due to comprehensively considering the urban spatial development and O-integration of distribution innovations; (2) The concept of SIUIT is able to reduce the land-use conflicts and negative environmental externalities; (3) The 2.x MSUFN system is developed based on systematic predictions of the possible future freight vehicles (T-integration), which enhance the flexibility of urban logistics transformation. However, this work remains some research limitations. Given that, the next chapter introduces these limitations and discusses future research directions.

Conclusion

7

Large cities and megacities are influential in the global economy (UN-Habitat 2016), and urban freight transport plays a critical role in urban economic growth (Dablanc 2011). Urban logistics is a complex process that involves several factors such as urban geographic environment, city road network, location of freight destination, delivery range, and capacity of transport modes. These elements need to strategically organize inside the urban areas to sustain this process. In recent decades, the local authorities have continually promoted the agendas of sustainable urban development. These agendas motivate logistics providers to launch sustainable urban freight planning, particularly for large cities and megacities. It is noteworthy that the urban freight transport strategy should be embedded in an overall sustainable development strategy with a long-term perspective (approximately 20–30 years) (Wolfram 2004). Nevertheless, considerable research has paid scant attention to the links between urban development and city logistics planning (Cui et al. 2015). Concurrently, much research has focused on applying distribution innovations to promote sustainable urban logistics from a short-term perspective (He 2020). Given that, urban logistics providers in large/megacities need to organize long-term strategy on SUFT that takes into account these exogenous and endogenous trends: urban spatial development and the integrations of distribution innovations. For achieving sustainable development in future large and megacities, adopt the foresight research methods is essential to formula the long-term strategy of SUFT. For logistics providers, the integrations of urban distribution innovations increasingly become the primary solutions to promote sustainable urban freight, which also needs a strategic organization to formulate appropriate freight measures. Given that the urban spatial development and integrations of distribution innovations have challenged the flexibility of conventional urban freight network, it is necessary to design an innovative urban freight network structure to achieve a sustainable transition of SUFT within a long-term

Z. He, *Future Sustainable Urban Freight Network Design in the Large Cities and Megacities*, Sustainable Management, Wertschöpfung und Effizienz, https://doi.org/10.1007/978-3-658-34203-6_7

perspective. To this end, this research applying a method mix of trend exploration and literature review to systematically discuss the urban spatial development in large and megacities and integrations of distribution innovations. Subsequently, the morphological analysis method is used to designing the 2.x MSUFN system to improve the flexibility of urban logistics transformation in large and megacities. The scenario analysis shows that the 2.x MSUFN can decrease the land-use conflicts and infrastructure expansion costs, enhance the delivery range and freight frequency without adopting short-term solutions.

Four primary scientific contributions are presented in this work addressing the main research question: *How to design a sustainable and flexible urban freight network to face future challenges in the large/megacities?* The first contribution is developing the *research framework of sustainable and flexible future urban freight system* (Figure 2.6 in Section 2.5.2) through the systematic literature review. This framework enlarges the body of knowledge related to the research field of urban freight network design and urban distribution innovations. Meanwhile, this framework integrates the exogenous trends of UFT into the research of sustainable urban freight planning. According to the relevance cross-analysis between the article topics of urban freight network design and urban distribution innovations, four research gaps have been determined to encourage the relevant scholars to contribute to the field of future urban freight planning. Moreover, this framework identifies the primary components of long-term planning of future SUFT in large cities and megacities. These components include the trends extrapolation of urban spatial development, tendency analysis of urban distribution innovations, and urban freight network structure design.

The second significant contribution corresponds to the *theoretical framework of future sustainable urban freight transport* (Figure 3.10 in Section 3.7). The systematic literature review of foresight research exposes that the long-term planning of sustainable urban logistics is lacking. Given that, this work systematically discusses and selected three appropriate foresight research methods to strengthen the *research framework of sustainable and flexible future urban freight system*. Additionally, the feasibility of the methods mix is further analyzed. This analysis ensures that the selected methods are suitable for foresight research of SUFT.

The third primary contribution is formulating the *concept of sustainable inner-urban intermodal transportation* (Figure 4.6 in Section 4.6.2). Followed the above research frameworks, this research employs the GE multi-factor analysis method to discuss the application status of eleven distribution innovations from the academic and enterprise dimensions. Subsequently, applied restrictions of these innovations are analyzed. Combining the previous analysis, this work develops the conceptual model of SIUIT that uses standardized small-containers to achieve the operational integration between the distinct distribution innovations. This model aims to integrate the different distribution innovations to operate as a system, thereby strategically improving urban distribution efficiency and sustainability.

The fourth crucial contribution corresponds to the model of *2.x-tier modular & sustainable urban freight network* (Figure 5.13 in Section 5.7.2). Followed the proposed research framework, this research uses the selected methods to develop this network model and integrate the SIUIT concept into it. Firstly, the trends extrapolation method is used to analyze the impacts of large and megacities spatial development on the conventional urban freight network. After that, the applied impacts of distribution innovations on urban freight network structure are discussed. Combined with the previous discussions, this work employs the morphological analysis method to identify feasible operational integration solutions. Moreover, the technological integrations of distribution innovations are also discussed by morphological analysis. For technology manufactures, this analysis provides a systematic thinking model to develop future urban freight vehicles. In the end, this work classifies the feasible solutions of O-integration and T-integration to identify the composed modules of the future urban freight network. Connecting with the trend analysis of urban spatial development on large and megacities, the conceptual model of the 2.x-tier modular & sustainable urban freight network is developed to resolve the principal research question.

Limitations and Future Research Works

The scenario analysis indicates that this work remains some limitations. Although the proposed model integrates the applications of urban distribution innovations and spatial development trends of large and megacities, constructing this system in the real cities remains some limitations. To this end, the relevant research limitations are summarized as follows: The first limitation is the urban freight policy-making and laws for the 2.x MSUFN system. Given this system is involved in the delivery drones, robots, robotic vehicles, and integration of passenger and freight within urban areas, the extensive applications of these innovations need policy support from the local authorities. Concurrently, the relevant laws formulations also need to further consider other possible problems, such as human-made damage of drones, usage regulations of delivery robots. The second limitation is regarding the particular platform of information and communications technology (ICT) for the 2.x MSUFN system. ICT has played a critical role in city logistics. The urban logistics transformations and operation measures of distribution innovations need technological support from ICT. This observation implies that the extensive application of the 2.x MSUFN system needs to be based on the digitalization progress of urban logistics. For example, the control platform is essential to use delivery robots and drones in urban logistics. The third limitation is that the impacts of the partial technology innovations on urban freight network are not further discussed (e.g., 3D-printers). Indeed, partial technology innovations are able to change the consumers' behavior, restructuring stakeholders, and even challenge the cost-benefit of logistics providers. The fourth limitation is mentioned in the scenario analysis: the decision-support system and selecting module system are not discussed for the 2.x MSUFN. The scenario analysis indicates that external factors indeed influence the construction of the 2.x MSUFN system in large and megacities, such as urban geographic circumstances and architectural styles. Developing the decision-support system and module selection system contributes to the urban logistics providers construct the appropriate 2.x MSUFN system for different cities.

Based on the identified research limitations, this work determines six future research directions. The first direction is integrating the sustainable urban logistics planning into urban planning. Commonly, urban planning depends on local authorities that focus on urban passenger transport, and freight transport is rarely considered. This observation highlights that urban freight planning passively follows urban development. The scenario analysis demonstrates that the 2.x MSUFN system can promote the integration of passenger and freight within urban areas. This finding implies that integrating city logistics into urban planning is possible. Meanwhile, this integrated urban planning is a potential solution for further transitioning to a sustainable city. Additionally, the relevant literature exposes that urban agglomeration has increasingly become the next phase for megacity development. Therefore, the second research direction is integrating the freight network of different cities based on urban agglomeration. This direction aims to promote sustainable urban clusters and enhance the regional economy. The third research direction is developing the ICT platform for the 2.x MSUFN system. In recent decades, some innovative computing concepts have motivated urban logistics digitalization. For example, the blockchain can be used in horizontal collaboration to reduce the trust risk between stakeholders, and edge computing can enhance the response speed of decisions on using delivery drones and robots. Given this, the ICT platform of the 2.x MSUFN system needs to systematically consider innovative computing notions. The fourth research direction is regarding urban freight policy-making of the 2.x MSDN system. This direction is intent on further promoting the 2.x MSUFN system in large and megacities and providing freight-policy suggestions for the local authorities. Furthermore, the research limitations mention that partial technology innovations influence the urban freight network. For example, the application of the 3D-printer possibly changes the current business model related to the supply chain. Therefore, the fourth research direction is integrating 3D-printers into the

2.x MSUFN system. In the end, the sixth research direction is the standardization of future sustainable urban freight transport. As the best of my knowledge, thus far, the standardized framework of future sustainable urban logistics remains lacking. This research direction contributes to logistics providers constructing the operational strategy on the regional logistics network under urban agglomeration.

References

Agatz, N., Bouman, P., and Schmidt, M. (2018). Optimization approaches for the traveling salesman problem with drone. *Transportation Science*, 52(4):965–981.

Aggoune-Mtalaa, W., Habbas, Z., Ouahmed, A. A., and Khadraoui, D. (2015). Solving new urban freight distribution problems involving modular electric vehicles. *IET Intelligent Transport Systems*, 9(6):654–661.

Ahani, P., Arantes, A., and Melo, S. (2016). A portfolio approach for optimal fleet replacement toward sustainable urban freight transportation. *Transportation Research Part D: Transport and Environment*, 48:357–368.

Al-Thani, S. K., Skelhorn, C. P., Amato, A., Koc, M., and Al-Ghamdi, S. G. (2018). Smart technology impact on neighborhood form for a sustainable doha. *Sustainability*, 10(12):4764.

Albrechts, L. (2001). In pursuit of new approaches to strategic spatial planning. A european perspective. *International planning studies*, 6(3):293–310.

Albrechts, L., Healey, P., and Kunzmann, K. R. (2003). Strategic spatial planning and regional governance in europe. *Journal of the American Planning Association*, 69(2):113–129.

Ali, N. and Rahim, A. (2018). Scenario-based impediments for intelligent freight transportation in Pakistan. In *2018 15th International Conference on Smart Cities: Improving Quality of Life Using ICT & IoT (HONET-ICT)*, pages 97–101. IEEE.

Ali, S. H. and Keil, R. (2006). Global cities and the spread of infectious disease: the case of severe acute respiratory syndrome (sars) in toronto, canada. *Urban Studies*, 43(3):491–509.

ALICE/ERTRAC Urban mobility WG (2015). *Urban Freight research roadmap*. European Road Transport Research Advisory Council, Brussels.

Allen, J., Piecyk, M., Piotrowska, M., McLeod, F., Cherrett, T., Ghali, K., Nguyen, T., Bektas, T., Bates, O., Friday, A., et al. (2018). Understanding the impact of e-commerce on last-mile light goods vehicle activity in urban areas: The case of london. *Transportation Research Part D: Transport and Environment*, 61:325–338.

Amanatidou, E. (2008). "joint foresight": towards a mechanism for joint programming in europe? *Foresight*, 10(6):103–117.

Amazon Prime Air (n.d.). Amazon Prime Air. https://www.amazon.com/Amazon-Prime-Air/b?ie=UTF8&node=8037720011. Accessed on 3 of April, 2018.

Amsteus, M. (2011). Managerial foresight: measurement scale and estimation. *Foresight*, 13(1):58–76.

181
Z. He, *Future Sustainable Urban Freight Network Design in the Large Cities and Megacities*, Sustainable Management, Wertschöpfung und Effizienz,
https://doi.org/10.1007/978-3-658-34203-6

Andaloro, L., Napoli, G., Sergi, F., Micari, S., Agnello, G., and Antonucci, V. (2015). Development of a new concept electric vehicle for last mile transportations. *World Electric Vehicle Journal*, 7(3):342–348.

Anderluh, A., Hemmelmayr, V. C., and Nolz, P. C. (2017). Synchronizing vans and cargo bikes in a city distribution network. *Central European Journal of Operations Research*, 25(2):345–376.

Anderson, S., Allen, J., and Browne, M. (2005). Urban logistics-how can it meet policy makers' sustainability objectives? *Journal of transport geography*, 13(1):71–81.

Aniskin, Y., Moiseeva, N., Rygalin, D., and Sedova, O. (2017a). Formation of modules of the mechanism of managing innovative activity on the basis of the system integrator. *International Journal of Economic Research*, 14(4):469–479.

Aniskin, Y., Moiseeva, N., Rygalin, D., and Sedova, O. (2017b). Technique of formation of the organizational system integrator for interaction of participants of the program for the development of the radio electronic industry. *International Journal of Civil Engineering and Technology*, 8(12):906–915.

Apel, S., Prinz, T. M., and Schau, V. (2015). Challenging service extensions for electric vehicles in massively heterogenic system landscapes. In *CEUR Workshop Proceedings*, volume 1360, pages 44–50.

Arnold, F., Cardenas, I., Sörensen, K., and Dewulf, W. (2018). Simulation of B2C e-commerce distribution in Antwerp using cargo bikes and delivery points. *European transport research review*, 10(1):2.

Arvidsson, N. (2010). New perspectives on sustainable urban freight distribution: A potential zero emission concept using electric vehicles on trams. In *Proceedings of the 12th World Conference on Transport Research*, pages 11–15.

Arvidsson, N. and Pazirandeh, A. (2017). An ex ante evaluation of mobile depots in cities: A sustainability perspective. *International Journal of Sustainable Transportation*, 11(8):623–632.

Asih, A., Sopha, B., Khairunnisa, Y., Gunawan, H., and Karuniawati, Y. (2018). Heterogeneous vehicle routing delivery on collaborative distribution using genetic algorithm-The case of Yogyakarta city. In *2017 IEEE International Conference on Industrial Engineering and Engineering Management (IEEM)*, pages 1432–1436. IEEE Computer Society, Washington, D.C.

Asih, A. M. S., Jatiningrum, W. S., and Sopha, B. M. (2016). Collaborative distribution-application to the city of Yogyakarta, Indonesia. In *2016 IEEE International Conference on Industrial Engineering and Engineering Management (IEEM)*, pages 1141–1145. IEEE Computer Society, Washington, D.C.

Auto-Date (n.d.). Technical specifications and fuel economy of automobiles. https://www.auto-data.net/en/. Accessed on 5 November 2018.

Bamwesigye, D. and Hlavackova, P. (2019). Analysis of sustainable transport for smart cities. *Sustainability*, 11(7):2140.

Barker, K. E., Cox, D., and Sveinsdottir, T. (2011). Foresight on the future of public research metrology in europe. *Foresight*, 13(1):5–18.

Bates, O., Knowles, B., and Friday, A. (2017). Are people the key to enabling collaborative smart logistics? In *Proceedings of the 2017 CHI Conference Extended Abstracts on Human Factors in Computing Systems*, pages 1494–1499. ACM.

Battaia, G., Faure, L., Marques, G., Guillaume, R., and Montoya-Torres, J. R. (2014). A methodology to anticipate the activity level of collaborative networks: The case of urban consolidation centers. In *Supply Chain Forum: International Journal*, volume 15, page 6. Bordeaux Management School.

Behiri, W., Belmokhtar-Berraf, S., and Chu, C. (2018). Urban freight transport using passenger rail network: Scientific issues and quantitative analysis. *Transportation Research Part E: Logistics and Transportation Review*, 115:227–245.

Behiri, W., Ozturk, O., and Belmokhtar-Berraf, S. (2016). Urban freight by rail: A milp modeling for optimizing the transport of goods. In *The 6th International Conference on Information Systems, Logistics and Supply Chain*, pages 2–9.

Behrends, S. (2012). The significance of the urban context for the sustainability performance of intermodal road-rail transport. *Procedia-Social and Behavioral Sciences*, 54:375–386.

Behrends, S., Lindholm, M., and Woxenius, J. (2008). The impact of urban freight transport: A definition of sustainability from an actor's perspective. *Transportation planning and technology*, 31(6):693–713.

Behrendt, F. (2019). Cycling the smart and sustainable city: analyzing ec policy documents on internet of things, mobility and transport, and smart cities. *Sustainability*, 11(3):763.

Behörde für Wirtschaft und Innovation (2015). Modellprojekt: Nachhaltiges Lieferkonzept für die Innenstadt wird ausgeweitet. https://www.hamburg.de/pressearchiv-fhh/4442626/2015-01-28-bwvi-lieferkonzept/. Accessed February 11, 2019.

Beirigo, B. A., Schulte, F., and Negenborn, R. R. (2018). Integrating people and freight transportation using shared autonomous vehicles with compartments. *IFAC-PapersOnLine*, 51(9):392–397.

Benjelloun, A. and Crainic, T. G. (2009). Trends, challenges, and perspectives in city logistics. *Buletin AGIR,*, 4:269–284.

Birko, S., Dove, E. S., and Özdemir, V. (2015). Evaluation of nine consensus indices in delphi foresight research and their dependency on delphi survey characteristics: A simulation study and debate on delphi design and interpretation. *PloS one*, 10(8):1–14.

Björklund, M. and Johansson, H. (2018). Urban consolidation centre–a literature review, categorisation, and a future research agenda. *International Journal of Physical Distribution & Logistics Management*, 48(8):745–764.

Boccia, M., Crainic, T. G., Sforza, A., and Sterle, C. (2018). Multi-commodity location-routing: Flow intercepting formulation and branch-and-cut algorithm. *Computers & Operations Research*, 89:94–112.

Boysen, N., Briskorn, D., Fedtke, S., and Schwerdfeger, S. (2018). Drone delivery from trucks: Drone scheduling for given truck routes. *Networks*, 72(4):506–527.

Browne, M., Allen, J., and Alexander, P. (2016). Business improvement districts in urban freight sustainability initiatives: A case study approach. *Transportation Research Procedia*, 12:450–460.

Browne, M., Allen, J., Woodburn, A., and Piotrowska, M. (2014). The potential for non-road modes to support environmentally friendly urban logistics. *Procedia-Social and Behavioral Sciences*, 151:29–36.

Brundtland, G. H., Khalid, M., Agnelli, S., Al-Athel, S., and Chidzero, B. (1987). Our common future. *New York*, 8.

Bureau of Transportation and Statistics, Research and Innovation Technology (2009). *Commodity Flow Survey*. United States, Department of Transportation, Washington.

Cagliano, A. C., Carlin, A., Mangano, G., and Rafele, C. (2017). Analyzing the diffusion of eco-friendly vans for urban freight distribution. *The International Journal of Logistics Management*, 28(4):1218–1242.

Cardenas, I. D., Dewulf, W., Vanelslander, T., Smet, C., and Beckers, J. (2017). The e-commerce parcel delivery market and the implications of home B2C deliveries vs pick-up points. *International Journal of Transport Economics*, 44(2):235–256.

Carsten Stahl, B. (2011). It for a better future: how to integrate ethics, politics and innovation. *Journal of Information, Communication and Ethics in Society*, 9(3):140–156.

Castillo, V. E., Bell, J. E., Rose, W. J., and Rodrigues, A. M. (2018). Crowdsourcing last mile delivery: strategic implications and future research directions. *Journal of Business Logistics*, 39(1):7–25.

Cepolina, E. M. (2016). The packages clustering optimisation in the logistics of the last mile freight distribution. *International Journal of Simulation and Process Modelling*, 11(6):468–476.

Cepolina, E. M. and Farina, A. (2013). An optimization methodology for the consolidation of urban freight boxes. In *15th International Conference on Harbour, Maritime and Multimodal Logistics Modelling and Simulation*, pages 46–52. Bruzzone, Gronalt, Merkuryev, Piera Eds.

Chan, L. and Daim, T. (2012). Exploring the impact of technology foresight studies on innovation: Case of bric countries. *Futures*, 44(6):618–630.

Chen, C. and Pan, S. (2016). Using the crowd of taxis to last mile delivery in e-commerce: a methodological research. In *Studies in Computational Intelligence*, volume 640, pages 61–70. Springer.

Cho, Y. and Kim, M. (2014). Entropy and gravity concepts as new methodological indexes to investigate technological convergence: patent network-based approach. *PloS one*, 9(6):1–17.

Choubassi, C., Seedah, D. P., Jiang, N., and Walton, C. M. (2016). Economic analysis of cargo cycles for urban mail delivery. *Transportation Research Record*, 2547(1):102–110.

Comi, A., Buttarazzi, B., Schiraldi, M., Innarella, R., Varisco, M., and Traini, P. (2018). An advanced planner for urban freight delivering. *Archives of Transport*, 4:27–40.

Conway, A., Fatisson, P.-E., Eickemeyer, P., Cheng, J., and Peters, D. (2012). Urban micro-consolidation and last mile goods delivery by freight-tricycle in manhattan: Opportunities and challenges. In *Proceedings of the 91st Transportation Research Board Annual Meeting, Washington, DC, USA*, pages 22–26.

Conway, M. (2015). Foresight: an introduction. *Thinking Futures, Melbourne*.

Conway, M. and Voros, J. (2003). Foresight: Learning from the future. *Journal of Institutional Research*, 12(1):1–15.

Cornish, E. (2004). *Futuring: The exploration of the future*. World Future Society.

Cossu, P. (2016). Clean Last mile transport and logistics management for smart and Efficient local Governments in Europe. *Transportation Research Procedia*, 14:1523–1532.

Crainic, T. G., Errico, F., Rei, W., and Ricciardi, N. (2015). Modeling demand uncertainty in two-tier city logistics tactical planning. *Transportation Science*, 50(2):559–578.

Crainic, T. G., Ricciardi, N., and Storchi, G. (2004). Advanced freight transportation systems for congested urban areas. *Transportation Research Part C: Emerging Technologies*, 12(2):119–137.

Crainic, T. G. and Sgalambro, A. (2014). Service network design models for two-tier city logistics. *Optimization Letters*, 8(4):1375–1387.

Cui, J., Dodson, J., and Hall, P. V. (2015). Planning for urban freight transport: An overview. *Transport Reviews*, 35(5):583–598.

Cuncev, I. (2004). The management of intermodality in urban transportation. In *Proceedings of the CODATU XI: World Congress: Towards More Attractive Urban Transportation, Bucarest, Romanian*, pages 22–24.

Dablanc, L. (2007). Goods transport in large European cities: Difficult to organize, difficult to modernize. *Transportation Research Part A: Policy and Practice*, 41(3):280–285.

Dablanc, L. (2011). City distribution, a key element of the urban economy: guidelines for practitioners. *City distribution and urban freight transport: Multiple perspectives*, pages 13–36.

Dablanc, L. (2013). City logistics. In *The SAGE Handbook of Transport Studies*, page 119. SAGE.

Dablanc, L., Morganti, E., Arvidsson, N., Woxenius, J., Browne, M., and Saidi, N. (2017). The rise of on-demand 'Instant Deliveries' in European cities. In *Supply Chain Forum: An International Journal*, volume 18, pages 203–217. Taylor & Francis.

Dampier, A. and Marinov, M. (2015). A study of the feasibility and potential implementation of metro-based freight transportation in Newcastle upon Tyne. *Urban Rail Transit*, 1(3):164–182.

Damrongchai, N. and Michelson, E. S. (2009). The future of science and technology and pro-poor applications. *Foresight*, 11(4):51–65.

Daniela, P., Paolo, F., Gianfranco, F., Graham, P., and Miriam, R. (2014). Reduced urban traffic and emissions within urban consolidation centre schemes: The case of Bristol. *Transportation Research Procedia*, 3:508–517.

Danko, T., Kalinina, I., Maslennikov, V., Kiselev, V., Sekerin, V., and Gorokhova, A. (2018). Foresight in management as a tool for the design transformation of marketing management of the potentials of small and medium-sized businesses. *International Journal of Civil Engineering and Technology*, 9(13):1105–1113.

De Decker, K. (2012). Cargo cyclists replace truck drivers on european city streets. *Low-Tech Magazine. Np, nd Web*, 24.

De Langhe, K. (2017). The importance of external costs for assessing the potential of trams and trains for urban freight distribution. *Research in Transportation Business & Management*, 24:114–122.

De Marco, A., Mangano, G., Zenezini, G., Cagliano, A. C., Perboli, G., Rosano, M., and Musso, S. (2017). Business modeling of a city logistics ICT platform. In *2017 IEEE 41st Annual Computer Software and Applications Conference (COMPSAC)*, volume 2, pages 783–789. IEEE Computer Society, Washington, D.C.

De Oliveira, L. K., De Oliveira, R. L. M., and De Avelar Rueda, L. S. T. (2017). Transshipment station for urban solid waste: An analysis considering city logistics concepts. *WIT Transactions on Ecology and the Environment*, 223:559–569.

Denyer, D. and Tranfield, D. (2009). Producing a systematic review. *The Sage handbook of organizational research methods*, pages 671–689.

Deutsch, Y. and Golany, B. (2018). A parcel locker network as a solution to the logistics last mile problem. *International Journal of Production Research*, 56(1-2):251–261.

Deutsche Post DHL Group (2017). DHL Cubicycles City Hub Frankfurt 02. https://www.dpdhl.com/en/media-relations/media-center/tv-footage/dhl-cubicycles-city-hub-frankfurt-02.html. Accessed on February 11, 2019.

Deutsche Post DHL Group (2018a). DHL Parcelcopter. https://www.dpdhl.com/en/media-relations/specials/dhl-parcelcopter.html. Accessed on 3 of April, 2018.

Deutsche Post DHL Group (2018b). Rapid Response from the Air: Medicines Successfully Delivered Using a Parcel Drone in East Africa. https://www.dpdhl.com/en/media-relations/press-releases/2018/rapid-response-from-the-air-medicines-successfully-delivered-using-a-parcel-drone-in-east-africa.html. Accessed on 3 December 2018.

DHL (n.d.). City Logistics DHL Express. https://www.dhlexpress.nl/sites/default/files/City%20Logistics%20DHL%20Express.pdf. Accessed on 3 December 2018.

Dinale, A., Molfino, R., Huang, P., and Zoppi, M. (2013). A new robotized vehicle for urban freight transport. In *Proceedings of the 15th International Conference on Harbour, Maritime & Multimodal Logistics Modelling and Simulation, HMS 2013*, pages 32–37.

Dinwoodie, J. (2006). Rail freight and sustainable urban distribution: Potential and practice. *Journal of Transport Geography*, 14(4):309–320.

Dobbs, R., Smit, S., Remes, J., Manyika, J., Roxburgh, C., and Restrepo, A. (2011). Urban world: Mapping the economic power of cities. *McKinsey Global Institute*, 62.

Dobrzańska-Danikiewicz, A. (2010). E-foresight of materials surface engineering. *Archives of Materials Science*, 44(1):43–50.

Dobrzańska-Danikiewicz, A., Dobrzański, L., Mazurkiewicz, J., Tomiczek, B., et al. (2011). E-transfer of materials surface engineering e-foresight results. *Archives of Materials Science and Engineering*, 52(2):87–100.

Dobrzańska-Danikiewicz, A. and Lukaszkowicz, K. (2010). Technology validation of coatings deposition onto the brass substrate. *Archives of Materials Science Engineering*, 46(1):5–38.

Dobrzańska-Danikiewicz, A., Tański, T., Malara, S., and Domagała-Dubiel, J. (2010). Assessment of strategic development perspectives of laser treatment of casting magnesium alloys. *Archives of Materials Science Engineering*, 45(1):5–39.

Doherty, S. and Hoyle, S. (2009). Supply chain decarbonization: The role of logistics and transport in reducing supply chain carbon emissions. In *World Economic Forum, Geneva*.

Dong, J., Hu, W., Yan, S., Ren, R., and Zhao, X. (2018). Network planning method for capacitated metro-based underground logistics system. *Advances in Civil Engineering*, 2018:1–14.

Ducret, R. (2014). Parcel deliveries and urban logistics: Changes and challenges in the courier express and parcel sector in Europe-The French case. *Research in Transportation Business & Management*, 11:15–22.

Dudin, M. N., Protsenko, I. O., Frolova, E. E., Posokhov, S. P., and Voikova, N. A. (2017). Managing the development of high-tech enterprises based on foresighting. *Academy of Strategic Management Journal*, 16(Special issue 2).

Duinker, P. N. and Greig, L. A. (2007). Scenario analysis in environmental impact assessment: Improving explorations of the future. *Environmental impact assessment review*, 27(3):206–219.

Ehmke, J. (2012). *Integration of information and optimization models for routing in city logistics*. Springer Science & Business Media, Berlin/Heidelberg, Germany.

Eidhammer, O., Andersen, J., and Johansen, B. G. (2016). Private public collaboration on logistics in Norwegian cities. *Transportation Research Procedia*, 16:81–88.

Ejdys, J. and Szpilko, D. (2013). Problems of the strategic tourism management in the regions of poland. *Actual Problems of Economics*, 146(8):284–294.

Erik Karlsen, J., Øverland, E. F., and Karlsen, H. (2010). Sociological contributions to futures' theory building. *Foresight*, 12(3):59–72.

Estrada, M. and Roca-Riu, M. (2017). Stakeholder's profitability of carrier-led consolidation strategies in urban goods distribution. *Transportation Research Part E: Logistics and Transportation Review*, 104:165–188.

European Commission (2011). Roadmap to a single european transport area-towards a competitive and resource efficient transport system. *White Paper COM(2011)144*. Luxembourg: Office for Official Publications of the European Commission.

Ewedairo, K., Chhetri, P., and Jie, F. (2018). Estimating transportation network impedance to last-mile delivery: A case study of Maribyrnong city in Melbourne. *The International Journal of Logistics Management*, 29(1):110–130.

Faccio, M. and Gamberi, M. (2015). New city logistics paradigm: From the "last mile" to the "last 50 miles" sustainable distribution. *Sustainability*, 7(11):14873–14894.

Farrelly, L. (2014). Redefining, reinventing and realigning design for demographic change. *Architectural Design*, 2(84):8–13.

Fatnassi, E., Chaouachi, J., and Klibi, W. (2015). Planning and operating a shared goods and passengers on-demand rapid transit system for sustainable city-logistics. *Transportation Research Part B: Methodological*, 81:440–460.

Ferraris, A., Santoro, G., and Papa, A. (2018). The cities of the future: Hybrid alliances for open innovation projects. *Futures*, 103:51–60.

Fiorini, M. and Lin, J.-C. (2015). *Clean mobility and intelligent transport systems*. The Institution of Engineering and Technology (IET), London, UK.

Franceschetti, A., Honhon, D., Laporte, G., Van Woensel, T., and Fransoo, J. C. (2017). Strategic fleet planning for city logistics. *Transportation Research Part B: Methodological*, 95:19–40.

Francis, H. (2016). Australia post tests drones for parcel delivery. http://www.smh.com.au/technology/innovation/australia-post-tests-drones-for-parcel-delivery-20160415-go77a4.html. Accessed February 11, 2019.

Freudendal-Pedersen, M., Kesselring, S., and Servou, E. (2019). What is smart for the future city? mobilities and automation. *Sustainability*, 11(1):221.

Gao, C., Yang, J., Xu, J., Chu, P., and Zhang, L. (2018). The design and analysis of the matching system for the urban freight taxis. In *CICTP 2017: Transportation Reform and Change-Equity, Inclusiveness, Sharing, and Innovation*, pages 1447–1452. American Society of Civil Engineers, Reston, VA.

Gayialis, S. P., Konstantakopoulos, G. D., Papadopoulos, G. A., Kechagias, E., and Ponis, S. T. (2018). Developing an advanced cloud-based vehicle routing and scheduling system for urban freight transportation. In *IFIP International Conference on Advances in Production Management Systems*, pages 190–197. Springer.

Geels, F. W. (2005). The dynamics of transitions in socio-technical systems: a multi-level analysis of the transition pathway from horse-drawn carriages to automobiles (1860–1930). *Technology Analysis & Strategic Management*, 17(4):445–476.

Geels, F. W. (2011). The multi-level perspective on sustainability transitions: Responses to seven criticisms. *Environmental innovation and societal transitions*, 1(1):24–40.

Geels, F. W. and Schot, J. (2007). Typology of sociotechnical transition pathways. *Research policy*, 36(3):399–417.

Gianessi, P., Alfandari, L., Létocart, L., and Wolfler Calvo, R. (2015). The multicommodity-ring location routing problem. *Transportation Science*, 50(2):541–558.

Giordano, A., Fischbeck, P., and Matthews, H. S. (2018). Environmental and economic comparison of diesel and battery electric delivery vans to inform city logistics fleet replacement strategies. *Transportation Research Part D: Transport and Environment*, 64:216–229.

Glenn, J. C. (1994). Introduction to the futures research methodology series. *Washington, DC: United Nations University. (Part of Glenn 1994a)*.

Global Reporting Initiative (2013). G4 sustainability reporting guidelines: Reporting principles and standard disclosures. *Global Reporting Initiative, Amsterdam*, pages 7–14.

Gonzalez-Feliu, J. (2016a). A joint freight catchment and cost benefit analysis to assess rail urban logistics scenarios. In *International Conference on Information Systems, Logistics and Supply Chain*, pages 14–27. Springer.

Gonzalez-Feliu, J. (2016b). Viability and potential demand capitation of urban freight tramway systemss via demand-supply modelling and cost benefit analysis. In *Proceedings of the 6th International Conference on Information Systems, Logistics and Supply Chain (ILS 2016), Bordeaux, France*, pages 1–4.

Gragnani, S., Valenti, G., and Valentini, M. P. (2004). City logistics in Italy: a national project. In *Logistics Systems for Sustainable Cities: Proceedings of the 3rd International Conference on City Logistics (Madeira, Portugal, 25–27 June, 2003)*, pages 279–293.

Gruber, J. and Kihm, A. (2016). Reject or embrace? messengers and electric cargo bikes. *Transportation research procedia*, 12:900–910.

Gruber, J., Kihm, A., and Lenz, B. (2014). A new vehicle for urban freight? an ex-ante evaluation of electric cargo bikes in courier services. *Research in Transportation Business & Management*, 11:53–62.

Gruber, J., Rudolph, C., and Kolarova, V. (2015). Factors determining the introduction of cargo bikes in urban commercial transport. *Zeitschrift für Wirtschaftsgeographie*, 59(2):115–129.

Gudanowska, A. E. (2014). Technology mapping as a tool for technology analysis in foresight studies. In *2014 IEEE International Technology Management Conference*, pages 1–4. IEEE.

Gudanowska, A. E. et al. (2016). Technology mapping–proposal of a method of technology analysis in foresight studies. *Verslas: teorija ir praktika*, 17(3):243–250.

Guerlain, C., Cortina, S., and Renault, S. (2016). Towards a collaborative geographical information system to support collective decision making for urban logistics initiative. *Transportation Research Procedia*, 12:634–643.

Haas, I. and Friedrich, B. (2017). Developing a micro-simulation tool for autonomous connected vehicle platoons used in city logistics. *Transportation Research Procedia*, 27:1203–1210.

Hammad, A. W., Akbarnezhad, A., Haddad, A., and Vazquez, E. G. (2019). Sustainable zoning, land-use allocation and facility location optimisation in smart cities. *Energies*, 12(7):1318.

Hammad, A. W., Akbarnezhad, A., and Rey, D. (2017). Sustainable urban facility location: Minimising noise pollution and network congestion. *Transportation research part E: logistics and transportation review*, 107:38–59.

Hayward, P. (2003). Resolving the moral impediments to foresight action. *Foresight*, 5(1):4–10.

He, Y. and Yang, Z. (2018). Parcel delivery by collaborative use of truck fleets and bus-transit vehicles. *Transportation Journal*, 57(4):399–428.

He, Z. (2020). The challenges in sustainability of urban freight network design and distribution innovations: a systematic literature review. *International Journal of Physical Distribution & Logistics Management*, 50(6):601–640.

He, Z. and Haasis, H.-D. (2019). Integration of urban freight innovations: Sustainable inner-urban intermodal transportation in the retail/postal industry. *Sustainability*, 11(6):1749.

He, Z. and Haasis, H.-D. (2020). A theoretical research framework of future sustainable urban freight transport for smart cities. *Sustainability*, 12(5):1975.

Hickman, R., Saxena, S., Banister, D., and Ashiru, O. (2012). Examining transport futures with scenario analysis and mca. *Transportation Research Part A: Policy and Practice*, 46(3):560–575.

Iannò, D., Polimeni, A., and Vitetta, A. (2013). An integrated approach for road, transit design in a city logistic plan: a case study. *WIT Transactions on the Built Environment*, 130:811–822.

Iden, J., Methlie, L. B., and Christensen, G. E. (2017). The nature of strategic foresight research: A systematic literature review. *Technological Forecasting and Social Change*, 116:87–97.

Iwan, S., Kijewska, K., and Lemke, J. (2016). Analysis of parcel lockers' efficiency as the last mile delivery solution–the results of the research in Poland. *Transportation Research Procedia*, 12:644–655.

Janjevic, M., Lebeau, P., Ndiaye, A. B., Macharis, C., Van Mierlo, J., and Nsamzinshuti, A. (2016). Strategic scenarios for sustainable urban distribution in the brussels-capital region using urban consolidation centres. *Transportation Research Procedia*, 12:598–612.

Janjevic, M. and Ndiaye, A. B. (2014). Inland waterways transport for city logistics: a review of experiences and the role of local public authorities. In *WIT Transactions on the Built Environment*, volume 138, pages 279–290. WIT Press, Southampton, UK.

Japan for Sustainability (2011). Yamato starts using streetcars for low-carbon parcel transport. https://www.japanfs.org/en/news/archives/news_id031255.html. Accessed on 23 November, 2019.

Jari, K.-o. and Theresa, L. (2017). Knowledge management and triangulation logic in the foresight research and analyses in business process management. In *International Conference on Knowledge Management in Organizations*, pages 228–238. Springer.

Jarke, M., Bui, X. T., and Carroll, J. M. (1998). Scenario management: An interdisciplinary approach. *Requirements Engineering*, 3(3-4):155–173.

Kaivo-Oja, J. (2014). Three theoretical approaches to pirate entrepreneurship: Towards future studies of pirate entrepreneurship. *International Journal of Entrepreneurship and Small Business*, 22(4):449–465.

Kaivo-oja, J. (2017). Towards better participatory processes in technology foresight: How to link participatory foresight research to the methodological machinery of qualitative research and phenomenology? *Futures*, 86:94–106.

KEBA (n.d.). Reliable self-service parcel lockers. https://www.keba.com/en/logistics-solutions/products/lockers/lockers. Accessed on 4 December 2018.

Kelly, J. and Marinov, M. (2017). Innovative interior designs for urban freight distribution using light rail systems. *Urban Rail Transit*, 3(4):238–254.

Kersten, W., Seiter, M., von See, B., Hackius, N., and Maurer, T. (2017). Trends and strategies in logistics and supply chain management–digital transformation opportunities. BVL International, Bremen, Germany.

Khan, K. S., Kunz, R., Kleijnen, J., and Antes, G. (2003). Five steps to conducting a systematic review. *Journal of the royal society of medicine*, 96(3):118–121.

Kikuta, J., Ito, T., Tomiyama, I., Yamamoto, S., and Yamada, T. (2012). New subway-integrated city logistics system. *Procedia-Social and Behavioral Sciences*, 39:476–489.

Kleinman, Z. (2017). Ocado Trials Driverless Delivery Van in London. http://www.bbc.com/news/technology-40421100. Accessed on 3 December 2018.

Koháni, M., Czimmermann, P., Váňa, M., Cebecauer, M., and Buzna, L. (2017). Location-scheduling optimization problem to design private charging infrastructure for electric vehicles. In *International Conference on Operations Research and Enterprise Systems*, pages 151–169. Springer.

Kok, M. (2013). Mobile Depot TNT Express. https://docs.google.com/file/d/0B7oEyNF3009ld2FoS2xfUjdaeEk/edit. Accessed February 11, 2019.

Koning, M. and Conway, A. (2016). The good impacts of biking for goods: Lessons from Paris city. *Case studies on transport policy*, 4(4):259–268.

Kononiuk, A., Sacio-Szymańska, A., and Gáspár, J. (2017). How do companies envisage the future? functional foresight approaches. *Engineering Management in Production and Services*, 9(4):21–33.

Köster, F., Ulmer, M. W., and Mattfeld, D. C. (2015). Cooperative traffic control management for city logistic routing. *Transportation Research Procedia*, 10:673–682.

Kováříková, L., Grosová, S., and Baran, D. (2017). Critical factors impacting the adoption of foresight by companies. *Foresight*, 19(6):541–558.

Kramers, A., Höjer, M., Lövehagen, N., and Wangel, J. (2014). Smart sustainable cities–exploring ICT solutions for reduced energy use in cities. *Environmental Modelling & Software*, 56:52–62.

Kunze, O. (2016). Replicators, ground drones and crowd logistics a vision of urban logistics in the year 2030. *Transportation Research Procedia*, 19:286–299.

Kupiainen, E., Mäntylä, M. V., and Itkonen, J. (2015). Using metrics in agile and lean software development–a systematic literature review of industrial studies. *Information and Software Technology*, 62:143–163.

Kuzmenko, Y., Levina, A., Savelyeva, I., and Aliukov, S. (2017). Logistic integration of trading service facilities: Spatial aspect. In *Proceedings of the World Congress on Engineering*, volume 2, pages 704–708. Newswood Academic Publishing, Hong Kong.

Labanauskas, G. (2016). Development of inland waterway transport for Kaunas city logistics. In *Proceedings of 20th International Scientific on Conference Transport Means 2016*, pages 1131–1134. Kaunas University of Technology, Kaunas, Lithuania.

Lagorio, A., Pinto, R., and Golini, R. (2016). Research in urban logistics: a systematic literature review. *International Journal of Physical Distribution & Logistics Management*, 46(10):908–931.

Lebeau, P., De Cauwer, C., Van Mierlo, J., Macharis, C., Verbeke, W., and Coosemans, T. (2015a). Conventional, hybrid, or electric vehicles: which technology for an urban distribution centre? *The Scientific World Journal*, 2015. Article ID 302867.

Lebeau, P., Macharis, C., and Mierlo, J. V. (2015b). The choice of battery electric vehicles for urban logistics: A conjoint based choice analysis. In *28th International Electric Vehicle Symposium and Exhibition (EVS28)*, pages 3–6.

Lebeau, P., Macharis, C., and Van Mierlo, J. (2016). Exploring the choice of battery electric vehicles in city logistics: A conjoint-based choice analysis. *Transportation Research Part E: Logistics and Transportation Review*, 91:245–258.

Lebeau, P., Macharis, C., Van Mierlo, J., and Janjevic, M. (2018). Improving policy support in city logistics: The contributions of a multi-actor multi-criteria analysis. *Case Studies on Transport Policy*, 6(4):554–563.

Lebeau, P., Macharis, C., Van Mierlo, J., and Lebeau, K. (2015c). Electrifying light commercial vehicles for city logistics? a total cost of ownership analysis. *European Journal of Transport and Infrastructure Research*, 2015(4):551–569.

Lebeau, P., Macharis, C., Van Mierlo, J., and Maes, G. (2013). Implementing electric vehicles in urban distribution: A discrete event simulation. *World Electric Vehicle Journal*, 6(1):38–47.

Lee, C.-H., Chen, C.-H., Lee, Y.-C., Xu, G., Li, F., and Zhao, X. (2015). Accelerating retail-innovation design for smart services via foresight approach and case-based design. *Transdisciplinary Engineering: A Paradigm Shift*, 5:813–820.

Lee, T.-L. and Chuang, M.-C. (2012). Foresight for public policy of solar energy industry in taiwan: An application of delphi method and q methodology. In *2012 Proceedings of PICMET'12: Technology Management for Emerging Technologies*, pages 60–67. IEEE.

Lee, Y.-Y., Tsou, C.-S., Lin, H.-C., Ien, C.-H., and Wu, Y.-T. (2008). Global perspective of health related edible plants from the agricultural point of view. *Asia Pacific journal of clinical nutrition*, 17:95–98.

Lemke, J., Iwan, S., and Korczak, J. (2016). Usability of the parcel lockers from the customer perspective–the research in Polish Cities. *Transportation Research Procedia*, 16:272–287.

Lenz, B. and Riehle, E. (2013). Bikes for urban freight? Experience in Europe. *Transportation Research Record*, 2379(1):39–45.

Leonardi, J., Browne, M., and Allen, J. (2012). Before-after assessment of a logistics trial with clean urban freight vehicles: A case study in london. *Procedia-Social and Behavioral Sciences*, 39:146–157.

Lewandowski, K. (2014). Reliability of the delivery in the last 100 meters. In *Safety and Reliability: Methodology and Applications-Proceedings of the European Safety and Reliability Conference, ESREL 2014 2015*, pages 2377–2386. CRC Press, Balkema.

Li, B., Krushinsky, D., Reijers, H. A., and Van Woensel, T. (2014). The share-a-ride problem: People and parcels sharing taxis. *European Journal of Operational Research*, 238(1):31–40.

Li, H., Liu, Y., Chen, K., and Lin, Q. (2018). The two-echelon city logistics system with on-street satellites. *Computers & Industrial Engineering*, 139. Article ID 105577.

Liakos, P., Angelidis, I., and Delis, A. (2016). Cooperative routing and scheduling of an electric vehicle fleet managing dynamic customer requests. In *Lecture Notes in Computer Science*, volume 10033 LNCS, pages 118–135. Springer.

Lin, J., Chen, Q., and Kawamura, K. (2016). Sustainability SI: logistics cost and environmental impact analyses of urban delivery consolidation strategies. *Networks and Spatial Economics*, 16(1):227–253.

Lindawati and De Souza, R. (2017). Determining urban freight facility locations using post-evaluation deliberation. In *Proceedings – 18th IEEE International Conference on High Per-*

formance Computing and Communications, 14th IEEE International Conference on Smart City and 2nd IEEE International Conference on Data Science and Systems, pages 1297–1303. IEEE, HPCC, DSS 2016, SmartCity.

Lindholm, M. and Behrends, S. (2012). Challenges in urban freight transport planning–a review in the baltic sea region. *Journal of Transport Geography*, 22:129–136.

Liu, S., Xu, J., Shi, X., Li, G., and Liu, D. (2018). Sustainable distribution organization based on the supply–demand coordination in large Chinese Cities. *Sustainability*, 10(9):3042.

Lopez, O. N. (2018). Urban vehicle access regulations. In *Sustainable Freight Transport*, pages 139–163. Springer.

Lu, M. (2014). Innovative solutions for sustainable urban freight transport. In *Proceedings of the 21st World Congress on Inteligent Transport Systems: Reinventing Transportation in Our Connected World, Detroit, MI, USA*, pages 7–11.

Macharis, C., Lebeau, P., Van Mierlo, J., and Lebeau, K. (2013). Electric versus conventional vehicles for logistics: A total cost of ownership. In *2013 World Electric Vehicle Symposium and Exhibition (EVS27)*, pages 1–10. IEEE, New York.

Maes, J., Sys, C., and Vanelslander, T. (2015). City logistics by water: Good practices and scope for expansion. *Operations Research/ Computer Science Interfaces Series*, 58:413–437.

Magruk, A. (2017). Concept of uncertainty in relation to the foresight research. *Engineering Management in Production and Services*, 9(1):46–55.

Magruk, A. et al. (2011). Innovative classification of technology foresight methods. *Technological and Economic Development of Economy*, (4):700–715.

Malanowski, N. and Zweck, A. (2007). Bridging the gap between foresight and market research: Integrating methods to assess the economic potential of nanotechnology. *Technological Forecasting and Social Change*, 74(9):1805–1822.

Mancini, S. (2013). Multi-echelon distribution systems in city logistics. *European Transport – Trasporti Europei*, (54):1–24.

Manier, H., Manier, M.-A., and Al Chami, Z. (2016). Shippers' collaboration in city logistics. *IFAC-PapersOnLine*, 49(12):1880–1885.

Marujo, L. G., Goes, G. V., D'Agosto, M. A., Ferreira, A. F., Winkenbach, M., and Bandeira, R. A. (2018). Assessing the sustainability of mobile depots: The case of urban freight distribution in Rio de Janeiro. *Transportation Research Part D: Transport and Environment*, 62:256–267.

Masson, R., Trentini, A., Lehuédé, F., Malhéné, N., Péton, O., and Tlahig, H. (2017). Optimization of a city logistics transportation system with mixed passengers and goods. *EURO Journal on Transportation and Logistics*, 6(1):81–109.

May, A., Jarvi-Nykanen, T., Minken, H., Ramjerdi, F., Matthews, B., and Monzon, A. (2001). Cities' decision-making requirements–prospects deliverable 1. *Institute of Transport Studies, University of Leeds, Leeds*.

Mazurkiewicz, A. and Poteralska, B. (2018). Methodology of innovation generation as an instrument for effective management of technological innovations. In *Proceedings of the 13th European Conference on Innovation and Entrepreneurship ECIE*, pages 467–476. Academic Conferences and Publishing International Limited Reading, UK.

Mbiadou Saleu, R. G., Deroussi, L., Feillet, D., Grangeon, N., and Quilliot, A. (2018). An iterative two-step heuristic for the parallel drone scheduling traveling salesman problem. *Networks*, 72(4):459–474.

Mckinnon, A. C. (2016). The possible impact of 3D printing and drones on last-mile logistics: An exploratory study. *Built Environment*, 42(4):617–629.

Melo, S. and Baptista, P. (2017). Evaluating the impacts of using cargo cycles on urban logistics: integrating traffic, environmental and operational boundaries. *European Transport Research Review*, 9(2):30.

Melo, S., Baptista, P., and Costa, A. (2014). The cost and effectiveness of sustainable city logistics policies using small electric vehicles. *Transport and Sustainability*, 6:295–314.

Mendonça, S., e Cunha, M. P., Ruff, F., and Kaivo-oja, J. (2009). Venturing into the wilderness: Preparing for wild cards in the civil aircraft and asset-management industries. *Long Range Planning*, 42(1):23–41.

Menge, J. and Horn, B. (2014). *Das Fahrrad im Wirtschaftsverkehr*. Wichmann, Berlin.

Mercedes-Benz (2016). Intelligently network delivery vehicle of the future. https://www. mercedes-benz.com/en/mercedes-benz/vehicles/transporter/vision-van/. Accessed on 3 December 2018.

Mercedes-Benz (n.d.). Taxi und mietwagen. https://www.mercedes-benz.de/passengercars/ buy/fleet-and-business/fb/taxi.html. Accessed on 3 December 2019.

Merchan, D., Blanco, E. E., and Winkenbach, M. (2016). Transshipment networks for last-mile delivery in congested urban areas. In *6th International Conference on Information Systems, Logistics and Supply Chain (ILS 2016), Bordeaux, France, 1-4 June*. International Conference on Information Systems, Logistics and Supply Chain.

Meyrick and Associates (2006). National intermodal terminal study. *Australian Department of Transport and Regional Services*. Meyrick Reference: 10781.

Mikołajewicz-Woz'Niak, A. and Scheibe, A. (2015). Virtual currency schemes-The future of financial services. *Foresight*, 17(4):365–377.

Mirhedayatian, S. M. and Yan, S. (2018). A framework to evaluate policy options for support-ing electric vehicles in urban freight transport. *Transportation Research Part D: Transport and Environment*, 58:22–38.

Mitrea, O. and Kyamakya, K. (2017). (How) will autonomous driving influence the future shape of city logistics? *Journal of Applied Engineering Science*, 15(1):45–52.

Mokum Mariteam (2012). Mokum mariteam: Vracht door de gracht. Accessed on February 11, 2019. https://www.mokummariteam.nl/.

Molfino, R., Zoppi, M., Dinale, A., and Muscolo, G. (2014). A robotic vehicle for freight deliv-ery in urban areas. In *16th International Conference on Harbor, Maritime and Multimodal Logistics Modelling and Simulation, HMS 2014*, pages 154–159.

Morganti, E. and Browne, M. (2018). Technical and operational obstacles to the adoption of electric vans in France and the UK: An operator perspective. *Transport Policy*, 63:90–97.

Motraghi, A. and Marinov, M. V. (2012). Analysis of urban freight by rail using event based simulation. *Simulation Modelling Practice and Theory*, 25:73–89.

Moutaoukil, A., Neubert, G., and Derrouiche, R. (2015). Urban freight distribution: The impact of delivery time on sustainability. *IFAC-PapersOnLine*, 48(3):2368–2373.

Mozuni, M. and Jonas, W. (2016). A morphological analysis tool for complex future-oriented scenario researches. In *Relating Systems Thinking and Design Symposium (RSD),Toronto, Canada*, pages 13–15.

Munim, Z. H. and Haralambides, H. (2018). Competition and cooperation for intermodal con-tainer transhipment: A network optimization approach. *Research in transportation business & management*, 26:87–99.

Muñoz-Villamizar, A., Quintero-Araújo, C. L., Montoya-Torres, J. R., and Faulin, J. (2019). Short-and mid-term evaluation of the use of electric vehicles in urban freight transport collaborative networks: a case study. *International Journal of Logistics Research and Applications*, 22(3):229–252.

Muscolo, G. G., Moregola, G., and Molfino, R. (2018). A preliminary study to optimise safety conditions on a freight urban robotic vehicle. *International Journal of Vehicle Safety*, 10(1):1–23.

Nadarajah, S. and Bookbinder, J. H. (2013). Less-than-truckload carrier collaboration problem: modeling framework and solution approach. *Journal of heuristics*, 19(6):917–942.

Navarro, C., Roca-Riu, M., Furió, S., and Estrada, M. (2016). Designing new models for energy efficiency in urban freight transport for smart cities and its application to the Spanish case. *Transportation Research Procedia*, 12:314–324.

Neghabadi, P. D., Samuel, K. E., and Espinouse, M.-L. (2016). City logistics: a review and research framework. In *RIRL 2016 EPFL, Lausanne, Switzerland*. hal-01420815.

Nguyen, D. T., Lau, H. C., and Kumar, A. (2015). Decomposition techniques for urban consolidation problems. In *2015 IEEE International Conference on Automation Science and Engineering (CASE)*, pages 57–62. IEEE.

Nugroho, Y. and Saritas, O. (2009). Incorporating network perspectives in foresight: a methodological proposal. *Foresight*, 11(6):21–41.

Nuzzolo, A. and Comi, A. (2015). Modelling the demand for rail in an urbancontext: Some methodological aspects. *European Transport – Trasporti Europei*, (57).

Olsson, J. and Woxenius, J. (2014). Localisation of freight consolidation centres serving small road hauliers in a wider urban area: barriers for more efficient freight deliveries in Gothenburg. *Journal of Transport Geography*, 34:25–33.

önke Behrends, S. (2012). The urban context of intermodal road-rail transport–threat or opportunity for modal shift? *Procedia-Social and Behavioral Sciences*, 39:463–475.

Oppolzer, T., Kretzschmar, J., Mauch, M., Schau, V., and Rossak, W. (2017). Agent based mixed fleet management in city logistics. In *14th Workshop on "Location-Based Applications and Services"*, volume 2020, pages 81–91. CEUR-WS.

Ouhader, H. and El Kyal, M. (2017a). Combining facility location and routing decisions in sustainable urban freight distribution under horizontal collaboration: How can shippers be benefited? *Mathematical Problems in Engineering*, 2017. Article ID 8687515.

Ouhader, H. and El Kyal, M. (2017b). The impact of horizontal collaboration on CO2 emissions due to road transportation. In *Proceedings of the international conference on industrial engineering and operations management*, pages 1959–1970. IEOM Society, Michigan, Southfield.

Ozturk, O. and Patrick, J. (2018). An optimization model for freight transport using urban rail transit. *European Journal of Operational Research*, 267(3):1110–1121.

Paananen, A. and J. Mäkinen, S. (2013). Bibliometrics-based foresight on renewable energy production. *Foresight*, 15(6):465–476.

Paddeu, D. (2017). The Bristol-Bath Urban freight Consolidation Centre from the perspective of its users. *Case Studies on Transport Policy*, 5(3):483–491.

PAL-V International B.V. (2018). PAL-V Liberty. https://www.pal-v.com/en/. Accessed on 3 May, 2019p.

Pamučar, D., Vasin, L., Atanasković, P., and Miličić, M. (2016). Planning the city logistics terminal location by applying the green-median model and type-2 neurofuzzy network. *Computational Intelligence and Neuroscience*, 2016. 6972818.

Pan, S., Giannikas, V., Han, Y., Grover-Silva, E., and Qiao, B. (2017). Using customer-related data to enhance e-grocery home delivery. *Industrial Management & Data Systems*, 117(9):1917–1933.

Pelletier, S., Jabali, O., and Laporte, G. (2018). Charge scheduling for electric freight vehicles. *Transportation Research Part B: Methodological*, 115:246–269.

Perboli, G. and Rosano, M. (2018). A decision support system for optimizing the last-mile by mixing traditional and green logistics. In *International Conference on Information Systems, Logistics and Supply Chain*, pages 28–46. Springer.

Pimentel, C. and Alvelos, F. (2018). Integrated urban freight logistics combining passenger and freight flows–mathematical model proposal. *Transportation research procedia*, 30:80–89.

Popper, R. (2008). How are foresight methods selected? *Foresight*, 10(6):62–89.

Porter, M. E. and Kramer, M. R. (2002). The competitive advantage of corporate.

Puga, A. (2007). A latvian experience addressing issues of the foresight innovation. *International Journal of Foresight and Innovation Policy*, 3(4):369–387.

Pysar, N., Dergachova, V., Kyvliuk, O., and Svyrydenko, D. (2018). Strategies for development of ukrainian energy market under conditions of geopolitical challenges. *Naukovyi Visnyk Natsionalnoho Hirnychoho Universytetu*, (5):148–154.

Quak, H., Nesterova, N., van Rooijen, T., and Dong, Y. (2016). Zero emission city logistics: current practices in freight electromobility and feasibility in the near future. *Transportation Research Procedia*, 14:1506–1515.

Ramos, J., Mansfield, T., and Priday, G. (2012). Foresight in a network era: Peer-producing alternative futures. *Journal of Futures Studies*, 17(1):71–90.

Rao, C., Goh, M., Zhao, Y., and Zheng, J. (2015). Location selection of city logistics centers under sustainability. *Transportation Research Part D: Transport and Environment*, 36:29–44.

Rassafi, A. and Vaziri, M. (2005). Sustainable transport indicators: definition and integration. *International Journal of Environmental Science & Technology*, 2(1):83–96.

Regué, R. and Bristow, A. L. (2013). Appraising freight tram schemes: A case study of Barcelona. *European Journal of Transport and Infrastructure Research*, 13(1):56–78.

Rezgui, D., Aggoune-Mtalaa, W., and Bouziri, H. (2015). Towards the electrification of urban freight delivery using modular vehicles. In *2015 IEEE International Conference on Service Operations And Logistics, And Informatics (SOLI)*, pages 154–159. IEEE, New York.

Rezgui, D., Siala, J. C., Aggoune-Mtalaa, W., and Bouziri, H. (2018). Towards smart urban freight distribution using fleets of modular electric vehicles. In *Proceedings of the Mediterranean Symposium on Smart City Applications*, pages 602–612. Springer.

Ritchey, T. (1998). General morphological analysis: a general method for non-quantified modelling. In *16th EURO Conference on Operational Analysis, Brussels*.

Rizet, C., Cruz, C., and Vromant, M. (2016). The constraints of vehicle range and congestion for the use of electric vehicles for urban freight in France. *Transportation Research Procedia*, 12:500–507.

Robinson, M. and Mortimer, P. (2004). Urban freight and rail-the state of the art. *Logistics and Transport Focus*, 6(1):46–47.

Rodrigue, J.-P., Comtois, C., and Slack, B. (2016). *The geography of transport systems*. Routledge.

Rohrbeck, R., Battistella, C., and Huizingh, E. (2015). Corporate foresight: An emerging field with a rich tradition. *Technological Forecasting and Social Change*, 101:1–9.

Rosano, M., Demartini, C. G., Lamberti, F., and Perboli, G. (2018). A mobile platform for collaborative urban freight transportation. *Transportation Research Procedia*, 30:14–22.

Rose, W. J., Bell, J. E., Autry, C. W., and Cherry, C. R. (2017). Urban logistics: Establishing key concepts and building a conceptual framework for future research. *Transportation Journal*, 56(4):357–394.

Roumboutsos, A., Kapros, S., and Vanelslander, T. (2014). Green city logistics: Systems of innovation to assess the potential of E-vehicles. *Research in Transportation Business & Management*, 11:43–52.

Rudolph, C. and Gruber, J. (2017). Cargo cycles in commercial transport: Potentials, constraints, and recommendations. *Research in transportation business & management*, 24:26–36.

Saeedi, F., Teimoury, E., and Makui, A. (2018). Designing sustainable city logistics distribution network using a probabilistic bi-objective mathematical model. *Uncertain Supply Chain Management*, 6(4):357–374.

Saetta, S. A. and Caldarelli, V. (2016). Urban logistics: The role of urban consolidation centre for the sustainability of transportation systems. In *Proceedings of the 18th International Conference on Harbor, Maritime and Multimodal Logistics Modelling and Simulation (HMS 2016)*, pages 69–75. Dime University of Genoa, Genova.

Santonen, T., Kaivo-Oja, J., and Suomala, J. (2008). Brief introduction to national open innovation system (NOIS) paradigm: Integrating online social networks and the triple helix model. In *Proceedings of the 6th International Conference on Politics and Information Systems, Technologies and Applications: PISTA 2008*, volume III, pages 126–131. International Institute of Informatics and Systemics.

Saragih, N., Nur Bahagia, S., Syabri, I., et al. (2017). Single-tier city logistics model for single product. In *IOP Conference Series: Materials Science and Engineering*, volume 273. 012015.

Sárdi, D. L. and Bóna, K. (2018). Macroscopic simulation model of a multi-stage, dynamic cargo bike-based logistics system in the supply of shopping malls in Budapest. In *2018 Smart City Symposium Prague (SCSP)*, pages 1–7. IEEE.

Savelsbergh, M. and Van Woensel, T. (2016). City logistics: Challenges and opportunities. *Transportation Science*, 50(2):579–590.

Schartinger, D., Wilhelmer, D., Holste, D., and Kubeczko, K. (2012). Assessing immediate learning impacts of large foresight processes. *Foresight*, 14(1):41–55.

Schatzmann, J., Schäfer, R., and Eichelbaum, F. (2013). Foresight 2.0-definition, overview & evaluation. *European Journal of Futures Research*, 1(1):15.

Schau, V., Apel, S., Gebhard, K., Mauch, M., and Rossak, W. (2016a). ICT-systems for electric vehicles within simulated and community based environments. In *Communications in Computer and Information Science*, volume 648, pages 217–222. Springer.

Schau, V., Apel, S., Gebhardt, K., Kretzschmar, J., Stolcis, C., Mauch, M., and Buchholz, J. (2016b). Intelligent infrastructure for last-mile and short-distance freight transportation with electric vehicles in the domain of smart city logistic. In *Proceedings of the Inter-*

national Conference on Vehicle Technology and Intelligent Transport Systems (VEHITS 2016), pages 149–159.

Schau, V., Rossak, W., Hempel, H., and Späthe, S. (2015). Smart City Logistik erfurt (SCL): ICT-support for managing fully electric vehicles in the domain of inner city freight traffic. In *5th International Conference on Industrial Engineering and Operations Management (IEOM)*, pages 1–8. IEEE, New York.

Scherr, Y. O., Neumann-Saavedra, B. A., Hewitt, M., and Mattfeld, D. C. (2018a). Service network design for same day delivery with mixed autonomous fleets. *Transportation research procedia*, 30:23–32.

Scherr, Y. O., Neumann-Saavedra, B. A., Hewitt, M., and Mattfeld, D. C. (2018b). Service network design for same day delivery with mixed autonomous fleets. *Transportation research procedia*, 30:23–32.

Schier, M., Offermann, B., Weigl, J. D., Maag, T., Mayer, B., Rudolph, C., and Gruber, J. (2016). Innovative two wheeler technologies for future mobility concepts. In *2016 Eleventh International Conference on Ecological Vehicles and Renewable Energies (EVER)*, pages 1–7. IEEE, New York.

Schliwa, G., Armitage, R., Aziz, S., Evans, J., and Rhoades, J. (2015). Sustainable city logistics-making cargo cycles viable for urban freight transport. *Research in Transportation Business & Management*, 15:50–57.

Scholz, R. W. and Tietje, O. (2002). *Embedded case study methods: Integrating quantitative and qualitative knowledge*. SAGA Publications.

Schwartz, P. (2012). *The art of the long view: planning for the future in an uncertain world*. Currency Press.

Seidlová, A., Šourek, D., and Ledvinová, M. Distribution models using waterway transport for city logistics. In *Proceedings of 21st International Scientific on Conference Transport Means 2017*, pages 220–225.

Serafini, S., Nigro, M., Gatta, V., and Marcucci, E. (2018). Sustainable crowdshipping using public transport: A case study evaluation in Rome. *Transportation Research Procedia*, 30:101–110.

Shcherbinin, D. and Prokhorov, S. (2018). The history of science and technology during the transition to a digital economy. In *2018 International Conference on Engineering Technologies and Computer Science (EnT)*, pages 8–10. IEEE.

Shen, J., Qiu, F., Li, W., and Feng, P. (2015). A new urban logistics transport system based on a public transit service. In *CICTP 2015 – Efficient, Safe, and Green Multimodal Transportation – Proceedings of the 15th COTA International Conference of Transportation Professionals*, pages 650–661.

Shostak, I., Danova, M., and Kuznetsova, Y. (2017). Foresight-research for green it engineering development. In *Green IT Engineering: Concepts, Models, Complex Systems Architectures*, pages 21–41. Springer.

Sładkowski, A., Dantas, R., Micu, C., Sekar, G., Arena, A., and Singhania, V. (2014). Urban freight distribution: council warehouses & freight by rail. *Transport problems*, 9:29–43.

Spickermann, A., Zimmermann, M., and Heiko, A. (2014). Surface-and deep-level diversity in panel selection-exploring diversity effects on response behaviour in foresight. *Technological Forecasting and Social Change*, 85:105–120.

Stahl, B. C. (2013). Virtual suicide and other ethical issues of emerging information technologies. *Futures*, 50:35–43.

Starship (n.d.). The self-driving delivery robot. https://www.starship.xyz/business/. Accessed on 3 December 2018.

STRAIGHTSOL (2012). TNT Express in Brussels – City Logistics Mobile Depot. http://www.straightsol.eu/demonstration_B.htm. Accessed on 5 December, 2018.

Strale, M. (2014). The cargo tram: Current status and perspectives, the example of Brussels. *Transport and Sustainability*, 6:245–263.

Strzelczak, S. (2015). Towards ontology-aided manufacturing and supply chain management–insights from a foresight research. In *IFIP International Conference on Advances in Production Management Systems*, pages 502–510. Springer.

Strzelczak, S. (2017). Production internet-functional perspective. In *IFIP International Conference on Advances in Production Management Systems*, pages 48–56. Springer.

Su, H.-N. and Lee, P.-C. (2010). Mapping knowledge structure by keyword co-occurrence: a first look at journal papers in technology foresight. *Scientometrics*, 85(1):65–79.

Tadei, R., Fadda, E., Gobbato, L., Perboli, G., and Rosano, M. (2016). An ICT-based reference model for e-grocery in smart cities. In *International Conference on Smart Cities, Malaga, Spain*, pages 22–31. Springer.

Taefi, T. T. (2016). Viability of electric vehicles in combined day and night delivery: a total cost of ownership example in Germany. *European Journal of Transport and Infrastructure Research*, 16(4):512–553.

Taefi, T. T., Kreutzfeldt, J., and Fink, A. (2016). Yielding a treasure: A transition management approach to electric urban freight vehicles in Germany. In *EVS 2016 – 29th International Electric Vehicle Symposium, Palais des Congres de MontrealMontreal, Canada*.

Taefi, T. T., Kreutzfeldt, J., Held, T., and Fink, A. (2015). Strategies to increase the profitability of electric vehicles in urban freight transport. *Green Energy and Technology*, 203:367–388.

Taefi, T. T., Stütz, S., and Fink, A. (2017). Assessing the cost-optimal mileage of medium-duty electric vehicles with a numeric simulation approach. *Transportation Research Part D: Transport and Environment*, 56:271–285.

Taniguchi, E. (2015). City logistics for sustainable and liveable cities. In *Green Logistics and Transportation*, pages 49–60. Springer.

Taniguchi, E., Thompson, R. G., and Yamada, T. (1999). Modelling city logistics. In *International Conference on City Logistics, 1st, 1999, Cairns, Queensland, Australia*.

Taniguchi, E., Thompson, R. G., and Yamada, T. (2016). New opportunities and challenges for city logistics. *Transportation research procedia*, 12:5–13.

Teoh, T., Kunze, O., Teo, C.-C., and Wong, Y. (2018). Decarbonisation of urban freight transport using electric vehicles and opportunity charging. *Sustainability*, 10(9):3258.

Teye, C., Bell, M. G., and Bliemer, M. C. (2016). Optimal location of open access urban container terminals under elastic cargo demand. In *Australasian Transport Research Forum (ATRF), 38th, 2016, Melbourne, Victoria, Australia*.

TNT Express (2013). TNT Express Introduces Mobile Depot in Brussels. https://www.tnt.com/corporate/en/data/press/2013/05/tnt-express-introduces-mobile-depot-in-Brussels.html. Accessed on 11 February, 2019.

Tobey, M. B., Binder, R. B., Chang, S., Yoshida, T., Yamagata, Y., and Yang, P. P. (2019). Urban systems design: A conceptual framework for planning smart communities. *Smart Cities*, 2(4):522–537.

Tourki, Y., Keisler, J., and Linkov, I. (2013). Scenario analysis: a review of methods and applications for engineering and environmental systems. *Environment Systems & Decisions*, 33(1):3–20.

Triantafyllou, M. K., Cherrett, T. J., and Browne, M. (2014). Urban freight consolidation centers: Case study in the UK retail sector. *Transportation Research Record*, 2411(1):34–44.

UN DESA (2015a). *World Population Prospects: The 2015 Revision, Key Findings and Advance Tables, Working Paper No. ESA/P/WP. 241.* Department of Economic and Social Affairs, Population Division, United Nations, New York.

UN DESA (2015b). *World population prospects: The 2015 revision, The 2015 Revision, DVD Edition*. Department of Economic and Social Affairs, Population Division, United Nations, New York.

UN DESA (2018). *2018 Revision of World Urbanization Prospects*. Department of Economic and Social Affairs, Population Division, United Nations, New York.

UN-Habitat (2016). *World Cities Report 2016: Urbanization and Development-Emerging Futures*. UN-Habitat.

UNCTAD. Secreteriat (2001). *Implementation of Multimodal Transport Rules*. United Nations. GE.01-51881.

Van der Heijden, K. (2011). *Scenarios: the art of strategic conversation*. John Wiley & Sons.

Van Duin, J., Tavasszy, L. A., and Quak, H. (2013). Towards E(lectric)-urban freight: first promising steps in the electric vehicle revolution. *European Transport – Trasporti Europei*, (54). Paper number 9.

Velove Cororpation (n.d.). The Armadillo. http://velove.se/the-armadillo/. Accessed on February 11, 2019.

Verlinde, S. and Macharis, C. (2016). Innovation in urban freight transport: The triple helix model. *Transportation Research Procedia*, 14:1250–1259.

Verlinde, S., Macharis, C., Milan, L., and Kin, B. (2014). Does a mobile depot make urban deliveries faster, more sustainable and more economically viable: results of a pilot test in Brussels. *Transportation Research Procedia*, 4:361–373.

Vervoort, J. and Gupta, A. (2018). Anticipating climate futures in a 1.5 c era: The link between foresight and governance. *Current Opinion in Environmental Sustainability*, 31:104–111.

Vleugel, J. and Bal, F. (2018). More space and improved living conditions in cities with autonomous vehicles. *International Journal of Design & Nature and Ecodynamics*, 12(4):505–515.

Voronina, M. and Moroz, O. (2017). A substantiation of foresight research of development strategy of descriptive geometry, engineering geometry and computer graphics departments on the basis of industrial 4.0 ideology. *Man In India*, 97(3):375–389.

Wang, L. S. and Deng, Q. M. (2013). A portable subway logistics system for the transportation of small and medium-size cargo. *Advanced Materials Research*, 734-737:1604–1608.

Wang, X. (2015). The trend of urban freight regulatory path under the cloud. In *ICTE 2015 – Proceedings of the 5th International Conference on Transportation Engineering*, pages 2102–2108. American Society of Civil Engineers, Reston, VA.

Wang, Y., Ma, X., Liu, M., Gong, K., Liu, Y., Xu, M., and Wang, Y. (2017). Cooperation and profit allocation in two-echelon logistics joint distribution network optimization. *Applied Soft Computing*, 56:143–157.

Wang, Y., Zhang, J., Assogba, K., Liu, Y., Xu, M., and Wang, Y. (2018). Collaboration and transportation resource sharing in multiple centers vehicle routing optimization with delivery and pickup. *Knowledge-Based Systems*, 160:296–310.

Wątróbski, J., Małecki, K., Kijewska, K., Iwan, S., Karczmarczyk, A., and Thompson, R. (2017). Multi-criteria analysis of electric vans for city logistics. *Sustainability*, 9(8):1453.

Wikipedia (n.d.a). Ge multifactorial analysis. https://en.wikipedia.org/wiki/GE_multifactorial_analysis. Accessed on 11 February, 2019.

Wikipedia (n.d.b). Intermodal freight transportation. https://en.wikipedia.org/wiki/Intermodal_freight_transport. Accessed on 3 December, 2018.

Winkenbach, M., Kleindorfer, P. R., and Spinler, S. (2015). Enabling urban logistics services at la poste through multi-echelon location-routing. *Transportation Science*, 50(2):520–540.

Wittlöv, A. (2012). Urban freight transport: Challenges and opportunities. *Urban freight for livable cities: How to deal with collaboration and trade-offs*, pages 12–23.

Wolfram, M. (2004). Expert working group on sustainable urban transport plans. Final Report (Deliverable D4). Rupprecht Consult, Cologne, Germany.

Workhorse Group (2016). HorseFly UAV Delivery system. http://workhorse.com/aerospace. Accessed on 7 June, 2019.

Yang, J. and Gao, H. (2015). Impact of different carbon policies on city logistics network. In *MATEC Web of Conferences*, volume 22. EDP Sciences. 01052.

Yang, J., Guo, J., and Ma, S. (2016). Low-carbon city logistics distribution network design with resource deployment. *Journal of Cleaner Production*, 119:223–228.

Yang, W., Cheong, T., and Song, S. H. (2015). A multiperiod vehicle lease planning for urban freight consolidation network. *Mathematical Problems in Engineering*, 2015. 921482.

Yu, J. J. and Lam, A. Y. (2017). Autonomous vehicle logistic system: Joint routing and charging strategy. *IEEE Transactions on Intelligent Transportation Systems*, 19(7):2175–2187.

Yuan, B. J., Hsieh, C.-H., and Chang, C.-C. (2010). National technology foresight research: a literature review from 1984 to 2005. *International Journal of Foresight and Innovation Policy*, 6(1-3):5–35.

Zhang, R. and Wang, L. (2018). A study on price evaluation and management of urban freight taxi in Shanghai. In *CICTP 2017: Transportation Reform and Change-Equity, Inclusiveness, Sharing, and Innovation*, pages 1472–1480. American Society of Civil Engineers, Reston, VA.

Zhao, L., Li, H., Li, M., Sun, Y., Hu, Q., Mao, S., Li, J., and Xue, J. (2018). Location selection of intra-city distribution hubs in the metro-integrated logistics system. *Tunnelling and Underground Space Technology*, 80:246–256.

Zhou, L., Baldacci, R., Vigo, D., and Wang, X. (2018). A multi-depot two-echelon vehicle routing problem with delivery options arising in the last mile distribution. *European Journal of Operational Research*, 265(2):765–778.

Zolkifly, N. H. and Hussin, M. N. (2017). Digital display of car showroom: Proposing an emotional-environmental conceptual model. *Pertanika Journal of Social Sciences & Humanities*, 25(S):49–58.

Zwicky, F. (1969). *Discovery, invention, research through the morphological approach*. Macmillan Publishers.

Zwicky, F. and Wilson, A. G. (1967). *New Methods of Thought and Procedure: Contributions to the Symposium on Methodologies*. Springer.